I
Just Want
to
Be Perfect

a collection of essays by
Some Fine Ass Chicas

TABLE OF CONTENTS

1   *Introduction*

3   *The Breast Pump Corporate Travel Log*
By Kim Forde of The Fordeville Diaries

12   *How To Find The Perfect Swimsuit*
By Wendi Aarons

15   *Easy Breezy Brunch—A Search For The Perfect Mother's Day*
By Jennifer Lizza of Outsmarted Mommy

21   *Here Comes the Bride(smaid)*
By Janel Mills of 649.133: Girls, the Care and Maintenance Of.

28   *The Perfect Senior Portrait is a Myth*
By Chrissy Woj of Quirky Chrissy

35   *It Didn't Go So Smoothie*
By Tara Wood of Love Morning Wood

40   *Picture Perfect*
By Jen Simon

47   *At Least You Have Your Health*
By Stacey Gill of One Funny Motha

54   *How to Suck at Church*
By AK Turner

59   *The Burning Pain of Perfection*
By Allison Hart of Motherhood, WTF?

65   *Perfect Mom Friends*
By Deva Dalporto of MyLifeSuckers

69   *Comeuppance*
By Audrey Hayworth of Sass Mouth

77   *How The Perfect Beach Vacation Can Go Grossly, Horribly Wrong*
By Joelle Wisler of Running From Mountain Lions

81   *Threshold of Hell-ing It*
By Meredith Spidel of Mom of the Year

85   *The Best Damn Hippie This Side of the Sixties*
By Christine Organ

91   *Pizza Party From Hell*
By Suzanne Fleet of Toulouse and Tonic

99   *A Pantry Is Just a Closet with Food in It*
By Nicole Leigh Shaw

103   *Gladys Doesn't Live Here Anymore*
By Lisa René LeClair of Sassypiehole

108   *The Suburban Dress Code*
By Kelcey Kintner of The Mama Bird Diaries

112   *Vintage Dreams and a Modern Reality*
By Shya Gibbons

117   *Putting the Wrong Foot Forward*
By Ellen Williams and Erin Dymowski of Sisterhood of the
Sensible Moms

124   *Look into My Eyes: A Theme Song for the World's Worst Baseball Mom*
By Julianna W. Miner of Rants from Mommyland

133   *My Sexy Almost Died (And So Did My Stylist)*
By Lola Lolita of Sammiches and Psych Meds

139   *Pain is Beauty. Beauty is Stupid*
By Bethany Kriger Thies of Bad Parenting Moments

143   *On Failing to Become an MLM Millionaire*
By Jessica Azar of Herd Management

148   *The Rise and Fall of the Perfect Seductress*
By Hedia Anvar of Gunmetal Geisha

156   *Bikini Wax By Nadia*
By Meredith Gordon of Bad Sandy

166   *Bedpans, Barbies and Busted: One Nurse's Perfectly Public Humiliation*
By Christine Burke of Keeper of the Fruit Loops

171   *The Perfect Wife*
By Kathryn Leehane of Foxy Wine Pocket

177   *I'm Just Trying To Fit In*
By Harmony Hobbs of Modern Mommy Madness

181   *A Labor of Love*
By Ashley Fuchs of The Malleable Mom

188   *White Mamba*
By E. R. Catalano of Zoe vs. The Universe

194   *I Tried to Be the Perfect Mom Friend but My Butt Got in the Way*
By Kim Bongiorno of Let Me Start By Saying

199   *Diets, Death, and Shit*
By Alyson Herzig of The Shitastrophy

205   *Volunteering Makes Me Antsy*
By Susanne Kerns of The Dusty Parachute

211   *Getting Burned By Old Flames*
By Robyn Welling of Hollow Tree Ventures

216   *I Just Want Perfect Boobs*
By Jen Mann of People I Want to Punch in the Throat

224   *Notes from the Editor*

224   *Other Books Available*

INTRODUCTION

Welcome to Book Four of the I Just Want to Pee Alone series! When I had the idea to start an anthology series four years ago, I had no idea that it would catch on the way it has. I thought it would be a fun way to build a tribe of like-minded writers and help shine a light on their hilarious work and maybe our moms would buy a copy. I'm so grateful that so many readers have embraced this series and encouraged us to keep going.

If you've read this entire series, then you know that in the past we've done motherhood and relationships with the opposite sex and then back to motherhood. This time we wanted to try something new again.

This time it's the cult of perfection. As women we're constantly inundated with "helpful" and "ah-may-zing" tips to do it all and be it all. We're told to lean in, find a balance, be a great mom and a hot wife, cook like a chef, clean like a maid, and help our preschooler build a bust of George Washington out of papier mâché by Friday. We're told to speak up, but not too loudly or with profanity—a lady never raises her voice or drops f-bombs—and smile more!

Every woman I know has tried something to be more perfect, whether it's the hot new diet, the crazy fabulous workout everyone is doing, steaming, waxing, plucking, and buffing our nether regions, disfiguring our bodies with high heels and girdles, learning to pole dance, cooking classes with master chefs, competitive crafting, living mindfully, or clearing the clutter by thanking our ratty underwear for their service before we toss them.

This is a book about 37 women's paths to try and be perfect. Don't worry. Very few of them actually succeeded. If they succeeded, they didn't make it into the book. I really didn't want to hear success stories—UNLESS they succeeded in a hilarious way. ("Sure, I bleached my asshole, but in the end I realized I liked the way I felt with a bleached asshole.") What I really want to focus on were the times they tried to be perfect and it completely backfired in a hilarious (and usually cringe-worthy) way. ("Since I bleached my asshole, I have never been able to sit in a chair properly without my inflatable donut.")

This book is to let you know that you're not alone. We're not laughing at you, we're laughing with you.

Jen Mann
People I Want to Punch in the Throat

The Breast Pump Corporate Travel Log
By Kim Forde
The Fordeville Diaries

If I'm being honest, I excel at very few things overall. While I don't fail all of the time, I've rarely risen to the top of my class or separated myself from the pack. My life is really a series of B+ level performances. Could I do better? Sure. Do I bust my ass to be the very best? Meh.

And then, every once in a while, I unexpectedly stumble upon something that I happen to do really well. Like clipping PTO box tops or finding the most flattering photo filter on Instagram.

You know what else I never expected to be particularly good at? Pumping breast milk. Because, when you're young, you don't aspire to play a starring role in *Great Lactators of Our Time*. You don't dream about your milk output and how it can surpass your wildest expectations.

Sometimes, gifts are just bestowed upon us.

In true self-sabotaging fashion, I hated the very thing I was so good at. I never really minded the breastfeeding itself (beyond the initial pain and how-does-this-work factor). But if you've ever spent any time at all pumping, I don't have to tell you that there is really nothing less fabulous than being topless and hooked up to a machine during the few minutes you are not tethered to a newborn each day.

However, if you're lucky/talented like me, you're what they call an overproducer. And with this talent comes great responsibility.

I learned this as I returned to work full-time when my child was three months old.

Several times during each work day, I'd head over to the pumping room, hauling my distinctly unstylish black bag over my shoulder. You know the one. You've seen it. The one that screams, "I know this bag is supposed to be discreet and incognito, but clearly it's a breast pump. It means I'm never more than three hours away from being topless with plastic accessories hanging off of my body. And, you'll be totally fucking sorry if you mistake this black bag for your black bag when leaving the office tonight."

We were lucky to have dedicated pumping rooms in my workplace, for sure. I emailed on my Blackberry and even fielded phone calls, all to the *whirrrrr* of the pump. I'd will my body to produce a set amount of ounces of breast milk at each session, knowing what I needed to sustain my baby each day while I was working. I knew one side produced more than the other. I knew when I was slightly dehydrated. I knew how long it would take, down to the minute. *Whirrrrr* went the pump. Two or three times every day. Nights. Weekends. *Whirrrrr.*

My freezer at home became a point of pride. While most moms would bask in self-congratulatory praise over Pinteresting made-ahead meals stacked high, mine overflowed with bags of frozen breast milk. Piles and piles of them. *Why, look at that stash. How many ounces could I save? And who put a bag of vegetables in here? There is simply no room. I am overproducing and we will not waste a single drop.* I started to wonder if we'd end up donating some of it just to make room for actual adult human food.

All of this was well and good in the land of the lactating, until about two weeks after I returned to work and my boss informed me I'd need to travel for a meeting. To London. For a week.

I'm sure that many companies have come a long way in the last nine years, but back in the Corporate Breastfeeding Support Triassic Period of 2007, how the hell was this going to work? Would my place of employment be providing a residential-sized freezer in my hotel room, along with medical-grade dry ice and international shipping costs to get the liquid gold back home? They say the key to negotiations is always starting big.

My boss was a mother herself. I looked deep into her eyes for some flicker of empathy, but I could see that the figure-it-out approach was really the only one on the table. Ah, the pre-*Lean In* workplace era!

Giving up pumping was not an option, not on such short notice. Surely my body would spontaneously combust, and I had already maxed out all of my days off for the next 412 years while birthing a human. Plus, without pumping, what would I excel at? The options were shamefully few.

The working mother pressure/guilt got inside of my head. Surely, women can do it all! Or at least be forced to try.

I had to press on. Or pump on.

And, so, I needed a plan for the perfect pumping regimen overseas. I had so many questions.

- Will an electrical voltage adapter work on a pump?
- Will I have to pump on Eastern time to keep my body on the same schedule, bringing my total hours of sleep from few to zero?
- Will the *whirrrrr* of the pump take on a British accent while I'm there?
- What will I do with all of the milk?
- Why the fuck did I agree to any of this?
- Shouldn't I stop cursing so much now that I am a mother?
- Why did they all have to die at the end of *Lost*?
- WHAT ABOUT THE FUCKING FLIGHT?

Oh dear God, the flight. I am a crappy flier under the most ideal conditions. Add in leaving a new baby at home and figuring out international in-flight pumping, and I was a basket case.

But with very little notice and choice, off I went.

I feared many elements of this situation, but here's one I hadn't considered for a single moment: That the TSA would give me a hard time in the security line over the bag containing my pump that, in retrospect, probably resembled an amateur bomb more than a little on an X-ray machine. I could've blamed Medela, but I bet this didn't really come up at their R&D department meetings: "How can we ensure the pump doesn't get confused with an instrument of terrorism?"

I also hadn't really thought about how the TSA would want to, say, disassemble my pump while I stood by, incredulous and terrified at the prospect of it being confiscated. A non-functioning pump would be game over for this trip and, possibly, my job. All because I was on the cusp of being put on the No Fly List for trying to express breast milk over international waters.

After what seemed like a mental eternity, my pump was handed back to me, about eighty-five percent intact. At this point, I had no choice but to dig very deep in my soul and draw from life experiences that could be helpful in reassembling this fucking instrument of life at the gate with six minutes until boarding—like perhaps resurrecting The Ghost of IKEA Projects Past. YESSSSS. I could summon my strength from the many torturous Swedish direction manuals I'd survived. I envisioned the unhelpful-yet-seemingly-critical-and-ever-present free-floating screw in space graphic. And I knew what had to be done to put my FuuuuckenPuuuump (note to IKEA: idea for future brand name—call me) back together.

Did I mention that I'm not a great flier?

But at least that entire drama had taken my mind off of the pressing issue of pumping in-flight. I'm not a math savant, but I figured out early on that seven hours in the air was at least twice as many as my body was used to tolerating between pumping sessions. I had gone through all of the possible scenarios in advance with my husband, who basically served as Project Manager for my Prime Meridian Milk Crisis. In theory, I had the option to pump in my seat, but I knew I couldn't do it. My only other choice at 35,000 feet was a restroom pumping session.

It's worth underscoring at this point that nothing amplifies a woman's germaphobic tendencies more than having a newborn. I'd like to also mention that aircraft restrooms, in my mind, rank among the most disgusting public spaces on Earth. I have rendered myself into an in-flight camel many a time just to avoid entering that claustrophobic pit of filth. And so the visual of me proceeding to the two foot by two foot plague cubicle with my stylish black bag over my shoulder should tell you that I was dying five million deaths.

I mentally psyched myself up for what had to be done in the name of avoiding mastitis, and got my mission underway.

Now, under normal circumstances, you'd have to punch me clear in the skull before I'd agree to dump a full container of pumped milk down the sink. However, the thought of producing my child's food in a foul airplane bathroom mitigated any of that hesitation. That, and the expense of global shipping of bodily fluids. This act was purely to keep my supply up and prevent any breast tissue from exploding out of my body that would necessitate a visit to a British clinic. Down the drain the liquid gold would go.

But not before, at the single most inopportune time possible, the plane encountered moderate to heavy turbulence as I was fully compromised. My first thought was, of course, my usual fear of certain impending death. This was followed very closely by my absolute and total refusal to leave the disgusting bathroom to return to my seat, because there was no fucking way in hell I was going to start this whole traumatic process over again three minutes later when we were back to smooth sailing.

And so, despite the *ding-ding* of the seat belt indicator, I stayed put. *Whirrrrr* went the pump. Well, *whi-i-ir*, since it was operating on a battery pack, per my Project Manager/spouse's plan.

Ding-ding again, complete with the captain's announcement, in his best we're-not-going-to-die voice.

Nope. I was not leaving. If my body cooperated, I only needed about six more minutes (which, incidentally, equals fourteen hours and thirty-nine minutes in Disgusted Time).

A knock on the door from the friendly skies.

"Ma'am. I must insist you return to your seat. The captain has indicated the seat belts fastened sign."

Her voice was lovely and British and proper.

"Uhhhhh, I just need a minute here."

My voice was jittery and pissy and American.

A more insistent knock.

"Ma'am, I'm afraid not. You must return to your seat NOW."

Were we really in danger? I didn't know. I was too busy trying to pry the suction seal of the pump off of me and put my fucking shirt back on.

KNOCK, KNOCK, KNOCK.

"MA'AM. We are going to have to break down this door if you don't open it right away."

"No, wait, please! Can you just let me get my shirt back on?"

"EXCUSE ME, MA'AM?"

Oh, fuck. This woman probably thought I was a drug mule or some crazy shit. In I went with my black bag, which had already been flagged and disassembled by the TSA, and now I refused to come out. And I wasn't fully clothed. Perfect. I was about to become the "Based on a true story" reference in a Liam Neeson movie.

I stepped out, shirt buttons askew, probably the only person in the history of aviation to have this problem without the benefit of Mile High Club membership. I was sweaty and out of sorts, and I'm sure this very primped flight attendant thought I had several bags of heroin stashed in my nether regions.

When I arrived in London, I was sincerely stunned and grateful not to be greeted by an Interpol brigade on the runway. But I failed to realize that my lactation problems were just beginning.

My first morning in the London office, I discreetly approached the lovely executive assistant who was coordinating our meeting. I gestured to my black bag, which still had three large "TSA INSPECTED" stickers on it, and asked her where I might be able to pump in the building during my five-day stay.

Her lovely smile was betrayed by a look of utter confusion. She didn't seem to follow my line of questioning. She appeared to be of child-bearing age but had no idea how to address my problem.

And then it hit me.

Ohhhhhhh. Because other civilized countries let women stay home for more than five minutes after having a baby…

It was coming to me in waves.

They don't have to pump in the workplace very much because they can do that on a maternity leave that's longer than their labor and delivery. Their kids are eating steaks by the time the government makes them return to work.

So, there's nowhere to pump.

For the next five days.

OMG, I miss the airplane bathroom and my drug mule alter ego problem.

The lovely assistant finally realized what I needed and, trying to be helpful, she kindly directed me to a janitorial closet without a lock.

"Will this do?"

"Surrrrrrrre."

Hey, it was on terra firma and without the TSA's involvement. I was sure I could handle the infrequent knocks from a custodian who needed his supplies.

The fifteen men seated around the conference room table that week are probably still wondering what ever happened to that American female with the black bag who would disappear from their urgent quarterly meeting every three hours for exactly twenty-six minutes. She must have had a drug problem. Poor girl.

But, dutifully, I reported to my janitorial suite for my shifts. *Wh-i—i-i-i-ir-r-rrr* went my pump on its dying battery pack. Stashes and supply levels were maintained, only to be transported from the dark mop closet to the employee restroom, where I poured the contents down the sink—usually in full view of at least three people I'd never met before—while trying to make awkward small talk.

By day three, the routine was exhausting me but I felt the end was in sight. Until we were surprised with a team-building off-site activity day. At a country club.

Ohfortheloveofallthatisholy.

In my two decades of professional office life, I encountered precisely zero colleagues who enjoyed and found value in team-building activities. Let's call a spade a spade: These are exercises in humiliation and shame, designed to make you prove how much you want your job, fake just how collegial you can be, and demonstrate how far out of your comfort zone you're willing to go—all while acting like it's totally fucking normal to casually catch a falling co-worker in an act of trust, or to perform an original karaoke piece based on not-so-funny office buzz words and corporate inside jokes. Please.

This particular team-building day was not the karaoke kind, which was immediately evident upon arriving in the grand circular driveway of its location. I'm not a country club gal generally, but I knew enough to realize that this particular place was in a whole other stratosphere of status, wealth and privilege. Why, it was like being transported to the set of a Merchant Ivory film. Everyone on the premises bore a distinct resemblance to Jeremy Irons.

And there I was, black bag over my shoulder, ready to get topless and down to business.

I would bet ten million dollars (or whatever the equivalent in British Pounds is with today's exchange rate) that I was about to be the only woman to take off her shirt on this property in the history of forever.

Clearly this establishment was old-school, but I didn't really understand the magnitude of the situation until my only female colleague and I were politely informed that this is typically a gentleman's club and so there isn't a proper ladies' room.

Excuse me?

We were to use the singular "guest loo" near the coat check. Oh, shit. My mind was racing. Where the fuck would my black bag and I go to *whirrrrr* and produce without causing an international incident? Was I about to single-handedly break down diplomatic relations between the US and UK in one pumping session? I had never missed a custodial closet so much in my life and was suddenly wistful about my days pumping next to the mop bucket. Oh wait, was that also nostalgia I was feeling for the vile in-flight bathroom? Yes. Yes, it was.

I don't really know how I got through the day—I hear people can black out in times of trauma. I do remember persistent banging on the guest loo door from the grounds manager (I think his name was Jeeves), who made the flight attendant of five days prior seem like Mary Poppins. I managed not to be escorted out for suspicious activity only by cutting my session short. This led to my blouse's buttons visibly straining to stay intact. All while I was knee/breast deep in team-building hell, as Kenneth Branagh lookalikes served us tea.

I had to wonder how much more I could do in the name of lactation.

Sometimes, it's hard to articulate how motherhood will make you do anything for your child. It's not always a tangible feeling. Other times, it's crystal fucking clear when you're hauling a black bag across international borders, approaching No Fly status and risking every remaining shred of your dignity, five time zones away from home. All because you're an overproducer.

KIM FORDE writes about the art of domestic failure on her blog, The Fordeville Diaries. A former Manhattan resident, she is now a secret suburban convert at home with three young kids. Kim has appeared in the NYC production of "Listen to Your Mother," and has written for The Huffington Post *and Scary Mommy. She was twice named a Humor Voice of the Year by BlogHer and contributed to several humor anthologies, including* I Still Just Want to Pee Alone, I Just Want to Be Alone, You Have Lipstick on Your Teeth, *and* I Just Want to Pee Alone. *When not busy managing her Starbucks addiction and healthy fear of craft stores, she can often be found on archaeological digs in her own minivan. She also may spend more time on social media than she is prepared to admit.*

How To Find The Perfect Swimsuit
By Wendi Aarons

Step 1: Ascertain Your Body Type!

Ascertain is a fancy way of saying "figure shit out," and it's key to know what shape your body is. This is easily accomplished by slowly walking past a downtown construction site. If the no-necked men scream, "Hey, fat ass!" at you, then you know you're "pear-shaped." If they scream, "Yo, where ya boobies at, Flatima?" you're "small-busted." And getting hit in the head by a glob of wet cement simply means you're "Louie Anderson-esque" and the gentlemen would appreciate you enjoying the beach in a burqa or small circus tent. On to Step Two!

Step 2: One Piece or a Two Piece?

How much do you want to reveal? If your answer is "less than a married politician when asked what he was doing with that male hustler behind the bushes in the park at midnight," a one-piece suit is what you need. But if you're instead the type of person who regularly posts pictures of her toenails and rashes on Instagram, get yourself a rockin' bikini, baby! Who cares if it feels weird to show off your bare stomach? As any Real Housewife or man wearing a trench coat at the movies can tell you, there's *no such thing* as overexposure. Even if said overexposure means the losers down at the municipal pool now know you have a Whitesnake tattoo on your coccyx. Whatever.

Step 3: Don't Shop Online

While it may be tempting to have a new swimsuit sent right to your door, you *must* resist the lure of online shopping. You see, recent medical studies show that the abject humiliation and self-loathing one feels while standing under the harsh fluorescent lights of a public dressing room is crucial to a woman's health. Because it is this same humiliation and self-loathing that keeps women safe from harm at the beach. After all, does an unconfident woman ever jump into the deep end or body surf? Does she see a shark in the water and decide to fist fight it? Does she eat raw clams? No, she does not. Rather, she hides her thighs under a beach towel and lives until she's motherfucking ninety years old.

Step 4: Ask the Experts!
Walking into a store's swimwear department can be overwhelming. Therefore, one must immediately enlist the help of a professional. Said professional will always be named "Madison" or "Jenna" and they are always found leaning against the cash register, gossiping about their new assistant manager who's like, so majorly tasty but still kind of a dick, you know? Simply tell Madison/Jenna what body type you are (refer to Step One) and they'll quickly bring you armfuls of suits to try on in the dressing room. Then they'll be happy to give you their expert opinion on which one looks the best. How easy is that?

Note: If Madison/Jenna is under the age of thirty, their expert opinion will include eyerolls and a text sent to their friend over in Juniors Shoes that says, "Kill me hard f I ever become a dum housewif who wears fugly skirtinis LOL LOL LOL" and/or a GIF of a puking cat.

Note: If Madison/Jennifer is over the age of thirty, your new suit will cost two hundred dollars.

Step 5: Don't Believe In Miracles!
Due to recent advances in solar microtechnology, many swimsuit brands out there now claim their revolutionary material will make you "shrink two sizes" or "flatten your tummy." These suits are usually named "The Wonder Suit," "The Magic Suit," "The MuffinTop Terminator," or the "Fuck Off, Fat!" but unfortunately, most of them actually make you look like a boa constrictor that just swallowed a feral hog. Yikes!

For that reason, it's crucial to remember that even though a miracle suit may sound good, there's just no way a swimsuit can solve your many and vast figure flaws. Unless, of course, the face of Jesus suddenly appears on it. Your love handles will probably be a little less noticeable then because the Messiah is a total focus-puller.

Step 6: Take the Plunge!
After buying your new suit, there's just one more thing to do to make sure it's the perfect choice. Simply find a body of water, jump in and then immediately stand up. Now carefully look at yourself: is the top sagging down to your waist, therefore baring your boobs and making you look like a cast member from *Periomenopausal Girls Gone Wild*? Has the bottom inched itself up into a painful DIY thong? Is water pouring out of it like you're the Unsinkable Molly Brown and it's the goddamn one-piece *Titanic*? If the answer is "No," then congratulations! You've found the right swimsuit. But if the answer is "Yes," then sorry, but you'll need to go back to Step One and start over, friend.

Or just sit inside your house eating tubs of Cool Whip until September. That works, too.

WENDI AARONS is an award-winning humor writer and blogger who lives in Austin, Texas with her husband and two sons. Her humor has been seen at McSweeneys, US Weekly *Fashion Police, Someecards, AlphaMom, LifetimeTV,* The Wall Street Journal, The New York Times, *BlogHer, andNickMom. She was one of the creators of the much-lauded political parody Twitter feed @paulryangoslingand the three-time director of Listen to Your Mother Austin. Her blog wendiaarons.com was named "Editors Choice Funniest Mom Blog" by Parents Magazine, and she is a sought-after speaker on humor.*

Easy Breezy Brunch—A Search For The Perfect Mother's Day
By Jennifer Lizza
Outsmarted Mommy

I have a confession to make. I have always been someone with expectations that never quite match my reality. Some people might call me a romantic, or an optimist, perhaps even a dreamer, while others just call me an idiot. Call me what you will but in all the years of my expectations not becoming my reality I have never let go of the idea that everything I do in life is going to turn out awesome. Fast forward to the day I became a mother.

Expectation: My hair and makeup would remain perfect throughout labor so that we could get one perfect photo of the three of us immediately following the delivery of our adorable baby.

Reality: After sweating, crying, and pooping more times than I would like to admit during delivery, I'm pretty sure I looked like I had just survived the sinking of the Titanic. Oh and my adorable son looked like he had just been in a boxing match that he didn't win. "Everyone say cheese!"

After our oldest son was born I started to realize that many of my expectations on motherhood were not in fact going to be my reality. Who are all these women in the magazines holding new babies anyway? They look well rested. They are showered and they are always smiling. Listen I am not an expert by any means but I know enough to call bullshit when I see it.

I spent the first six months of new motherhood utterly exhausted. I didn't always have time to shower and my house? Let's just say there were days even the dog seemed to be worried. Just when I started to have the whole motherhood thing down we welcomed our second son. Throwing another kid into the mix of our family actually went much smoother than I had expected, but it was still like throwing feathers into a fan. Shit. Everywhere.

To be perfectly honest I dreamed about being a mother for as long as I could remember and here I was a mother of two beautiful boys.

Then it hit me. I have boys. Mother's Day is going to be awesome!

Expectation: The boys will make breakfast with my husband every year. They will bring it to me in bed where I will still be peacefully sleeping at nine o'clock. There will be flowers and adorable homemade cards. They will surprise me with a spa day and birds will sing.

Reality: We will rush around like maniacs in the morning so that we can visit my mother-in-law for brunch. We will have to stop for flowers on the way. Oh, and cards. Crap we forgot cards. We will then rush home with two exhausted kids, beg them to nap for two unsuccessful hours, and then rush off again to see my mother and grandmother for dinner.

OK, so I have another confession to make: I really started to dislike Mother's Day. Don't get me wrong I want to see all of the women in my life who mean so much to me, but my expectation of Mother's Day had a lot more relaxing and a lot less running around. I wanted a perfect Mother's Day.

Then it happened, the Mother's Day that changed it all. We were doing our usual brunch routine with my in-laws but instead of going to their house we were going to a fancy restaurant. My husband offered to take care of getting the kids ready so that I could get ready in peace. Well all right! This was looking like a Mother's Day I could get on board with. I decided I was going to get dressed up. I had spent two weeks in Yoga Pants, zero makeup, and a ponytail.

I blow dried my hair, put on makeup and stood in my closet looking for the perfect outfit. I wanted something that said classy, stylish mom. I had to dig DEEP in the back but I found something. I decided on a red and white skirt. It was fitted at the waist and pleated at the bottom. I went with a plain white button down on top and nude heels. Yes I even broke out the heels. My feet weren't quite sure what was going on at first, but they got on board after the first couple steps. When I walked downstairs my older son and my husband told me how nice I looked. The baby smiled. Good enough. I was beaming. It was Mother's Day and I was going to enjoy every minute of it. This day was going to be perfect. I could feel it.

We arrived at the restaurant, pulled up to the valet and the attendant opened my door. Hmm this must be what all the mothers in Beverly Hills feel like. The boys looked adorable and my husband cleaned up pretty nicely if I do say so myself. We walked into the big room with crystal chandeliers and we sat at the table. It was a buffet brunch. My husband offered to go up to make the boys their plates. I think I started to hear birds singing. When he got up the baby started to act up a little so I took him out of his seat and he stood on my lap. I sang him a song and he wiggled and danced. When my husband got back with plates piled with pancakes, eggs, bacon, donuts, fruit, bagels, and crumb cake the baby happily sat back in his seat. And I realized this is why I normally make their plates.

I proceeded to get up and make my plate. As I walked around the room looking at all the amazing choices I couldn't help but smile. I felt good. I mean I felt really good. You know that feeling you get every once in a blue moon when all the planets align? When your hair comes out just right, your clothes actually fit, your kids are behaving like little angels and all seems right in the world? I was having an *all feels right in the world kind of day*. I might have even noticed a few glances, perhaps even a few smiles from people in the room. Mama's still got it, baby. I sat down and enjoyed my mimosa. I had a HOT cup of coffee and an omelet made just for me. This was the Mother's Day I had always dreamed of. It was heaven. It was perfect!

When we were finished with our meal my older son decided he had to use the bathroom. I volunteered to take him. We walked across the ballroom together and I couldn't help but flashback to all those perfectly showered, smiling mothers in the magazines. This was the closest I had ever felt to them. When we got into the bathroom we both went and then proceeded to wash our hands. As I finished I happened to turn around to look at myself in the mirror and that's when it happened. That's when I saw something out of the corner of my eye that didn't seem quite right. So I spun around again and suddenly I realized my reality was crashing into my expectations and knocking them clear out of the room AGAIN.

"Oh my God. Oh my God. OH MY GOD!!!! SHIT! SHIT! SHIT!"

"Mommy you said a bad word what's the matter?"

"Oh my GOD!! SHIT!"

"Um mom?"

"Yes honey. I know I said a bad word and I'm sorry. SHIT!"

"No. I can um. I can see your butt."

"OH MY GOD I KNOW!!!!"

Yes there I stood in all my classy mom glory with a giant tear in the seam of my skirt. Not a little tear. I'm talking a big giant catch the wind in your ass; give everyone a full moon at brunch tear. Tear is probably the wrong word. It was a hole. A big flipping hole and I had bent over at the omelet station! OK it wasn't a hole. The entire back of my skirt was gone. SHIT! It was directly on my ass cheek. It was not the best day to have chosen a thong. Nope. Not. At. All. I was panicking. I didn't have my cell phone with me and I had no idea how I was going to walk back into the ballroom like this. I was wearing a piece of Swiss cheese.

"OH MY GOD people weren't smiling at me. They were smiling at my bare ass.

OH MY GOD I just showed my ass to over 200 people. How did this happen?!"

"I don't know mommy. Maybe you should cover your butt with toilet paper?"

"I can't walk into a ballroom with toilet paper covering my butt honey."

"Yeah. OK. So I guess we just go back in with your butt out?"

"OH MY GOD!!! SHIT!"

I realized at that moment that my skirt must have ripped while I was holding the baby on my lap. He was twisting and turning while standing on my legs and that's when it must have happened. It happened so long ago. How did my husband not notice? How did my mother in law not notice? Oh my God my mother in-law. This should go over well. They should really serve mimosas in the bathroom.

At that moment I looked at my son and he looked at me and we started laughing. We laughed so hard that we cried. His face was red from laughing. My face was red from laughing. A woman walked into the bathroom and said "Oh I must have missed a really good joke."

"No. My mom's butt is showing and the whole restaurant saw it." Cue an eye roll from her and more laughter from us.

Finally I realized we couldn't stay in the bathroom for the rest of brunch so we made a plan. I was going to turn my skirt so that the rip was no longer smack in the middle of my ass and he was going to run into the ballroom and tell my husband what happened and that it was time to get the check. Yes, I was counting on a five year old to pull the emergency parachute for me. I had great faith in him. I had no choice.

We left the bathroom and I stood up against a wall in the lobby. My son was on a mission.

"Hey Mom?"

"Yeah, buddy?"

"I love you!"

"I love you too. Now hurry up and get Daddy."

He gave me the thumbs up as he ran to my rescue. Five minutes passed. Ten minutes. Twenty minutes.

OH COME ON PEOPLE!!!! I was starting to sweat, which was kind of weird since I had a nice cool breeze through the vent that used to be my skirt.

Finally my husband came out in a panic.

"What's the matter? You got sick in the bathroom? You shit yourself?"

"What? No! My skirt ripped and my ass has been hanging out for a better portion of this brunch. I said shit one thousand times. Can we focus on the real issue? I'm practically nude at brunch. Don't laugh. You can laugh when we get in the car. For now just get the check and let's get out of here. Wait, you thought I shit myself and it took you twenty minutes to come out here?"

"Honey, not now. You are practically nude—let's focus." He paid the check. He told his entire family that my skirt had ripped and they all proceeded to come out of brunch laughing.

We got into the car and we laughed so hard we had tears rolling down our faces. It was at that moment that I realized my expectations on motherhood were exhausting. My reality on the other hand was hilarious. The laugh I shared with my son that day was one of the best Mother's Days I have ever had. A perfect Mother's Day will never be in the cards for me. After all I walked around a giant ballroom with my entire ass hanging out. Perfection is not mine to own. Pants on the other hand sound like a smart purchase, big, baggy pants.

JENNIFER LIZZA is a wife, mom, writer, runner, sleep enthusiast, and blogger at Outsmarted Mommy. Her two boys outsmart her daily, although in her defense it could be the lack of sleep. When she's not cracking people up on Twitter she can be found making them cry with her sentimental writing online in The Huffington Post, Club Mid, Scary Mommy, Today Parents, Mamapedia, *and* What The Flicka? *Her kids are not the least bit impressed; they just want to know what's for dinner. Jennifer and her firefighting husband call New Jersey home and when she is not writing, running or daydreaming about a nap you can often find her out with her family eating pizza and ice cream. Follow their journey on Facebook and Instagram and come laugh and cry with her at outsmartedmommy.com.*

Here Comes the Bride(smaid)

By Janel Mills

649.133: Girls, the Care and Maintenance Of.

If you had asked me a year ago if I had ever been a bridesmaid, I would have said, "No. The only wedding I've ever been in was my own." Then I would have stared blankly off into space, with this kind of sad, mournful look on my face, making our whole interaction feel kind of awkward and uncomfortable. After the silent weeping started and you finally resorted to faking a very important phone call to escape our disaster of a conversation, you'd probably wonder, "Wow, how did someone so remarkably stable manage to never be asked to stand up in a wedding?"

Well, shit, I don't know. There are probably a couple of reasons. First, I don't have a ton of female family members. No sisters, and all of my girl cousins were either much older or much younger than me. Second, and this is probably the bigger factor, girls kind of freak me out. My close friends in high school and college were guys, and their girlfriends sure as hell weren't asking *me* to be in their wedding. But I just assumed at some point, *somebody* would ask me to be in their wedding. I mean, that happens to every girl, right? Nobody goes through life without being important enough to someone to stand up with them on the most important day of their life, right? *Right*?!

I held fast to this belief that one day, it would happen for me. In the meantime, I continued attending everyone else's wedding, but as a lowly guest. I always made sure to wear a really bitchin' dress (to show other potential brides that I was obviously high-quality bridesmaid material). I looked on happily at the bridesmaids sashaying down the aisle, but in my head I would just seethe at that smug bitch wearing the sea foam green, mermaid-cut dress because THAT SHOULD BE ME, GODDAMMIT. I mean, *put me in, coach!*

As I entered my thirties and realized that the clock was ticking on my window of opportunity to wear shitty dresses and plan bomb-ass showers, I started getting desperate. Whenever I made a new girlfriend, I was unusually helpful and encouraging in the dating department. If things looked good, I would move it to Phase Two. "You know, if you and Steve ever get married, I should be in the wedding! You know, since I was the one that got you guys hooked up in the first place. Hahahahahaha!" Kidding, not kidding. Planting the seed.

But all this got me was a half-hearted, "Yeah, hahahaha!" and then an invitation in the mail a few years later, letting me know where to show up to watch the women who actually made the cut. Whomp whomp.

As I coasted into my mid-thirties, still dress-less, I started to accept the idea that it wasn't going to happen for me. "That's OK," I told myself as I inhaled a bag of chips while watching cat videos at work. "It's not a big deal. I bet lots of women don't get to be in weddings. Besides, it's their loss, because I would be *such* a kick-ass bridesmaid."

Then, miracle of miracles, the impossible happened: my work BFF met a guy, started dating him for awhile, and then went and got fucking engaged. This, in and of itself, was a miracle. Not because there's anything wrong with her, mind you; quite the opposite. She's such a shining, sparkling unicorn of a woman that it's amazing that there was someone in the metropolitan area worthy of marrying her. But, the even bigger miracle:

She asked me to be a bridesmaid in her wedding.

I played it cool on the outside (sort of) while she explained some of the details of the wedding, but on the inside, my brain started playing every single party song I had ever heard during my lifetime, all at once. She's talking about ordering my dress, and I'm just smiling and nodding while meanwhile Montell Jordan's singing *This is How We Do It* in my head. I couldn't even believe it. I was going to be a bridesmaid, and not just that—I was going to be the BEST bridesmaid. I would win at it. I would overachieve the *fuck* out of this honor.

And overachieve I did. I showed up to bridesmaid work days to help get centerpieces ready and do other arts and crafts bullshit with a good attitude and snacks and drinks! I ordered my bridesmaid dress immediately, earning me bonus points when the maid of honor dragged her feet and ended up having to wait months for her size to come back in stock. My friend, the bride, even asked me to pick out and order her cupcakes and wedding cake from the local supermarket chain, because she doesn't give a shit about wedding details like that. Not only did I figure out which location had the best decorator, I sent pictures to my friend (the bride), drove to the store three different times, and called twice to confirm and make sure the order was correct.

I was so good at bridesmaiding it *hurt*.

Then one day, I got an email from the maid of honor about the bachelorette party. Here's the itinerary she sent:

3:00 pm: Mani/pedis at the local day spa

5:00 pm: Dinner

7:00 pm: Drinks on the town

OK, dinner—I got that. I'm good at eating, I eat like every goddamn day, so I've got that part in the bag. Drinks on the town— easy. I don't drink, so that's where I get to overachieve by being the designated driver. Perfect. But that first part? Shit. This is where my early history comes back to bite me in the ass. I've never had my nails done professionally. Not for prom, not for my wedding, not for fun. I've successfully dodged all invitations to go with a bunch of women to do this, because it seems really scary and full of those unspoken girl rules that I'll inevitably not know about and then screw up and get really embarrassed. And a *pedicure?!* Someone touching my feet while I just sit there and awkwardly wait for them to finish? Uh uh. That's fucking weird.

My friend, the bride, called me. "Did you get Naysha's email?"

"Yeah, I did. Already wrote the date on the calendar!"

"Yay! I can't wait, I haven't had a pedicure in so long."

"Yeeeeeahhhhhhhhh, about that. Like, do I *have* to get a pedicure?"

"What do you mean? Why wouldn't you want to get a pedicure?"

"Because the idea of someone touching my feet just kind of freaks me out."

"Well, I mean, you don't *have* to get a pedicure. You could just hang out while we get one, but you're going to be the only person not getting a pedicure, probably, and it might be boring waiting for us to finish…"

I could hear the slide-whistle sound of all the Bridesmaid Points I had accumulated over the past few months slowly draining away as my friend's voice trailed off. Nope. There was no way I was going out like that. I hung up, and spent the next few days mentally preparing myself to face the last feminine frontier I had yet to face as a woman: the mani/pedi.

So, we go to the day spa, and the first thing I realize is that I have no idea how this works. Everyone else seemed to already know what to do, so I did what I always do when encountering a new girl experience: I just floated along and pretended to be doing what everyone else was doing. Everyone seemed to be looking at nail polish, so I did that. They have entire walls dedicated to nail polish bottles! Amazing! Since everyone else seemed to be admiring the colors, I did the same thing. But then everyone kind of drifted away to the great big chairs, and I suddenly realized *oh fuck*, I was supposed to be picking a color. Everyone had a nail polish bottle in their hands! I grabbed a bottle of blue nail polish (because one time my student assistant at work told me my nails looked cool when I came to work with blue nail polish from the weekend's manicure from my four-year-old) and sat down in the biggest goddamn chair I've ever seen in my entire life. I had to hoist myself up into the chair like I was mounting a horse, carefully avoiding the enormous foot bucket attached to the front of the chair. But crisis averted! I was in the chair, with my nail polish.

The woman who would very shortly be mortified at the thought of touching my weird feet smiled at me, and then reached her hand out for the nail polish I was holding. She looked at it, frowned, and said, "Um, not this bottle." (Oh, at this point I should probably mention that this lady didn't seem to speak a whole lot of English, and the English she did speak was heavily accented. This is critical, because I am completely unable to understand any accents outside of

Fargo-esque Midwestern English. Seriously—I can't even understand people speaking English with a British accent. I tried watching *Absolutely Fabulous* with my friends in college, and all I could gather from it was the old white ladies with big hair shouting "Daaaaaaahling" and drinking straight from the wine bottle. They also smoked a lot. Suffice it to say that anything beyond a Canadian lilt sounds like mouth noise to me. So now I am in a completely new social situation, this poor woman is trying to tell me something is wrong with the nail polish I chose at random, and I have to figure out what I did wrong without sounding like a racist bougie moron when I talk to her.)

The bridesmaid next to me said, "Oh yeah, you can't use that bottle. You have to choose one from the *other* rack." There were literally just two big-ass racks of nail polish, with no labels or signage explaining the difference. Just as I suspected—I had fallen into some kind of *Mean Girls*-esque trap set up by the salon, meant to expose the women who have never had a pedicure before. So I walked over to the rack, put the nail polish back, and grabbed a bottle from the other rack. I have no fucking clue to this day what the difference was between those two bottles, and I don't really care. The foot lady seemed happy, and that was good enough for me.

It was right after I mounted my chair again and bent down to slip off my shoes when I noticed *I didn't shave my legs*. But I didn't think this was a big deal, because she's just going to be working on my feet, right? Oh nooooooooooooooooo, incorrect! Because apparently the thing that is just sooooo cooooooooooooooooooooool about pedicures is that they put this cold ultrasound goo on your feet and calves, and then they fucking rub their hands up and down your legs like they're trying to sell them in an infomercial. This is supposed to feel good and not be embarrassing at all to have a woman sit below you on a stool at your feet while you try to remember how many days it's been since you shaved, and whether or not this poor woman will talk about your prickly legs in the back room when you leave, or wait until she gets home to dry heave. Or maybe she'll just try to emotionally block the memory of your hairy legs completely from her mind, until she sees you one day walking down the street and then it all comes flooding back and she *pretends* things are fine, but really THEY ARE NOT and she calmly walks back to her car and just sobs uncontrollably over the haunting memory of your unshaven calves until she can't cry anymore.

So yeah, I was feeling pretty good about how things were unfolding.

During the course of the whole foot washing and massaging portion of the pedicure, it was painfully obvious to my poor technician that I had no fucking clue what was happening. I know this is true because she was constantly tapping my feet to get me to do what she wanted, similar to how you would tap on a horse's foot to get him to lift it up. At first I thought it was part of the procedure, like she was checking my reflexes or curious about whether these were actually my feet or if they were some kind of practical joke feet made out of rubber or that special effects silicone they use to make movie monsters. Then I looked at her and she was giving me that smile I give my kids when I'm trying to be patient with them, but I'm actually trying to figure out exactly how dumb they really are. So I lifted my foot up, and then she tapped my other foot, and I put that foot down into the water. This made her happy, so I kept moving my feet around whenever she tapped on them. I looked at the other bridesmaids down the line of gargantuan chairs, and no one else was getting the tap taps—just me. I looked across the aisle at the opposite row of huge chairs and saw an eight year old girl, sipping a can of orange juice and moving her feet back and forth like she knew exactly what to do. I resisted the urge to see if I could bounce my plastic champagne glass off her head, ultimately deciding that throwing garbage at a child wasn't exactly "perfect bridesmaid" behavior. Plus, my aim is shit.

After my toenails were painted a lovely shade of electric blue, I managed to execute a perfect dismount from my massage throne and waddled over to where the other women seemed to be wandering. I found my flip-flops and put them back on. My friend, the bride, moseyed over.

"Hey, look at you, wearing the right shoes to a pedicure!"

"Yup, I did manage to figure that out." I didn't. My husband stopped me on my way out the door to suggest I wear them.

"How was your first pedicure?"

"You know, it wasn't so bad."

"Wanna come back next week?"

"Absolutely not."

"Fair enough. Let's go eat."

Finally, something I knew how to do.

Much *much* later, during a post-wedding visit to the neighborhood bar, my BFF, the bride, told me that I was the bridal party MVP, to which the rest of the (slightly intoxicated) bridal party happily nodded and agreed. Now, I'm not saying that I went home and printed out and framed a certificate declaring me a Bridesmaid MVP, complete with a picture of me and my BFF along with a laminated wallet-size version that could be presented to future potential brides that I may meet later in life.

But I'm not *not* saying that I did that.

JANEL MILLS is the librarian/thug behind the blog 649.133: Girls, the Care and Maintenance Of, where she writes about raising a princess, a wild child, and the sassiest redhead on Earth using as many curse words as possible. Janel was a contributor to NickMom, and is also a contributor to several wildly successful anthologies including the I Just Want to Pee Alone *series. She's also been featured on* The Mighty, Scary Mommy, *and* The Huffington Post. *You can find her on Facebook or on all the other things at @649point133. When not blogging or librarian-ing, she keeps busy raising three beautiful little girls with her beardedly gifted husband in the wilds of metro Detroit.*

The Perfect Senior Portrait is a Myth
By Chrissy Woj
Quirky Chrissy

Around three in the morning, I woke up in a panic. I knew immediately something was wrong. My eyes popped open, but I couldn't see. Not because it was dark, but because there was something wrong with my eyes. I spun my head from side to side. My heart began racing. My breathing was short. Gasping. Invisible pins stung every inch of my body. I was delirious and terrified.

I tried to get out of bed, but quickly realized I had no control over my legs. I fell to the floor, blind and feeling the intractable pain of a sunburn. I crawled toward my parents' bedroom, which was directly next to mine. I howled outside their room like a dog that hadn't been fed, pushing against the door with my body.

"Mommy!" My teenage voice wailed.

Within seconds, my mother rushed to the door, flipping on the hall light, "What! What's going on? What happened?"

"I can't see anything! I think I'm dying!" I sobbed. "I'm going to die! I don't know what to do!"

Once the light was on, it was evident I had blurred vision, but I was not, in fact, blind. Knowing my tendency to dramatize every malady, Mom assured me I wasn't actually dying as she felt my forehead, but she jetted around the house looking for something to bring down my fever.

She guided me to the foot of her bed, where she helped me up and sat down next to me. She handed me two pills and a glass of water, telling me to drink the whole glass before I could sleep. She rubbed aloe on my back as I drank. Dr. Mom could sense my troubles were the effects of sun poisoning and dehydration.

Earlier the previous morning—three days before my high school senior picture appointment—I thought I'd sneak in some poolside pampering and work on my color. I had the ultimate outfits set aside for the photo session: new frocks from the Girlfriends L.A. catalog to show off my serious style. I just needed to improve on my pasty complexion.

I was seventeen, and perfection started with a tan base. Glistening, shaded tones of brown prevented the onslaught of hormonal acne and gave my skin the alluring glow I assumed all high school girls dream of. Of course, tans don't always work the way you plan.

A tan makes you look skinny. And the senior yearbook photos are full color.

I filled a travel mug with ice water, grabbed my hot pink beach towel, and chose a Harlequin romance novel from my growing collection.

This is going to be the best day! And then, I'll look fabulous in my pictures. Just a few hours under my solar savior and I'll be ready for my close up.

I debated whether to wear sunscreen, noting the only sun protection in Mom's medicine cabinet was SPF 35 and smelled like sweat and baby powder. I took a quick whiff and knew I had already made my decision.

Ugh. I probably don't need it, anyway. It'll only prevent me from achieving a flawless tan.

I headed to the backyard just before 10:00 am, wearing a brightly colored two-piece bathing suit. My parents were taking my boyfriend and me to the White Sox game that evening, so I figured I had at least three or four hours of reading and relaxing ahead of me before I needed to get ready. I laid the towel out on the small deck, turned on my favorite alternative rock station, and plopped down on the towel.

That afternoon, I spent far more time lying on my stomach with my nose in a book than I did on my back. Occasionally, I'd feel the thermal heat of the sun pounding on my shoulders and jump into my family's above-ground pool. On my last dip in the pool, I situated myself on a raft, and grabbed the book for a little in-pool reading.

As the clock neared one, I realized I hadn't eaten lunch and was feeling a little parched. I vacated my inflated perch and made my way back to the kitchen. My brother's friends were over, and as soon as I stepped inside, I heard their sniggering. My sidelong glance provided all the confirmation I needed. Yes, they were laughing at me.

"What?" I snapped.

My sun-despising brother offered some sage advice: "Uhh…Chrissy…you may not want to go back out there today."

"Why not?"

"You're really freaking red." My brother's friend restrained himself from laughing out loud, but I could sense his amusement. I glared at him, my thoughts seething as I considered my own wicked ways to end his joy.

I settled for an exasperated "Fuck off" with both my middle fingers lifted to the ceiling before I looked down at the growing crimson on my arms, shoulders, and legs. I had yet to see the dangerous shades of red forming on my back. To make matters worse, there was a large square of Irish white skin on my chest, a patch that closely resembled the shape of an open copy of *The Sheikh's Seduction*.

"Oh, fuck." Internally, I was crumbling. Memories of sunburns past haunted my brain as I quickly worked through all potential repercussions:

Pain, limited mobility, a few weeks donning varying shades of reds and oranges on my skin, and itching. I can get through this.

"Ahahahahahaha! Dude. You're so burned. And what the fuck is up with the big white splotch?"

"It's from my book," I muttered to my audience of three, who erupted in laughter.

I stormed off, my creased brow leaving semi-permanent indentations on my taut, charred forehead.

What am I going to do? The baseball game tonight. Oh God, my pictures! Motherfuck.

I began to search for the economy-sized bottle of aloe so I could slather myself in delicious, delicious moisture.

How the hell did this happen? I don't usually burn this badly.

I thought back to my morning.

OK, I woke up and shimmied into my bathing suit. I consumed a filling meal of cheesy eggs with toast. After breakfast, I grabbed my outdoor essentials and bathed myself in the sun's rays. I missed All My Children *because I was deep into one of my lady porn novels — oh shit!*

Skipping *All My Children* meant I had been out in the sun for nearly three hours. And during the peak sun time, too! Combined with my decision to forgo sunscreen, it was the perfect storm for a horrifying sunburn.

With just a couple hours until my boyfriend arrived, I started psyching myself up for the game.

You've dealt with worse burns than this. You've walked through Disney World burnt to a crisp, Chrissy. Your parents went out of their way to invite you and your man to this game. With those seats, you may even be on TV. Oh shit! We may. Be on. TV. Maybe I shouldn't go. My swollen, raw face has no business in public. Except…no. Time with the boyfriend is so worth it. Get through the game, and you'll be able to snuggle up with him afterward.

I tried to dress for the Sox game, but everything hurt. I opted to let the girls fly braless, threw on a supportive tank top and the softest pair of lounge pants on the planet.

The burn progressed from a deep orange-red to crimson to near-purple. I felt like an Oompa Loompa turned Violet Beauregarde. Late in the afternoon, when my boyfriend arrived, I braced myself for his reaction. After I winced from his hug, he wisely held back any commentary and asked how I was feeling.

"Oh, you know…It sucks. I'm in pain, but fine. Ish."

By the time we left for the game, I was already having difficulty walking. My legs were fried behind my knees. I could feel the skin tightening and pulling with every step. Even my comfy pants betrayed me — they felt more like a cilice than velvety, cotton loungewear. But I wasn't going to be deterred from those front row seats along the first base line.

At the game, I found solace in sitting. My mom and boyfriend ran for food while I stayed put in my seat. It hurt to move. I couldn't stand up and cheer when Mark Buehrle hit a home run. And I was thankful the burn and dehydration limited my need to pee.

Near the fourth inning, my mom started making fun of people on the Jumbotron.

"Everyone always looks at the Jumbotron instead of the cameras. If we were ever on it, we would direct our eyes to the cameras, right?"

"Yep, Mom. Sure thing."

By the seventh-inning stretch, standing up to sing *Take Me Out to the Ball Game* was out of the question, and now, I was freezing. It wasn't cold out, but the sunburn chills had set in.

Shortly after the start of the eighth inning, I looked up to see my shivering tomato face on the big screen and cried out to my parents and boyfriend. They jumped up and started pointing at the Jumbotron, excitedly waving without looking for the camera. I trembled in my seat, trying to hide my face. It was as if the camera guy knew I was dying a sluggish, agonizing death and intended to capture my last hours for posterity. I yearned to disappear, so I lifted my jacket and tucked my head down into my armpit. No one wants to see a human lobster on the big screen.

Jumbotron or not, put a fork in me; I'm done.

After the game, I drove my boyfriend home. We parked a half block from the front of his house and attempted to enjoy the requisite teenage make out session, but with my sunburn, I could move about as much as a cold, fried fish. I apologized for my lack of involvement, and we said goodnight.

I went home exhausted and congratulated myself on getting through the day.

That wasn't so bad. Tomorrow, it will be so much better. You know how burns work. Once you sleep on it, the burn starts to fade. Sleeping is healing, Chrissy.

With that last thought, I passed out on my bed for a few quiet hours of sleep before my alarming panic attack at three in the morning.

Several hours after my mom poured water down my throat and rubbed aloe on my back, the sun peeked into the room, and my eyes blinked open to the sound of my dad's snores. I took in my surroundings to discover I was, in fact, still at the foot of my parents' bed. But I could see. And I could walk...slightly.

Oh sweet cheeses. I spent the whole night in my parents' bed?! But I did almost die, and that makes it OK, right?

Everyone ends up with a sizzling, searing sunburn at least once in life, but mine left me sleeping with my parents instead of my boyfriend.

My senior photos were scheduled two days later, and I knew I wouldn't be up for adorable poses in my trendy, new duds. I rescheduled my appointment for later during the summer and spent the next week in bed, watching soap operas and talk shows on my remoteless thirteen-inch television. Because I couldn't change the channel, I refer to my sunburn healing time as The Week I was Forced to Watch *The Rosie O'Donnell Show*.

Thankfully, I was able to distract myself in the weeks to follow when the peeling part of the healing process set in. As each flake of skin began to show itself on my arms and legs, I took secret delight in one of my summertime guilty pleasures. Like a snake, I sloughed an entire layer of skin, which resulted in my dry discomfort. I begged for back scratches to relieve the itching so frequently, my mom bought me a back scratcher to shut me up.

As the sunburn faded and the peeling subsided, my skin was left with a delicate tan just in time for my rescheduled senior portrait appointment. After weeks of suffering though the itching and burning pain, my complexion was camera ready. Forget the sniggering collective of my brother's friends. Forget the Jumbotron nightmare. Forget the bad daytime TV. This picture—the product of a laborious summer tan gone awry—was going to be incredible.

Unfortunately, my shoot was shortly after The Worst Haircut Ever. I'd been rocking the radar dome since early childhood, but the new cut was a short football-helmet-shaped bob—treading dangerously in pixie-cut waters—paired with my forehead full of Vulcan bangs. My mother wouldn't let me reschedule a second time. Despite the parlous pain and grievous tribulation I went through for the perfect tan, it seems I was never meant to have a beautiful senior picture.

CHRISSY WOJ *is a writer and humorist, sometimes pairing the two as she would her favorite bottle of cheap wine and expensive cheese. She writes at her personal, no-niche, full-nonsense blog, Quirky Chrissy, where you'll find her passionately raving about cheese, her hilarious soon-to-be husband, and the obscene number of times she falls down. Her work has been featured on* The Huffington Post, Scary Mommy, *and* Dirty, Sexy, Funny with Jenny McCarthy. *Chrissy is a full-time editor for a creative content marketing agency and has a master's degree in education. You can spot her practicing yoga on Instagram or sharing random and ridiculous thoughts on Facebook, and Twitter.*

It Didn't Go So Smoothie
By Tara Wood
Love Morning Wood

I've never been a wispy girl. I wasn't genetically blessed with long, lean limbs, high metabolism, or above average height.

Instead, I was gifted with meaty thighs, birthin' hips, and pockets of underarm fat that might easily be mistaken for me having four titties. My height is not much greater than that of a Hobbit.

I had no idea that there was anything out of the ordinary about my body until, in fourth grade, I passed a boy a note. I'd had a crush on him and simply wanted to know if he'd be my boyfriend. I gave him the typical choices: check the box 'Yes' or 'No'. Within a couple of minutes he passed the note back and, although he checked the 'Yes' box, he put a qualifier on it: "Only if you lose some weight. I don't like how chubby you are." What a little fucker.

Still, I wasn't too troubled by my superfluous adipose tissue until I reached high school. That's when I noticed that I was seemingly invisible to boys while my wafer thin and average sized friends were busy making lists to weigh the pros and cons of several of the boys that had asked them on dates.

By my junior year, I'd started smoking and found I could substitute food with cigarettes and the pounds just melted off. Sure there was the offensive odor, persistent, hacking cough, and constant logistical fuckery of finding someone of age to purchase what quickly became my little box of meal replacements, but within about two months, I'd lost twenty pounds.

Cigarettes kept my weight in check until my early twenties when I fell hard and fast for beer and bar food. Although I was still smoking, I no longer relied on tobacco and nicotine as substitutes for chewing actual food. Instead, three or four nights a week, I'd nosh on plates of loaded nachos, mozzarella sticks, and taquitos washing them down with pitchers of piss-warm beer.

Before long, I'd regained that twenty pounds I'd smoked off in high school and added about ten more just for good, extra inches, measure.

While I was never one to exercise or give one single shit about fitness or health in any capacity, I somehow managed to marry a man who, on purpose, went to the gym every day. In fact, he bought a Soloflex to keep in our teeny tiny first house so that he could get in some pull-downs and chest presses if his busy work schedule didn't accommodate a gym visit on any particular day. Although it sat, mocking me, in the corner of our bedroom, the only value I saw in this awkward monstrosity was it providing me an extra place to hang my wet towels. I sometimes put my ashtray on the bench seat, but that was about as close as I came to using the torture device.

When we decided to start a family, I made a commitment to quit smoking and drinking. I'd take better care of myself and be more mindful of what I put into my body. I willingly joined a gym and actually showed up for group classes. I had to begrudgingly admit that I felt better than I ever knew I could. No more junk food for me, either. I ate loads of salads and veggies and more breasts of plain-ass baked chicken than I care to remember.

I maintained this new standard of health for many years and through seven pregnancies, never returning to my old friends smoking, drinking, or mozzarella sticks. I mean, I do sometimes eat mozzarella sticks because, come on, fried cheese is fucking delicious.

A few of years ago, my husband started making and drinking thick shakes as meal replacements. A scoop of protein powder added to fruits, vegetables, seeds, and weird-sounding supplements all mixed together in an absurdly expensive, high powered blender would serve to nourish his body a couple of times a day. He would only need his teeth for one meal as his diet was mostly liquified and required little to no jaw interaction.

I would look at him askance as he poured his freaky cocktail into a glass and gulped it down. It didn't take long for him to try to get me on board his new, super clean food train, but I was having none of it.

As far as I was concerned, meals were to be consumed while in a seated position, preferably at a table, on a plate or in a bowl but not slurped from a cup all thick and wet and already mixed together.

"Try it." he said. "It really isn't bad. You mostly just taste the sweetness of the fruit." I resisted for a long time years, in fact. I grew accustomed to and learned to live with the several-times-a-day whirring of the blender, packets and jars of oils and seeds cluttering the kitchen counter, and bags upon bags of kale and sprouts while never crossing the threshold to dark green leafy vegetable side.

While the allure of drinking liquid, premixed meals eluded and disgusted me, I couldn't help but notice the convenience they provided. Having several kids at this point, I was always looking for ways find the time to keep a tidy house, exercise, or slip into pants without an elastic waistband.

I could make several shakes every morning and just grab them and go without having to prep, cook, or chew my food potentially saving myself thirty to forty-five minutes per day to do other crap!

I was hosting several pounds of unwanted pregnancy weight and, although I was working out at the gym several times a week, still wasn't fitting into pants with buttons and looking the way Hollywood Moms did. The thought of dropping the extra weight by mindlessly mixing fruits and veggies into a rapidly consumable liquid instead of spending hours at an exercise facility that made me feel inadequate and homicidal finally convinced me give pulverized produce a try.

The first couple of days went well. I woke up earlier than I typically do in order to be mindful and deliberate about the the ingredients that I'd be swallowing three times a day. I was confident these green concoctions would usher me into a brand new world of looking and feeling great-ish.

I would grab a pre-made shake out of the fridge and gulp it down on the way to drop the kids off at school in the morning. At lunch time, I didn't trouble myself with making some dumb sandwich behold! there was a gigantic insulated cup chock full of spinach, apple, carrot, flax seed and raw, organic extra virgin cocofuckingnut oil just waiting to travel down my gullet.

The convenience of drinking my meals on the go could not be denied. However, after the third day or so, I did start to miss actually chewing food. In addition to a longing to use my teeth and jaws again, I began to experience something that took me by surprise.

While I've never necessarily been able to set my watch by my defecation schedule, upon suddenly introducing all this ruffage into my body, there was no longer any rhyme or reason to poop poop time. When my sigmoid colon decided it was ready to evacuate its contents, the feeling was sudden and emergent. There was no warning. No matter where I was the shower curtain aisle at Target, getting my oil changed, in stirrups for my yearly cervical swab when it was time for shit to get real, it did.

Save for an occasional stomach bug, I'd never experienced the dizzying and acute fear that I just might have apocalyptic diarrhea while sitting in car line at my kid's school. What was I to do when the first asshole quiver hit? There are cars in front of me, behind me, and on either side. I couldn't get out of the car and try to power walk into the school I'd surely blow out the back of my pants with an audience of moms and dads there to witness the devastation.

I tried to give my digestive tract a week or so to accept all of the goodness I was forcing upon it, but it remained unhappy. I couldn't blame it for rioting a little. I had, after all, completely snatched away anything from a box or bag and replaced it with only things that grew from the ground or trees or artisan recycled glass jars. After becoming a self-imposed prisoner in my own home and forcing my children to ride the bus while my colon adjusted, it became clear that I'd have to abandon what I'd hoped would be the solution to avoiding the gym, but still being able to look amazing in skinny jeans like all those starlets with trainers and chefs and cocaine habits.

I started chewing food again and went back to the gym.

The likelihood of my bunghole abruptly transforming into an explosive salad shooter while waiting in line at Old Navy was just too much pressure.

If a protein shake were to write me a note asking me to be its girlfriend, I'd have to check the 'No' box. I would remind it that we tried but we just weren't compatible. I'll choose a few extra pounds and having a general idea of when I'll need to find a bathroom over shitting my pants in an elementary school parking lot any day.

TARA WOOD is a humor writer and creator of the porn-free blog Love Morning Wood. She is the wife of one easily amused man, and mother of seven children who do not find her to be at all funny or even mildly entertaining which is a damn shame because she is fucking hilarious. She does not suffer fools gladly but always tries to be loving and compassionate when she has to tell someone they're being an utter wanker. Follow her on Facebook and Instagram.

Picture Perfect
By Jen Simon

The Christmas tree hit the floor with a crash, its faux branches no match for the three boys who leaped on it.

"Watch your kids!" I wanted to yell at their negligent parents but I couldn't—the wild beasts belonged to my sister and me.

My sister's sons, Eli, four and a half, and Jonah, eighteen months, and my son Noah, four, were too startled to move. Although they managed to avoid being tangled in the lights and tinsel, several ornaments popped off the tree and rolled around.

"This is going great," I said to my mom as I propped Ryan, my infant, up to my shoulder. He promptly spit up on my neck. What a shitshow.

My husband, sons, and I had flown from Brooklyn to Kansas City, where I grew up, to visit my family for Thanksgiving. My sister had declared that she was done with babies after her second son was born. I issued the same proclamation when my second was born also. Our individual families were complete; our whole family was complete. The best way to commemorate a milestone? Pictures. The perfect pictures.

Unfortunately, the only day we could do it was the absolute worst day to do it: the Saturday after Thanksgiving. Half of the young families of Kansas joined us at Portrait Innovations to get their own perfect pictures for their perfect Christmas cards. The studio was overrun with girls in velvet dresses and Mary Janes and boys sporting red vests and clip-on ties. They were adorable. They were everywhere. They were better behaved than our little monsters.

Portrait Innovations was a step up from Sears Portrait Studio. One enters into a large, main waiting area with plush couches for the adults and a Lego table for the kids. Behind the waiting area lay two rooms for the photography, each open to the main room. One was decked out in a Christmas scene complete with a decorated tree and a fireplace background scrim. The other room offered a choice of backgrounds — some solid colors and several with winter scenes. OK, maybe it was only half a step up from Sears.

The night before The Big Day, the boys did their best to sabotage the outing: Ryan woke up a handful of times (a few more than usual) and Noah got up at five in the morning (a little earlier than usual), but I was determined (far more than usual) not to be derailed on our day's quest. We would get great pictures of our great family. Nay, we would get perfect pictures of our perfect family!

The first blow to our plan came that morning, ironically in picture form via text from my sister.

At first, I couldn't tell what it was. I turned it around and squinted until I made out a blurry picture of her husband's pinkish eye—OH NO! Pink eye! She answered as soon as I dialed.

"Tell me it isn't true," I gasped.

"Oh yes," she confirmed. "He woke up with pink eye this morning. It was crusted together but now it's all gooey. I'm not sure which is worse."

"Grooooossss. I guess he's out." I sighed. "We won't be able to take a picture of all ten of us."

"What?" my husband asked. "We're not doing it? I don't have to go?" He was about as eager to get pictures taken as he was to watch me give birth again. He'd probably rather have pink eye than take family pictures.

"You're coming!" I barked and went back to packing.

If there was even a small chance we would need something, I brought it. In addition to the regular child-management items like diapers, wipes, and spit-up rags, I augmented my diaper bag with: a change of clothes for each kid, Ryan's lovey, Noah's favorite stuffed animal, several books for each kid, a Superman, a Spiderman, sundry other toys (some that beeped or made noise, some that didn't), a water bottle for each kid and each adult, and four kinds of snacks for both my older son (he'd need bribes to sit still) and my husband (he'd need sugar to stay patient). I packed more than I did when I went overseas for a week. I packed more than my relatives did when they emigrated from The Old Country.

Come hell or high-water, we were going to do this. And it was going to be *almost* perfect now that we had one man down. Dammit.

The second blow to my perfect plan came upon our arrival at the studio. "We're running about twenty minutes behind, so please just make yourselves comfortable in the main room while we get a studio ready for you," the receptionist told me as my parents, husband and boys checked in. Great. We had chosen the perfect time for our appointment—between Ryan's two naps and before Jonah's sole nap. Our already narrow window of minimal crankiness closed to a mere crack.

A few minutes later, my sister arrived with her boys and we set up camp, taking over an entire couch and an oversized club chair. Our rambunctious boys started running after each other, screaming more than usual. According to the master plan for the perfect pictures, we quickly directed them to the small playspace with the Lego table to occupy them during the wait. There, the third blow fell. What I believed would be some pleasant Lego building immediately became a violent turf war. Two boys were already there when my gang of pre-school toughs arrived. These pint-sized Jets and Sharks sized each other up across the short, green studded table. One boy began hoarding the red Legos, sticking them in his pockets. Another boy had his tower promptly knocked over by Jonah.

"Moooooooooom!" Jonah's new nemesis wailed. Without waiting for a response, he leaned over and pinched Jonah on the cheek. My sister dropped to his side, worried Jonah was hurt. I was worried too; worried the pinch would leave a red welt. Or worse; a bruise. How dare this kid mess with my nephew's face? Didn't he know that messing with my nephew's face was a direct attack against me? Against my picture taking experience! Maybe, just maybe, we could get the pictures done before a welt or bruise appeared.

Once he recovered from the shocking cheek pinch, Jonah dove back into the fray, this time darting after his brother Eli and my son Noah as they made a break for it—right into the room with the Christmas tree. The twinkling lights, sparkling streamers, and luminous ornaments proved too irresistible to resist. Eli launched himself toward the tree, the other two close behind. The adults in the family leapt into action. Too late to stop the tree from falling, but fast enough to stop the kids from totally tearing it apart, my husband, sister, and father rushed the room, each grabbing a kid. My husband and father picked up the tree, with little damage done, except to our reputation as civilized people.

Oh, and that's not all. At this point, the chaos was at least limited to noise and property damage, and perhaps some busted blood vessels in Jonah's face, but nothing that would seriously impact our near perfect pictures. I turned to my mother to tell her it could have been worse, and with impeccable timing, my infant spat up on me. OK, I thought, this is mostly on my back, and it won't be in the picture if I stand at just the right angle.

Just then, another waiting baby chose that moment to add a piercing scream to the pandemonium. Of course I had nursed before I left the house, but it was no match for the force of nature that was a crying baby. Nipples perked and engaged, my milk started to let down. *Feed that baby* my breasts commanded me. *Nooooo* I silently screamed, as I handed Ryan to my mom and pressed my hands over my breasts, willing them to stop. *Stupid boobs! That's not your baby!*

I ran to the bathroom and stuffed tissues into my bra but it was too late—two distinct wet spots had appeared, the right twice as big as the left. My right boob was the workhorse, even for a false alarm. While I had thought of extra clothes for the kids, I didn't bring anything I could change into. Of course. So even though the baby spit-up had landed on my back, I now had wet nipple spots to conceal.

With the delay, I might have had some time to clean up a little more, but our miniature heathens were so horrible, we got bumped to the front of the line and were called to take pictures soon after. There are some perks to rowdy boys. Atrocious behavior for the win!

My family of four was up first. I strategically placed one boy, then the other in front of me and my wet orbs. Aside from some fussing from the baby, silliness from Noah, and griping from my husband, things went pretty well. It was the calm before the storm.

The next step was all four boys. As soon as Stacey brought her boys into our room, Noah jumped up and tackled Eli. Then, in a coordinated but unspoken attack, they rushed the white background screen, trying to climb it.

"They can't do that!" The photographer shouted. My husband and sister each grabbed a laughing, kicking, squirming kid.

"Sorry," the photographer said, a little calmer, "they could get it dirty or even pull it down."

"No, you don't need to apologize," I said. "You're right; I'm sorry—we'll be on top of them more." As soon as I said that, I looked up to see Jonah sprinting toward the front door.

"Jonah on the loose!" I cried. My sister dropped Eli and gave chase. As she snagged him, he, an expert at the art of going boneless, went limp. His arms shot up as he buckled his knees and slid to the floor. Once on the floor, he started crawling away again.

What was going on with these kids? Were they trying to ruin my dream? If so, they were doing a pretty good job of it.

"Let's get the four of them together before something else happens," I said, teeth clenched, still determined.

The photographer brought out a white bench so we could line them up.

"I want to hold baby Ryan!" Eli called.

"No, he's my baby!" shouted Noah, expressing more interest in his brother than he had in the previous five months.

While the boys squabbled, Jonah headed to the corner. Uh oh. I knew that move.

"Jonah, what are you doing?" My sister asked.

"Mama! Away!" he scolded her. Great. Nothing like actual shit to remind you how shitty your day is going.

While Jonah was indisposed, I revised the plan and settled my two boys into a small chair together. As per his desire only moments before, I put Ryan on Noah's lap.

"Why don't you kiss your brother," the photographer suggested to Noah. He looked up at my husband and me, his beautiful face angelic. My heart swelled as he bent down and kissed his brother.

This is it, I thought. *This is the sweetest moment ever. I'm so glad we get to memorialize this.* And then Noah attacked, biting Ryan's forehead.

"Aaaaaaaah!" I screamed louder than Ryan. Snatching him from Noah's arms, I glared at my first-born. My husband pulled him out of the chair for a time out and we all decided to take a short break. Well, the boys decided for us that we were taking a break.

"This is fun?" My husband sighed under his breath.

"No one said this was fun," I hissed incredulously. "This isn't fun—this is work. We have to work at things to make sure they're right. To make sure they're perfect!"

"Good luck with that." He shook his head and moved away from me.

After my nephew finished pooping and my sister coaxed him to the bathroom, she returned with a grim but determined look. "He refuses to put his pants back on."

No. no no no no no! I wanted to stomp my feet and pout, but I had to be the adult.

"Jonah, the big boys are wearing pants. Don't you want to be like Eli and Noah?"

"No! No, no, no, no, no!" he shouted, echoing my sentiment.

"We wear pants in public," my sister said. Jonah just went boneless again.

I gave up.

"OK. I don't know what to do anymore. Eli, you get to hold baby Ryan."

"I want to hold something. Why don't I get to hold something? I want a ball," Noah whined, pointing to the props in the corner basket.

"Ball, ball," shouted Jonah, eyeing the balls.

We lined up the boys—Eli holding Ryan, Noah and Jonah each holding balls—and the photographer snapped away.

When it was time to order prints, we chose the best one all four boys. Eli's shirt was twisted and half of his collar was tucked in. Ryan was mid-spit-up. One of Noah's eyes was half-closed. And, of course, Jonah was pants-less. But it was true to our life. It was as perfect as it was going to get.

JEN SIMON writes about motherhood, postpartum depression, sex, relationships, pop culture, and feminism. Jen has been published on Cosmopolitan, Yahoo, Redbook, The Huffington Post, *Babble,* Scary Mommy, Ms., *and more than two dozen other websites. This is her fifth anthology.*

While she writes about serious topics, Jen's also a pretty funny lady. Her tweets and Facebook statuses have been included in the funniest round-ups on Today Parents, The Huffington Post, *Babble, and* Romper.

Although she was not born a redhead, she has been fixing that mistake for nearly two decades. After growing up in Kansas City, she lived in New York City and Brooklyn for thirteen years before giving in to the suburbs of New Jersey.

Follow her on Facebook at Facebook.com/JenSimonWriter, on Twitter at @NoSleepInBklyn, on Instagram at JenSimonWriter and see her writing on her website, JenSimonWriter.com.

At Least You Have Your Health
By Stacey Gill
One Funny Motha

For close to two years I've had pain in my lower back. But because I like to ignore things for as long as possible and because during the same visit in which my doctor theorized I most likely had arthritis, she also treated me for high cholesterol and I couldn't take any more medical ailments for a body that, apparently, was in an advanced state of premature aging, I put off seeking medical treatment. When I returned the following year still in mild but consistent pain, my doctor sent me for x-rays. They confirmed her hypothesis, and with an actual diagnosis I could no longer ignore, I agreed it was finally time to get my health in order.

Like most moms with kids to care for, a career to manage, and a household to run, I'd always left my needs for last. But with this unexpected and somewhat alarming diagnosis, I resolved this was the year I was going to make myself a priority. This was the year I was going to take charge of my long overdue needs and make the necessary time for myself in order to improve my health and overall well-being. Plus, I feared if left unchecked the arthritis would have me hunched over, hobbling down the street, my gnarled, sun-spotted fingers gripping a wooden cane, by the time I was forty-five.

Supplied with a bunch of phone numbers for area physical therapists, I ran down the list and noticed an out-of-state number. While odd, it was a Brooklyn number, and since I'd lived in Brooklyn back in the day I felt a sort of kinship with this physical therapist who clearly was behind in updating his business number. But that wasn't the main reason I chose to call the practice. The main reason was that the office was exceptionally convenient, two minutes from my house, which is pretty much how I choose all my medical professionals.

Punching the digits into my phone, I listened to a few rings before someone picked up.

"Hi, this is John."

"Um, hi." I hesitated, slightly confused. "I'm trying to reach Advanced Physical Therapy?"

"Yes, you've reached Advanced PT."

Then why did you answer with "Hi, this is John?"

Overlooking the odd greeting, I explained my problem and said I was calling to schedule an appointment. John, though, didn't have his appointment book with him. He'd have to call me back.

When the phone rang later that afternoon I was just pulling into the pick up line at school. Reaching over to the passenger seat as I turned into the drive, I frantically dug through my purse, searching for the buzzing phone. Seizing it, I pulled it out and checked the number. Then I debated what to do. Conducting a call while driving through the school parking lot just as the inmates were released was not ideal. Still, I didn't want to miss John's call. On the last ring I picked up.

"Hello?" With the phone in one hand, I steered through marauding packs of middle-schoolers with the other as John rattled off a steady stream of appointment times into my ear. I didn't catch any of them. Instead, I was deeply engaged in avoiding fatalities. As I swerved around one swarm of wholly oblivious kids and then another, I realized it wasn't actually possible to schedule an appointment while also operating a moving vehicle. I told John I'd call him back later and quickly hung up.

When I returned the call that evening, John answered his phone the exact same way he had the first time only this time there was the added bonus of techno music blaring in the background. Pretending to ignore the thumping beat, I explained again who I was and why I was calling although what I would've liked to have said was, *Where are you? And why did you answer your phone?*

I could barely make him out over the pulsating beat, but I managed to discern that he did in fact have his appointment book this time. I just had to hold on while he located it. After a long pause wherein I listened to rhythmic stylings of DJ Snake and Flo Rider he returned and proceeded to schedule the appointment. I have to hand it to him, though. He never once skipped a beat. In fact, it was like he wasn't even in a nightclub. He acted completely normal as if he was just sitting in the office filing paperwork. I think the most impressive part of the whole conversation was that he was able to hear me over the blaring music.

Given that it was five o'clock on a Wednesday night, I don't think he was actually in the club. More likely he was at the gym, and while I don't want to tell anyone their business, don't answer your phone when you're at the gym. Especially if you're using your personal phone as your business phone, and you don't recognize the number. Screen your calls. And return them when there isn't dance music pumping in the background, OK?

That's what I was thinking as I strained to hear John from my position crouched on the sidewalk outside my son's Tae Kwon Do class with my purse splayed on the cement as I clawed through in search of a pen with which to write down the appointment.

I typically conduct my personal business on the sidewalk outside the dojo because that's my forty minutes of down time, and I like to make the most of my day. I take my business outside because I like to be discreet and have some privacy, and while that typically works out just fine, on this particular day another parent of a little ninja thought it would be fun to stand right *next* to me and scream into her cell phone. Between the woman shouting beside me and the techno music on the other end of the line, it was rather difficult to conduct the phone call, but as this was our third attempt at arranging an appointment, the appointment book had been secured and my back was long overdue for some treatment, I felt compelled to forge on.

From my squatting position I glared up at the woman and jammed a finger into my ear. Then I proceeded on with the call like any other reasonable person would do. Since this would be our first appointment there were some details to go over so I remained huddled on the sidewalk under the streetlight answering question after question as the woman raged on next to me. Not once did she step away or march down to the other end of the sidewalk so that maybe we could both conduct our personal affairs in private. It was a long ten minutes trying to pretend like any of this was normal, but eventually I arranged the appointment and hung up.

I can't say I had complete confidence in Advanced Physical Therapy, but since it took me nearly three months to get around to making an appointment after a couple of years dragging my feet, now that I actually *had* one, I didn't know if I wanted to cancel it. Still, I had some concerns over what exactly I was walking into. When I got home I told my husband about the whole affair.

"Am I gonna have to go with you?" he demanded.

"No, no," I insisted. "I'm sure it'll be fine."

I was not sure it would be fine. It *probably* would be fine. I'd either return home arthritis-free or I get murdered, stuffed into a body bag and heaved into a dumpster out back. There was no way to tell, but I didn't want to overreact. Plus, my appointment was at 6:15 pm, which was before Kevin would be home from work.

The following week on a dark, wintery night I drove across town to the small, brick, two-story office building that looked like it had formerly housed apartments. Upon entering, I checked the directory on the ground floor for the office number. John had mentioned his office was on the second floor, but I was unsure of the actual number. Scanning the directory several times, I was unable to find a listing for him. *Strange.* But the office building was small so I decided to head up the narrow staircase to look for the door marked with his practice's name.

Upstairs I walked the length of the short hallway, peering at each of the plaques. There were only four doors. FOUR. But his name wasn't on any of them. I began racing up and down the corridor reading all the placards again before stopping short in the middle of the hallway and looking back and forth, in a growing state of panic and confusion. With anxiety welling up in my body, I remembered the paper I'd written the address on, and I grabbed at my purse, snatching the note from the bottom. Reviewing the address, I confirmed I was, in fact, in the correct building. But that didn't explain where the hell his office was. The whole scene was slightly *Twilight Zone*-ish.

As I stood there thinking maybe this was my get-out-of-murder free pass, I noticed a little piece of paper on the door opposite me taped below the official nameplate. It read: Advanced Physical Therapy.

Oh, there it is. Finally. Thank God. Although you might have mentioned this little detail, John.

Entering the silent waiting room, I wondered if I'd made the right decision. The office was completely empty. There were no patients, no receptionist, nobody there save for John and me. It was slightly eerie being the only person in an office at night with a strange man who answered his business phone while listening to techno music.

John, who was young and trim with wavy, brown hair and a broad smile, led me down a narrow hall to a small, spare room with nothing in it save some card board boxes and a massage table. He gathered some information about my back, and then he proceeded to do what I assume were some sort of assessments. But first he wanted me to disrobe. Well, not entirely. He had instructed me to come in loose-fitting clothing, which I did, but apparently my sweatshirt was a little too bulky. He wanted to know if I had anything on underneath.

Again, mass murderer/rapist ran through my mind, and the chain of events fit exactly with how you'd expect a mass murderer/rapist would act. John might have seemed friendly and personable, but how did I know he wasn't going to throw me to the floor and straddle me? Who would hear?

I had a tank top on underneath so I slowly removed my sweatshirt and stood in front of him, feeling naked without even the false modesty a flimsy paper robe would've provided. Then John positioned me directly in front of him with my back facing him and instructed me to bend over. *Excuse me?* I was not at all comfortable with this.

I get that he's a medical professional, but I don't care who you are it will always feel inappropriate to bend over in front of another person of the opposite sex when they are standing approximately six inches behind you, watching you and perhaps eyeing your ass. Plus, how did I know this was a proper assessment?

With medical doctors exams are pretty standard stuff, typically involving stethoscopes and white coats and paper-covered tables. It all feels very clinical and official. The physical therapy office employs none of the trappings of a medical office, and to the suspicious layperson the maneuvers of a physical therapist and your average sexual deviant are pretty similar, especially if you're in an unmarked office alone at night with your assailant who's instructed you to undress.

Then John moved closer and placed his hands on my hips. It was an awkward position to say the least. He then ran his hands along my spine all the way down to the base, which let's face it, is my ass. Given I had a lower back issue, it made sense, but it was also like, "Whoa, watch where you're putting your hands, mister."

When I stood back up John came up behind me and wrapped his arm around my torso, grabbing my shoulder and dipping me backward. It was somewhat startling. Confined in a headlock, I wondered if this was standard diagnostic procedure. It seemed a difficult assessment to perform on every patient. What if the person was taller? What if he or she was big, husky linebacker?

The only other time I'd been in a position like that was in a self-defense class twenty years ago. And those long-forgotten techniques would no longer help me. Plus John was rather muscular while I had a bad back. Rather convenient circumstances for someone looking to torture and dismember a body.

I didn't get murdered that night, but I did have to go back the following week for a second appointment. While I didn't get murdered that time either, John's assessment of my condition and his solution to cure it were perhaps a fate worse than death. The problem, it appeared, stemmed from the stationary nature of my work. I sat at my desk too long. John's solution was simple. To not sit. Or to only sit for thirty-minute intervals, which to anyone who has to work at a desk for a living is the equivalent of not sitting. John delivered this news with an entirely straight face as if he was being completely reasonable, as if this was even possible. I wanted to shake him and shout, "Are you out of your mind? Do you even know what you're saying?"

Since I'm a writer sitting is pretty much all I do. I'm fairly good at it, and as it's practically a job requirement that's a real plus for me. I sit all day long. I sit until the job's done, which often is never. What exactly, I wanted to ask him, am I supposed to accomplish in thirty minutes? I certainly can't write a book in thirty minutes. I can't even compose a Facebook status update in thirty minutes half the time.

John had other suggestions for me, too, but they were equally as absurd. He said I needed to learn the correct way to sit at a desk. Which, he explained, was to sit with my back straight, shoulders back, head upright and feet flat on the floor. And not move. Ever. According to John that was all I had to do. Just concentrate on holding that uncomfortable position for eight hours a day while composing brilliant copy, which I suppose John assumed didn't require any thought at all.

John didn't seem to recognize the problem with any of this. I, however, was devastated. In fixing my back, my life had been ruined. The proposed solution was an impossible one, and I knew I could either have a writing career or a pain-free existence but not both. I knew if I was to concentrate on my sitting position, I couldn't concentrate on my work. And, I knew for the benefit of my health, my dreams would have to be sacrificed.

Telling you this story is my final act of writing. These are the last words I will ever pen.

STACEY GILL is an award-winning journalist, the mastermind behind the humor blog, One Funny Motha, and contributor to I Still Just Want to Pee Alone, the third book in The New York Times bestselling series. Her work has appeared on such sites as The Washington Post, The Huffington Post, Good Housekeeping, Babble, Brain, Child, and Scary Mommy. Perhaps most importantly, she's the proud founder of the Detached Parenting Movement, a child-rearing model she single-handedly developed without any guidance or advanced degrees in child psychology. She's currently at work on a memoir based on this theory. For a good time, find her on Facebook, Pinterest, and Twitter.

How to Suck at Church
By AK Turner

A tingling swells in my throat. *Walk in strong,* I tell myself. *You can do this. Just sit back in the corner and melt away. Be still and silent as a pebble on the sea floor; no one will even know you're there.* But a warm flood of moisture sweeps over my eyes. I try to blink the tide away. *They're going to eat me alive.*

I have a vague notion that this must be how grown-ups feel when entering prison. They probably hope to push-up their way to chiseled physiques and get a lot of reading done, but there's also the fear that someone will stab them with a sharpened spoon. Right now I wish someone would stab me with a sharpened spoon. Then I could go to the hospital and escape what's to come. And maybe the President would give me a medal for my bravery. Sadly, no one is going to stab me. I can't even find a pencil with which to stab myself.

It can't be helped, so I breathe deep and smile, as if my welling tears are nothing more than allergies. I enter fooling no one, because no one *smiles* when showing up here. My uncharacteristic expression gives me away.

It has begun.

For the next forty minutes I am at the mercy of my greatest fear: Sunday School.

This room is a clutter of Popsicle stick crosses and pictures of lambs and Jesus. I hear the phrase "lamb of God" a lot. I've never heard anyone refer to God as a farmer, so I assume God's lamb was more of a pet. Since the pictures always show Jesus with a lamb, I guess that Jesus was lamb-sitting because God had lots of godly work to do.

My plan to fade into the back of the room is foiled by the tiny chairs arranged in a circle. There *is* no back of the room. I sit facing others and the normal childhood angst that accompanies not fitting in is magnified. The differences between me and these other children are incandescent.

Physically, I'm Raggedy Ann in a room of Barbies and Kens. I am pudgy, worn, and with hair made of yarn amid golden braids and starched collars. I hear my stepmother's voice from earlier that morning, chiding my father directly and me with passive-aggression. "Bill, do *something* with your daughter's hair."

Mentally, I cannot compete. I know not a single Bible verse, nor the difference between verse and hymn. During trivia, which is supposed to be fun, I betray my vow of silence and blurt "Jesus" when the answer is "God," and vice versa. The family tree of these men baffles me. I have a sneaking suspicion that Joseph was Jesus' stepfather, but there's no one I can ask to be sure.

I'm emotionally stunted, as well. These children *feel* something I do not, like a sixth sense they share, from which I am excluded. It's a blindness from birth on my part; I'm surrounded by those who see that which I cannot fathom. This makes me wonder what else occurs in the world that everyone knows about but me. Or are they all just really good actors?

I am paranoid at ten years old. Maybe it's temporary. Maybe I'll be enlightened in time. I am ashamed.

* * *

"Let's first turn to Deuteronomy," the professor says. I have not the slightest clue what that means. I'm an eighteen-year-old college student and I've never felt greater ignorance. I enrolled in the class to sort through the confusion still swirling in my head from my religiously fractured youth. It wasn't easy pretending to be Lutheran every other weekend and Seventh-Day Adventist with grandparents. Being Lutheran required the dreaded Sunday School, but being Seventh-Day Adventist meant a childhood devoid of Saturday morning cartoons (*And what fresh hell is this?*). Only at home with my mother could I take a heathenish breath. That freedom was heavenly.

My fellow students all turn to the same place in their texts. I open the Bible in my hands and marvel at the fragile pages. *I'll just check the table of contents*, I think, but I can't seem to find it. *This is a mistake. Dear God, what am I doing here?*

Last week we studied the Gnostic Gospels and I nodded dumbly through the ninety-minute discussion, with the familiar fear rising and a suspicion that no one around me was speaking English. In an act of cruelty reminiscent of Sunday School, the class takes place in a circle of chairs, so I'm again prevented from hiding in the back. I feel sweat in my armpits. Soon, I will smell bad. *Where is the table of contents?* I flip casually through the book hoping to stumble on Deuteronomy. *Can't we just speak in page numbers? Why is there no table of contents?* I check again and again, wondering if only my copy is defective. I resign myself to scribbling notes, as if to show my engagement. I want the professor to think that I could *of course* turn to Deuteronomy if I wanted, but there's just so much *learning* going on in my young mind that my pen can hardly keep pace.

My final paper is a ramble of incoherence, speckled with random references to the curriculum. I get a B in the class, because I showed up and nodded dumbly. I am ridiculous.

* * *

With the identities of wife, mother, and thirty-something, I return with my family to the places of my childhood. My father retrieves us at the airport. He drives toward his home where my stepmother prepares dinner. She is an excellent cook, a Martha Stewart follower, a sleek image of elegance and grace in the kitchen. After two decades, her voice is still in my head. "Bill, do *something* with your daughter's hair." I can't help but run my hand along the crown of my head in the hopes of smoothing the strands that have gone wayward and rogue.

We arrive and she slurs a greeting. Smalltalk ping-pongs between my husband and father, while I focus on my one-year-old daughter. "Dinner is almost ready," my stepmother announces. She opens the oven and attempts to remove a baking sheet. Tater Tots bounce across the kitchen floor. "Whoops!" She laughs and sways. My dad skitters to help.

Accompanying the five-second-rule tots are meatball sandwiches. It is an unexpected meal from this kitchen; no truffle oil in sight. The wine flows because we all need it to get through, but it appears my stepmother started long before our arrival. After tots and meatballs she launches an interrogation of why I have not baptized my daughter and when I plan to do so. "That's not really high on my list," I mumble, disappointed in my own cowardice. She isn't satisfied; she pushes; she won't let it go. Had I learned nothing from Sunday School? She can't fathom that I've let my daughter live a year of her life in danger of purgatory. I study the floor, sheathed in dog hair and miscellaneous matter, and decide the five-second rule is bullshit.

My husband tries to change the subject, but she brings it back.

"We have to get her baptized!"

"You do know that *I* was never baptized," I say.

She makes an odd sound, a *pfft* paired with a roll of the eyes. I take this to mean that I've been dismissed as a lost cause years ago. My one-year-old bundle of innocence is what matters now.

Her face reddens and we've gone beyond discussion or disagreement. She's engulfed in good old-fashioned anger at this point. Of Biblical proportions. She begins to stand and I think she's about to slam her fist on the table when gravity betrays her. In a glorious, slow-motion fall from grace, she travels the length of the room, unable to right herself but unwilling to topple completely, balancing impossibly with each successive stumble as if channeling Buster Keaton. Her arms flail and my father's eyes widen with panic. The wave of momentum can't be indefinite. It crashes violently when she reaches a wall and comes to rest in a mangled heap in a corner of the kitchen that was home to twelve-packs of soda. Two cans roll lazily into the middle of the floor.

My father rushes to her side and helps her to her feet, with the admission that "Maybe we've had a bit too much wine." As he leads her into another room to "rest," she glares at me as if I'd pushed her. The fall is somehow my fault and there's a hatred in her eyes that is damning and righteous. Her venom baffles me. The next day she'll wake with wonder at how she got so bruised.

* * *

I gain no understanding of this foreign world; I am as lost as I was at the age of ten. My religious ignorance plays out at dinner parties instead of Sunday School, but it's as strong as ever. When the topic of faith comes up, I try to steer the conversation to safer ground, like abortion laws or second amendment rights. My evasive tactics fail and I resort to fantasizing about a sudden and gruesome injury that will require immediate medical attention and thereby end the discussion. My mind races with questions to add to the discourse, but yields only such gems as "Best guess on the end times—do you have a date in mind or is it pretty much wide open?" or "How about that lamb of God?" I bite my tongue to keep from giving voice to these idiocies. They are my private confirmation, my personal revelation, that I am an expert on how to suck at church.

AK Turner is the New York Times *bestselling author of* This Little Piggy Went to the Liquor Store, Mommy Had a Little Flask, *and* Hair of the Corn Dog. *Her forthcoming series* Vagabonding with Kids *follows her attempts to maintain sanity and a smidge of dignity while traveling around the world with her husband and two young daughters. Learn more at AKTurner.com and VagabondingWithKids.com. Follow her on Facebook, Twitter, Instagram, and Pinterest.*

The Burning Pain of Perfection
By Allison Hart
Motherhood, WTF?

All endeavors towards perfection are doomed to fail. But lessons are hard won and even epic failures don't always teach us to abandon the quest. Despite some doozies, throughout my life I continued to strive for shallow self-improvement, mostly using quick fixes, shortcuts, and bad ideas.

Once, bored with what I suddenly viewed as my little girl hair, I *knew* that my life would be perfect if only I had a cool, more sophisticated hairstyle. With visions of edgy eighties glam in mind, I took scissors to my long locks, ushering in the ugliest and most awkward phase of my life. No other girls in the fifth grade had boy-short hair, or an obviously homemade haircut. They stylishly sported Desperately Seeking Susan crimps or scrunchied side ponies. *What have I done?* Luckily, I somehow got my hands on a men's fedora and decided that fifth grade was the year I'd rock a fedora. How many ten-year-olds do you know that could rock a men's fedora? Yeah, I don't know any either.

Much later, as an impressionable, self-conscious teen, I tried and failed at bulimia. I knew it was unhealthy, but it seemed to work wonders for other girls! They looked terrific in clothes whereas I was squishy all over and wore clothes that were too small on me, constricting me in terribly unflattering ways. (But why buy jeans unless they're jeans to *aspire* to?) So I tried to make myself puke. No matter how far I jammed my finger down my throat, the contents of my stomach stayed put. Maybe I just needed to eat more to make it work? So I binged the shit out of myself. I ate and ate and ate. I ate all the things. I still never managed to pull the trigger. *I gained weight trying to be bulimic.*

Of all my calamitous misadventures on the road towards perfection, one stands out as the biggest disaster. This time, I had decided that my short, picked at, angsty nails were the barrier between me and that elusive golden ring. Enter a product called Nailtiques which promised to transform my ugly-ass nails into visions of feminine wonder and strength.

The regimen was simple: apply one coat of this stuff per day and my nails would reap the benefits of protein, keratin, vitamins, and magic, and before I knew it they'd be beyond reproach. Easy!

On day one I applied one coat. I felt better already. All day I admired my nails. *"You're on your way, you guys! Soon you'll be lovely and I promise I'll stop gnawing on you, and you and you and you and you..."* That night I applied another coat, because why not?

On day two I woke up and checked my nails. Huh. They looked much the same. No worries! These things take time! Rome wasn't built in a day, and if perfection was easy everyone would do it. I applied a coat of Nailtiques. And then another. A little while later I layered on another coat. That should do it. Maybe just one more for good measure.

That afternoon I applied one last coat. And then I felt something! *Oh, tingling! That has to be a good sign! Wow, that is a lot of tingling. An awful lot of tingling. Huh, that tingling is really something! It's a little more like burning now than tingling. Wow. It's really like burning. It's burning. It's burning! Holy hell it's burning!* I grabbed the nail polish remover. *I'll just take this off and all will be well.*

All was not well.

Nails of fire! Nails of fire! The searing, burning pain grew by the moment. This was getting serious—bad enough to tell my parents.

"Um, Dad? I used this stuff for my nails to make them grow and now it hurts."

"You should take it off."

"Yeah, I did. But it still hurts. I mean, it really, really hurts! It's burning. It's burning a lot."

"Did you read the directions?"

"Yes, of course I did! Jeez! I'm not an idiot!"

"Did you follow the directions?" (How well does this guy know me, right?)

"Not exactly. I *might* have applied a little more than I was supposed to. HELP! THIS HURTS! IT BURNS!!"

This is when I began to ugly-cry.

My dad suggested I soak my hands in cold water. *Great! I knew he'd be able to help!*

Cold water did not help. The burning continued to intensify. The whole world was afire. My entire life was burning nailbeds.

My father thought maybe soaking my hands in oil would do the trick. *Great! Surely there's some science-y thing that will happen and this burning nail nightmare will finally end.*

Oil did not end the nightmare. If the blinding pain had abated for even a moment, I might have appreciated how moisturizing the oil was for my hands and cuticles. But, alas, my nails were trying to kill me. Everything I had ever known vanished like a wisp of smoke. There was only painful misery now. This was everything.

As I slowly accepted that I would only ever exist in agony for all of eternity, my father read the back of the Nailtiques bottle. It listed the number for poison control in case of accidental ingestion. Out of other ideas, he dialed the number. I listened to his end of the conversation through my sobs.

"Hello. I'm calling because my daughter used too much of a product called Nailtiques and now she is in quite a bit of pain."

"It's a nail polish."

"No. No vomiting. She didn't drink it. Her nails hurt."

"That's right. She put it on her fingernails and now they are hurting her."

"Yes, she did take it off. She is still in a lot of pain though."

"Nailtiques. N-A-I-L-T-I-Q-U-E-S"

(Have you ever heard your father use a word like "Nailtiques"? It changes you.)

"Right. She applied it to her nails."

"No, she did not drink any of it."

"The directions say to apply one coat per day. She thought that more would be better."

(Fixes me with withering look.)

"She says it's burning. It seems to be getting worse."

"We tried soaking in cold water. Then we tried soaking in olive oil."

"Oh, it just seemed like a good idea at the time."

"Right. It didn't help."

"Yes, I'll wait."

The woman at poison control asked my dad to hold while she looked up Nailtiques. This was early 1990-something. How she "looked up" Nailtiques I'll never know. Encyclopedia? Microfiche?

There was no past, no future. Just burning nailbeds. Why had I never appreciated how functionally awesome my nails were before they were on fire? On fire nails are terrible. Short ugly ones are great! *I will never do anything like this again.*

Eventually she came back to the phone and my dad's end of the conversation resumed.

"Really? That makes sense. I should have thought of it. Thank you!"

The answer? Milk. The instant I submerged my anguished digits in the bowl of cold milk the burning began to subside. As I had grown accustomed to life as nothing more than an increasingly burning hell, words fail to capture the magnitude of my relief. I cried actual tears of joy. (They probably looked exactly like the tears I had been crying for quite some time at this point.)

As soon as my parents deemed me recovered enough to tease, the teasing started. It has not stopped since. They not only laughed at me about this episode, but for the remainder of my growing-up years, my parents referenced Nailtiques in their lectures to me as means to demonstrate my youth, impulsivity, capacity for large mistakes, failure to follow rules or directions, and general stupidity. In fact, they still do. It's a family favorite.

Occasionally, I still succumb to the lure of perfection only to find myself, once again, still myself. These quests have led to the collection of a myriad items and products designed to help me achieve my unachievable goal:

- *I'd be a perfect girl if I styled my hair daily!* Curling iron, flat iron, blow dryer, various mousses, gels, and sprays—all gathering dust. Turns out, I don't care enough about my hair to put in that kind of effort. Ever.
- *I'll be a perfect mom if I cook and bake with my kids!* Piles of kid-friendly cookbooks, cute wee aprons, and kitchen implements designed for little hands—all shoved in the back of my highest cupboard. With tremendous imperfection, I dislike cooking with my kids.
- *Health and fitness! That's the route to perfection!* Untold numbers of workout DVDs, weights, jump ropes, stretchy bands of varying lengths and stretchinesses, and abandoned nutritional supplements, including some promising to make my nails grow, fill the backs of closets and basement shelves. Reality check: I look like this because I'm lazy.

Now that I'm forty and "wise," I (mostly) accept that I am who I am, shameful cuticles and all. I will never be perfect, but I do have stories to tell and some notable accomplishments—I am a poison control hall of famer.

ALLISON HART was discovered wandering the streets of Boston strapped to an infant and muttering curse words to herself. She was brought to safety and placed in front of a keyboard and thus was born Motherhood, WTF?, her popular humor blog where she says the things other moms have the good sense to only think.

Since that fateful day in 2007, Allison has spent countless hours on the internet, on her site and others including Scary Mommy and The Huffington Post, *making people feel better about their parenting by sharing her daily struggles with a mix of humor, insanity, and cussing. The precise recipe is written with crayon on a random scrap of paper that Allison would never be able to find. She is also a contributor to the anthologies* I Just Want to be Alone *and* You Have Lipstick on Your Teeth.

I Just Want to Be Perfect

Allison spends her free time banging her head against the wall, repeating herself to her two children, and wondering why she came into this room. Four out of five doctors recommend you follow her on Facebook, Twitter, Pinterest, and, of course, her blog. The fifth doctor is a jerk.

Perfect Mom Friends
By Deva Dalporto
MyLifeSuckers

We moved from New York to a quaint California suburb when my daughter was seven-months-old. We found a perfect little house, down a perfect little driveway, in a perfect little town, and I was miserable. I was sleep-deprived. Depressed. Lonely. And desperate to fit in the with the local moms.

Now these moms weren't the kind of moms I was used to back in my neighborhood in New York. These moms wore jeans instead of yoga pants. These moms brushed their hair. These moms clearly showered *daily* and never left the house with leaky nipples or spit up on their shirts. These moms packed organic snacks and chlorine-free diapers in their trendy diaper bags and always had heirloom-quality wooden toys on hand to entertain their beautiful children with.

These moms were perfect.

Motherhood didn't come naturally to me. When I had my baby, I felt like I'd been hit by a bus. An adorable, screaming, pooping, seven pound bus. I always felt like a wreck. Exhausted. Dirty. On the verge of tears. But more than anything, I was desperately lonely. I just wanted to hang out with someone who could actually hold a conversation and didn't poop in my lap.

So after a few lonesome months, I invited a mom from Baby Gym out for lunch. We went to a cute little spot downtown and plopped our bundles of joy into their highchairs. Well, *she* plopped her baby into a highchair. I spent fifteen minutes trying to get my kid to sit down as she screamed, tangled her legs in the straps and went stiff as a board to prevent me from getting her to sit down. When I finally got her into the highchair, I was sweating and covered in some sticky greenish-brown substance that she'd smeared on me. I just prayed it wasn't poop.

We ordered and fed the babies. Well, *she* fed *her* baby. Her son sat happily eating homemade pureed peas and carrots while my daughter spit out her store-bought Gerber green beans all over the table and stared screaming, "Boob! Boob! Boob!" as she grabbed at my dirty shirt.

I started to babble after we ordered. I hadn't had a conversation with a friend in so long, it was like a spigot opened and everything I'd had to say over the past nine months—but had no one to say it to—came pouring out. I overshared. And I knew I was oversharing as stories about my boobs and my sex life came tumbling out of my mouth, but I couldn't shut up. It was painful. My new "friend" looked almost, well, okay *totally*, relieved when the check came.

I reached into my bag and felt around the mess of diapers and wipes to grab my wallet. Hmm—It had to be there somewhere—Right??? I couldn't have forgotten my wallet. Not now. Not today. Not in front of *her*!!!!! I started to panic and pulled my bag into my lap and frantically searched inside as my daughter pulled my hair and screamed in my ear. It wasn't there.

I felt my cheeks burning as the words came out of my mouth. "I, um, forgot my wallet."

Perfect mom smiled at me and flipped back her long blonde locks. "It's on me," she said.

I never heard from her again.

It took a while for me to get up the nerve to make another attempt at a mom friend after that. But nine months later, I was ready. I invited a mom from music class over for a play date. My daughter was talking and walking by then, and she was as ready for a friend as I was. When I extended the invitation, I felt like a fourteen-year-old boy asking a girl to a dance. But I did it. And she said yes. I was thrilled.

I spent hours prepping for their arrival. I wanted it to go perfectly. I cleaned the house. Dressed my daughter and myself in fresh clothes. (No stains! No yoga pants!) Hid all the plastic toys in the garage. Fanned out a stack of educational board books on the coffee table. I even put out a big spread of organic snacks. The playdate was going to be a smashing success.

They arrived right on time (what???) and the girls started to play with our newly-purchased heirloom-quality wooden toys as Music Class Mom and I chatted nearby.

"Oh yes," she said. "We're filling out preschool applications now. Sydney is gifted so we need to find the right school for her. Your daughter must be gifted too, she's such a good talker!"

I beamed. She *was* a good talker. She didn't sleep at all and refused to eat anything I made for her, but she was a great talker.

"Thank you," I said. "Would you like another cup of chai?"

"Yes, thank you."

I walked over to the kettle and smiled to myself. *This is going so well!* I thought. *Maybe I can hang with the perfect moms after all.*

And then I heard it. Her little voice piecing the air with excitement.

"There it is, Mom!" my daughter screamed. "There's that fucking cat!"

I felt like all of the air had been sucked out of the room.

"What, darling?" I said in my best June Cleaver voice. "Did you say something about a truck?" I smiled awkwardly at Music Class Mom and felt like I was going to puke.

"No," my daughter yelled. "That fucking cat who is always in our yard, he's back! Hi fucking cat! C'mere fucking, fucking, fucking cat! Oh, fucking cat!"

Music Class Mom rushed over to her daughter and put her hands over her ears. "We have to be going," she said, stuffing her kid's organic cotton sweater into her designer diaper bag. "It's nap time."

"It's only 11:30," I said.

"Right," she said as she raced out the door. "Bye."

I never heard from her again.

A few months later I sat on the rug in preschool orientation. I had given up on the perfect moms by that point and had settled into my un-showered, yogurt-coated, lonely existence. The teacher was rambling on about the benefits of a play-based education as the parents jotted notes and mentally patted themselves on the back for choosing such a wonderful program for their children.

The mom next to me leaned over her big pregnant belly and whispered, "I'm so tired."

I turned and looked at her yogurt-stained yoga pants and her messy mom bun and smiled.

"Me too," I said. "It's been a long three years."

She laughed.

"I'm Deva," I said extending my hand.

"Jacquie."

She shook my hand and I felt something sticky on her fingers. I just prayed it wasn't poop.

DEVA DALPORTO of MyLifeSuckers is the creator of the viral videos Suburban Funk, I Just Need Some Space, What Does the Kid Say, Let It Go – Mom Parody, *and many more. NBC called her the "Weird Al of YouTube Moms." Her videos have garnered over 70 million views and have been on Good Morning America,* The Today Show, People.com, *CNN, ABC,* Fox News, The Huffington Post, *PopSugar, Parents, trending on Yahoo several times and more. A former Senior Editor for Nickelodeon's ParentsConnect, Deva has also written for HuffPost, Yahoo!, PopSugar, Scary Mommy, Bio.com, What The Flicka and WeAreTeachers. She won a BlogHer Voice of the Year Award for Short Form Video and was nominated as Best Fan Cover Artist in ABC's Billboard Music Awards Special. She is a contributor to* I Just Want to Be Alone *and* The Bigger Book of Parenting Tweets. *Deva blogs at MyLifeSuckers.com and you can always find her on YouTube, Facebook and Instagram!*

Comeuppance
By Audrey Hayworth
Sass Mouth

I've always pursued perfection, which is impossible I know, but I'm a doer.

I don't know about you, but it seems as though the elusive pursuit of perfection is thwarted by my lady bits, both my breasts and vagina. Sometimes those bitches are not my friends, even though they are attached to my body and claim to be my friend, they are known liars.

Like I said, I'm a doer and I devoted the first twenty years of my life to the pursuit of perfection, starting with my boobs.

I had no boobs, literally just nipples attached to my ribcage, with butterfly ribs sticking out further than the nipples, which made it seem like my boobs were sticking out at the bottom of my rib cage.

I was, come hell or high water, going to fix that damn problem. And I finally did on a glorious day when I was twenty-one years old. No more ribs larger than my nipples, my full B cup did the job and I was deliriously grateful.

The new set either helped with my confidence, which helped land me more dates, or men are just really into perfect looking boobs, and were drawn to them. It was probably the latter. Regardless, in the years that followed the surgery, I went out on several dates with several different doctors. After the last date with one of them, I thought to myself, *I am never dating another doctor again.*

Six months later, I made the mistake on a Thursday of saying *out loud* I would never date another doctor. The following Wednesday, I went on a blind date with a doctor and then ten months later, I married him.

This, is the universe's comeuppance. If you say it out loud, the *exact opposite will happen.*

On our first date, my husband told me he could never date someone who had undergone plastic surgery. Marrying me was his comeuppance for that comment.

A funny thing happens when you marry a doctor—people mistakenly think you live a white-picket-fence life. This sentiment is both stifling to me and yet sickly appealing to my Type A perfectionist pursuing personality. It also sets me up for failure and exhaustion on a daily basis.

My husband and I went on to have two children over the course of the next five years, and to my glee and delight, my breasts looked even better after breastfeeding.

This was it, I thought, *I've finally achieved the perfect breasts. A boob job, two kids, breastfeeding and they are perfect.* I then made the mistake of uttering out loud to my husband that I actually liked my breasts better after breastfeeding.

That was on a Monday. I should've known better.

That Wednesday, at 7:30 in the morning, I was sitting at a red light while driving my screaming toddler to speech therapy. I was distracted by the screaming and my chest right below my collar bone was itching. I can clearly remembering staring at the red light, zoned out and not quite caffeinated enough, running my fingernails over the top of my chest.

Wait, I thought, one side feels *lower* than the other side. Both hands went up and each grabbed a breast.

One was smaller than the other.

Cars started honking at me and as soon as I pulled into the therapist's office, I couldn't hand my son off quick enough to run to the bathroom and lift my shirt. There, staring at me in the mirror, was a gaping hole in my chest, settling in next to my other perfect breast. One implant had ruptured, and because they were saline, my body absorbed it right up, sucking up my perfect breast with it. *This is what I get for talking shit about my old neighbor's bad boob job and being so obsessive about symmetry.*

I had moved to a new town since my surgery, so after polling everyone I knew, I got an appointment with a reputable plastic surgeon in town that Friday.

"Well," she started, "this isn't an emergency, so you can put it off indefinitely."

Bitch, please. I beg to differ, this is definitely an emergency. I have a damn hole in my chest and a chicken cutlet in its place.

I ended up going back to my old surgeon, driving four hours for the surgery, but he couldn't fit me in for four weeks. I had to carry around two chicken cutlets with me at all times, along with a bottle of baby powder, because the cutlets got sweaty, absorbed odor, and had to be frequently changed.

Around the same time, my uterus betrayed me, and I had to have her removed soon after my implant surgery. While in the hospital, it was discovered that because of scar tissue from abuse, my bladder couldn't empty itself and was causing a major infection. They explained it was like a half empty Capri Sun, the empty part slumped over and the bottom part full of urine it couldn't quite push out. This meant I was going to have to use catheters to empty my bladder from that day forward. Because I am married to a doctor, the nurses sent me home with a diagram and a starter catheter packet, assuming he would show me the ropes.

Ladies, the lowest point in my marriage was having to hold a flashlight in a dimly lit bathroom while your doctor husband instructs you on the proper way to insert a catheter into your urethra. The mystery is *gone*.

Success in catheterizing depends on K-Y Jelly, or the lubricating jelly of your choice. Which means that when you go out in public, you not only carry catheters, but a lubricator as well (think about going through airport security with that). Catheters need to be sterile, so I can't exactly dump KY into a travel container and carry around with me, the introduction of bacteria would mean a subsequent infection.

While I was trying to figure all of this out, I ran into Target to pick up a prescription right after they opened. After I paid for the medicine, I was strolling past the travel section, and lo and behold the heavens opened: travel size K-Y. Jackpot. I emptied that bin, taking their entire inventory and dumping all twenty bottles into the cart. *While I'm here,* I thought, *I better get some more K-Y for the house.* Two industrial size bottles went into the cart.

Now, normally I probably would not stroll around in public with a cart full of Kentucky Jelly, but I was in a desperate place. I went to checkout before I ran into someone I knew with a cart full of now twenty-two bottles of personal lubricant and nothing else.

There was only one lane open.

And the person behind the checkout was a damn male child. He may have been seventeen, but that's questionable.

I started to load up all of my K-Y onto the belt. I looked up to see his eyes got very large and he refused to look up as large beads of sweat started to drip down his forehead. As I was leaving, I'm fairly certain I heard him have a Freudian slip and say "Spank you" instead of "Thank you." I shop in Target at least twice a week and that was the first and last time I ever saw him. I'm convinced I'm the reason he quit, and I'm willing to bet he didn't finish his shift that day.

Shortly after the Target incident, Amazon came out with Amazon Prime. My catheters and K-Y Jelly now show up on my doorstep in an unlabeled box, and I can save face. Technology is *amazing*.

At home, in the master bathroom, our toilet is separated from the sink, in its own little room with a door. There is a window inside where the toilet is. It's just wide enough to put my box of catheters and K-Y. This part is important, so try to picture it. The catheters come in a green box with no identifying information on it anywhere. If anyone walked in there, most people probably wouldn't even notice it. Next to the box, I put the K-Y. When one gets low, I pull out another industrial size bottle and put it next to it, in a queue of sorts.

Now, most close friends know about the catheters, but even so, I hide the K-Y in the cabinet, because part of me is embarrassed. But to hide it, I have to take it out of that room and put it in a cabinet under the sink. It takes effort to remember, and frankly, sometimes I forget or just get lazy. Also, over the years, I've noticed that most people don't use the master bathroom during parties (and even then it's usually people we know), and I got complacent because I didn't think anyone would go in there to see it.

That is, most people didn't use the master bathroom, until the day I threw a bridal shower for a close friend of mine. Sixty-five people came, and I knew *maybe* five of them in attendance. Now, for the record, I can throw a shower, the kind that people drool over. I love every bit of it, and I try to one up my last party, making every damn last bit *flawless*.

The shower was amazing. I knew I had outdone myself. I was *smug*. I even had time to apply perfect makeup and put together an outfit without running around sweating like a maniac before the party started. I noticed that some of the older ladies were looking at me with lingering glances. *I just look that fantastic and relaxed*, I thought to myself, *I could pull it off without breaking a sweat*.

After the shower was over, I went into our master bathroom and sat down on the toilet to finally pee. I reached for a catheter and gasped. I had forgotten to put the bottles of lubricant up and staring back at me, there was not one, not two, but THREE industrial size K-Y bottles sitting on the window sill. As in, there was not an inch left of sill left because it was filled with lubricating jelly.

The room started to spin. I started to replay the stream of women using my bathroom. About sixty of the guests now think I am a freak in the bedroom. The aunts. My friends' mom. Her soon to be mother-in-law. The grandmothers. *The great-grandmothers*. All of the people that gave me the lingering looks did not, in fact, think I looked fantastic. They thought I looked like a nymphomaniac, one who would not be satisfied with just one bottle of personal lubricant.

The one person I knew personally that had used the bathroom I immediately called.

"Hey!"

"Hey! The shower was beautiful. Everything was perfect!"

"So listen, I realized after the shower that I left something out that I forgot to put—"

She interrupted me, "No need to explain, I mean, *good for you*. Ten years in and your sex life is still that hot!"

I didn't even have to tell her. She thinks I'm a freak, too, because *three industrial size* bottles of K-Y Jelly.

"Stooooooooooppppppppp. I mean, yes, our sex life is great, but that's not what it's is for!"

After a conversation where I was crying half from laughter and half from mortification, I got into my car, went to Target and bought a basket that fits on the window sill and holds all of the catheters and all of the lubricant.

Sometimes, if I forget to use catheters for more than a day, or if we travel more frequently, I get seriously bad urinary tract infections. I've always been able to tell when they come on, because I start running a high fever out of nowhere. This is usually no big deal, thanks to modern medicine, I can call up my general practitioner, pee in a cup and get on antibiotics.

It's usually no big deal, until the day it is. One night, while preparing the house for severe weather and tornadoes, I started having severe pains on my right side, but with no fever. I called my husband, the doctor, who was 2,000 miles away at a conference.

You probably have a bladder infection, he said.

I have no fever, I argued, *I think I have appendicitis, at least that's what WebMD says.*

You have a bladder infection, call the doctor in the morning and you can start antibiotics, he argued back, clearly exasperated.

The next day, tornadoes hit and everything was closed, including the doctor. *Okay, I can make it one more day,* I thought, as what felt like contractions started.

The next morning, I started peeing blood. I went to the doctor and started antibiotics, but by the time I started them, I was sick, high fever and vomiting from a raging bladder infection. My husband came in that afternoon from his trip, and three hours after landing, he started running fever. He had the flu. *The man flu.* I was on my own.

You know how you still do all the damn things because you are a mom? Even with 103 fever, contraction-like pains, and non-stop vomit?

Our oldest son is going to a new school for middle school, one where we don't know any of the families, and because of those tornadoes at the beginning of the week, the registration was rescheduled for the next morning, the morning after I started peeing blood. He could only be registered this particular morning, or he would lose his spot at this school.

I've got to pull it together long enough to do this, I thought. I walked to the bathroom, rinsed my face with cold water and applied mascara, in an attempt to hide my bloodshot eyes. *I've never met these people before and I can fake it for the next hour.*

I had to fake it because I am determined, always, to make an impeccable first impression. You only get one of those. I'm obsessive. If I know I am going to meet someone knew, or a group of new people, I do all the things—I make sure I'm wearing makeup, there's not one hair out of place, and my clothes are planned out and wrinkle free. I will even reluctantly admit that I plan getting my roots done a full week before something important on the calendar, so it looks more natural, and I bleach my teeth to remove the most recent coffee stains. I could go on, but I think I've already proven how ridiculous I can be.

Before I could go impress these new, fellow parents, I had to get both of our boys on the bus. As the bus pulled up, I was bent over, hurling all over our grass as all of our neighbors in our cookie cutter neighborhood drove by on their way to work. Not only was I still running fever, hunched over from pain and throwing up, I was now throwing up due to the strongest antibiotics on the market. I just prayed that none of my neighbors thought I was hungover.

I finally pulled it together long enough to drive to the school, pulling over twice to throw up. I pulled up into the parking lot, and I started getting nervous that I wouldn't make it through registration without throwing up. *I should've tried to eat something*, I thought, digging around in my car.

A blueberry protein bar. Perfect. I took two bites and started to gag. *I just have to hold it down for twenty minutes.*

In a move out of character for me, but because I was just struggling to make it ten more feet, I did not check myself in the rear view mirror. I got in line behind this very presentable, nice lady and we chatted for the length of the line. Another lady chimed in, and I left thinking, *I really hope our sons hit it off because I like them a lot. I mean, we're a somewhat normal, respectable family. I think I pulled it off and made a great impression. They'll want their kids to hang out with ours.*

Much to my relief, I made it through the rest of registration without throwing up and I made it to the car. When I put the car in reverse and checked my rear view mirror to move, I caught a glimpse of myself.

After I had thrown up and wiped the tears from under my eyes, apparently I smeared my mascara over one of my eyelids, all the way up to my eyebrow and under the other eye. I also had two very large blueberry bits in between several teeth that I did not know were there. The kicker? I had vomit on my shirt in three places and in my hair and didn't realize it.

I don't think they're going to let their kids come over to our house any time soon.

I spent my time recovering thinking about how I could rectify that first impression. I knew the mom's name, I could email her. No, that would seem weird. I'll just wait until the first parent's night and make sure I look like I had a makeover. I better go schedule my hair appointment now, so I can guarantee my hair gets done the week before. That reminds me, I probably need to get a push up bra because my once perfect breasts are finally starting to sag. Because, you know, comeuppance.

AUDREY HAYWORTH is a redheaded sass mouth who filters ninety percent of what she actually thinks. She lives in the South with her husband and two boys where all the good things are: family, friends, greasy food and an international airport in case she ever needs to flee the country. She loves glitter, unicorns, flamingos and cake for breakfast. You can find her at SassMouth.net, on Facebook, on Twitter, and on Instagram.

How The Perfect Beach Vacation Can Go Grossly, Horribly Wrong
By Joelle Wisler
Running From Mountain Lions

I was smug the day that it happened, I'm sure. We had just traded in three feet of snow at our home in Colorado for a warm sandy beach in Southern California for two weeks over Christmas break. We were going to soak in the sun and come back with enviable tans for our friends to admire and piles of photos documenting our perfect vacation. My Instagram feed was about to get seriously obnoxious. As it turns out, I still can't look at those pictures without wanting to heave the contents of my stomach into the nearest garbage receptacle.

It had recently rained in the part of California that we were visiting, after a long period of no moisture. The dry river beds that led to the ocean couldn't keep up with the amount of water coming down, so they let loose their contents. All of their contents. Organic, inorganic, all of it. The first few days we were there, the beach looked rough; sticks and decimated plants and the occasional dead bird or broken bottle littered the sand as far as we could see.

As my entire family marched out to the ocean that very first day (swimsuits, buckets, towels, sunscreen, checkity-check) we saw murky lakes sunken into the sand from the high tides. The kids didn't seem to care that the knee-deep water was brownish with bits of flotsam and algae swimming around. The shallow pools were warm and we thought, what the heck, the kids would be safer playing in there than trying to navigate the violent crashing waves. I remember actually feeling relieved. I could now just sit and watch, instead of having to run around like a lunatic to make sure that nobody was getting dragged, screaming, out to sea. On a side note, I'm super fun and relaxed on vacation.

My husband and I set up our spot near the edge of one of the little pools, flipping open the striped chairs and laying out towels that would be covered completely in sand before they even hit the earth.

The kids splashed and frolicked and built sand castles which displayed round rock doors and moats and seaweed paths. Meanwhile, I dug my feet into the wet sand and drew designs into the ground with sticks, zen-garden style, thinking that no moment could be better. The day was beautiful, the sky the color of happiness, and the white waves crashing in the background were like the soundtrack for all of my self-congratulatory feelings.

The day was everything we had hoped it would be. We walked back hours later, hungry, nicely exfoliated and, unknowingly, hosting a new group of friends.

The rest of the vacation went off without a hitch. The beach became clean again with the comings and goings of the tides. We all but forgot about the dirty warm pools and I was once again forced to chase children as my husband flung them like rag dolls into the waves. I was like a crazed Australian Shepherd, trying to herd my darlings away from every imaginary rip-tide or undertow or rogue kraken that I just knew was out there, waiting to snatch them away.

Christmas came and went. We opened presents and played games and annoyed the crap out of each other just like all of the other special moments of our life. Two weeks later we went home, and along with tanned bodies and relaxed souls, we also brought home our new friends that were most likely just traveling to our lungs to begin a brand new life cycle.

Fast forward to six weeks later. It was an ordinary morning. I usually wake up before everyone else to write or sometimes just listen to the sweet sound of my own thoughts for five seconds. The previous couple of days, I remember I had been feeling just slightly "off." I couldn't really explain it and the feeling wasn't strange enough that I had really given it more than a passing thought.

I got up that morning and went to the bathroom and that was when I experienced the moment that will most likely haunt me until the very last breath leaves my wrinkly old body. You see, one of the friends that had hitched a ride back to Colorado from our perfect beach vacation had just been unceremoniously evicted. As I sat on the toilet, I felt something … odd come out. And, sure enough, when I turned to look, there, floating in the porcelain bowl was what looked like a spaghetti noodle. The moment of truth arrived when the spaghetti noodle began to move.

The morning gets a little blurry after that. My first thought was that if there was one, there had to be others, and the worst part of knowing *that* was that the others were STILL INSIDE OF ME. I now know what it feels like to want to exit my own body in a blaze of glory. The strangest thoughts entered my mind during this existential crisis. I knew that they had to come out. How was I going to get them out? Fire? Whiskey? Jalapeños?

As these thoughts of mass murder raced through my head, I captured him (or her I'm still not sure) in a tupperware container and began to research the shit out of him. Which turned out to be a horrible mistake. As the rest of the house slept, I read everything I could find on *Ascaris Lumbricoides* who is most likely found in wet, warm areas like tepid pools on fantasy beach vacations.

Pictures rolled out on the internet with the intent, I was sure, of creating a horror reel of film that still pops into my mind at unsuspecting moments like when having french onion soup or rice noodles. It turned out that I had quite a healthy specimen, too. I was oddly proud. Not newborn-baby proud, but the fact was, I had indeed created life.

My husband stumbled into the kitchen, wiping the sleep from his eyes, weirdly calm at seeing his wife in blubbering, snotting hysterics, sitting in front of the computer, clutching a Tupperware container as if it were a live grenade. His calmness lasted only until I showed him my friend and informed him that, from my extensive research, he was probably in the same situation. As were the kids. I wish I could say that I cared about anybody other than myself at that moment. If someone would have offered only one antidote, I would have steamrolled over all of them to get it, including the three-year-old.

My doctor's appointment that afternoon came after hours of torment and intimate conversations with a poor, unsuspecting local pharmacist who I begged to just give me the drugs without a doctor's prescription. He felt for me, he really did, but mostly he tried to outgross me by telling me a story about a worm that he saw coming out of a guy's nose once. I don't think he anticipated that telling me this story would elicit the amount of crying that it did.

Three days of drugs for the entire family, some horrible moments with some stool sample containers, and we were all deemed free and clear of any alien visitors. I don't think I felt truly clean for months and any stray hemorrhoid is still a cause for panic. What I learned most from this whole situation is that no vacation will help make your life perfect, even if the pictures say otherwise.

What you can't see in those palm-tree-filled photos from your friends may make you wish that you had just stayed home and shoveled snow.

JOELLE WISLER is a writer and mom living in the mountains in Colorado who believes in sarcasm, winging it, and raising children who won't ever live in her basement. She once had to slide groceries up her driveway on a sled when there was over three feet of snow with her newborn baby strapped to her chest. Just like a freaking pioneer person. That was a random story but tells you a bit about what a princess she is because she won't stop talking about it. You can also find Joelle on Facebook, Instagram, and Twitter.

Threshold of Hell-ing It
By Meredith Spidel
Mom of the Year

Two years ago, we had what I lovingly refer to as The Weekend from Hell. When I think of it, I am instantly transported into the scene in *National Lampoon's Christmas Vacation* when Chevy Chase boldly declares, "Look around! We're standing on the threshold of hell!" while his eyes bug out of his head. Except that I could never, ever look as cute as Ellen in her eighties-esque ruffled open keyhole top and ginormous shiny sateen green skirt, so it's probably not even reasonable to identify so closely with the characters in that scene. Oh well.

You see, my daughter had just turned three months old. My grandmother had just died. My sister had just gotten married in a wonderful wedding. And my mother was in process of dying. So there were a lot of big life events going on. Good things, sad things, fun things, tough things, and whole lot of looking hellacious in bridesmaids' dresses and being covered in spit-up formula.

I felt like I was losing my mind, but I had this, right? Nothing like clinging to some positive energy and a whisper of hope to get you through those more challenging times. Surely, life was going to "settle down" soon?

And then one Friday night, my two-year-old son was innocently playing with his blocks when he twisted his body in a weird way and he crumbled to the floor, screaming in pain. I called my husband at work and told him I thought our son broke his leg. Naturally, my husband told me I was crazy.

Twelve hours later, a few ambulance rides, and a lot of hysterical tears on my part, our son had landed at Dupont Children's Hospital and bravely survived the first surgery of his young life. He had been put in a hip spica cast, a cast that extended from under his armpits to his toes. He would be in this cast for at least six weeks, and due to the perfectly straight positioning of his cast, he would not be able to ride in car seat or leave the house during that time without an intense harness system that caused me to instantly break into a panicked sweat every time I saw it. Also, my son would now require 24/7 supervision, so that would be fantastic. But hey, he could move his arms and there was a convenient square hole cut in the cast for diaper-changes. *So at least there was that.*

My husband and I had never really gone over protocol for how we would split duty should one child require hospitalization while we had a newborn at home. *Foolish, unprepared parents that we were.* He ended up manning the hospital scene while I stayed with our daughter, but I needed to get myself to the hospital and we somehow had to get my husband's car from the initial emergency room my husband had driven to. Queue up the in-laws, who in general, already think I'm an insane mess, but are usually nice to me anyway.

I am sure this weekend did boatloads to show them that I so clearly had my act together.

After a lot of fuss and a couple false starts to pick up the car with me forgetting vehicle keys which my in-laws handled patiently and gracefully, we got everyone sorted and to where they needed to be. Including my son, who was blessedly now home.

One small catch? Did I mention we were in the midst of a snowstorm and our power had shut off earlier that day? And my husband and I hadn't quite gotten around to buying a generator yet. We had only recently moved into our home, and you see, it was Halloween weekend. OCTOBER. Pennsylvania in October.

We weren't anticipating getting major storms that downed our power for three days. We weren't anticipating having a totally incapacitated toddler in frightful pain either, but hey, who was keeping track?

Our kind pastor lent us his generator, which we put to use running the fridge, linking space heaters to the kids' rooms with extension cords, and playing the current family favorite, *Mickey's Great Clubhouse Hunt,* on the laptop on repeat. We then walled off the living room with a heavy blanket and cozied up by the fireplace. With my casted and sedated son. With my three-month-old daughter. And with my in-laws. *Perfect.*

Really, all was going pretty pleasantly well. My crying hysterics had abated to a minimum, and I had even begun to toy with the idea of taking a break from heating water for my daughter's bottles over the propane camping stove to do something indulgent, like take a shower.

And then it happened.

I realized I had lost my wallet.

Relatively, I was at a point in my life where I was handling a lot. I still grasped at that false bravado that had been carrying me; *I could do this*. We called hospitals to see if anyone had reported it. We upended the box of sanitary napkins the nurse had given us to help pad my son's diapers (yes, I will actually be able to tell my son one day that he used cases of maxi pads—*amazing*). We checked every corner of the van.

It wasn't there. The wallet was just *gone*. The tears had started to well up again and my slim tether to sanity was starting to look a bit weak. But it was still cool; I believed this could be managed until...I realized losing my wallet meant I had lost my library card.

Breaking. Point.

Forget it. This mama was done.

Wailing and tantruming, I sobbed to my husband, "But I won't be able to check out any more books! How will I read?!"

You see, you can mess with a lot of things in my life. If God had called me to have a child with broken bones, a dying mother, and lots of bonus time watching *Mickey Mouse Easter* movies with my in-laws while bouncing a newborn baby to sleep on Halloween weekend, fine. I could be down with that. *But don't take my reading away*. No way, no how. It's all about priorities on this earth.

I wept, smearing gross snot from my nose, and pleaded with my husband, "It can't get worse than this, can it, J?"

He looked me dead-on and said, "No, Meredith, it absolutely cannot get any worse than you losing your library card."

And then...the bubble of laughter started. And rose. And overtook us both until we couldn't breathe.

Gasping for air, surrounded by our own Threshold of Hell, we knew in that moment that it could never get any worse. Or any better.

You see, *this*, in all its horrible glory, is actually the sweet stuff of life. One of the stories that we will grow old with. One that will make us shudder when we remember how magnificently awful that weekend was, yet how proud we were of ourselves when we managed to jam our son's monkey costume over his cast, lay him in a wagon and still take him out trick-or-treating. *And even remembered to feed our daughter too.*

Because *this* is how and why you can laugh at a time like this. Helps keep the tears at bay and reminds us of the truly important things in life—like secure library cards.

MEREDITH SPIDEL blogs at themomoftheyear.net, where she spoofily earns her Mom of the Year title one epic parenting fail at a time, striving to offer heart and hope with a sweet dose of humor for fellow parents of the world and all their empathizers. She has been part of several best-selling anthologies, featured on prominent sites such as The Huffington Post, In the Powder Room *and* BlogHer, *and loves her role as the Executive VP/Operations Manager of The BlogU Conference. When she's not breaking up fights over Legos and juice boxes, she remains fully committed to sharing a less serious look at the world of parenting. Follow along with Meredith on Facebook, Twitter, Pinterest and Instagram for more smart scoop on the stuff that keeps our heads spinning as parents.*

The Best Damn Hippie This Side of the Sixties
By Christine Organ

A few years ago I decided that I wanted to honor my inner hippie. Inspired by Barbara Kingsolver's book *Animal, Vegetable, Miracle,* and after reading one too many articles about sad cows and angry chickens and how Monsanto is the Devil's spawn, I decided it was time for me and my family to do our part to be more eco-conscious. I didn't plan to wear hemp skirts or shun modern medicine, but I wanted to do a little more to reduce our carbon footprint, so to speak. I wasn't exactly sure what "carbon footprint" meant, but I knew reducing it was a good thing.

For starters, I wanted to make sure my family wasn't eating beef from sad cows or eggs from angry chickens. We could use less plastic, compost, and grow our own vegetables watered with collected rain water. How hard could it be?

"I think we should try to eat less meat," I said to my husband one night while we cleaned up the kitchen after dinner. "I'm worried about how the animals are treated and all the environmental damage, you know?"

"Okay..." he said, dubious.

"When I was a kid, we ate meat from the butcher in town and vegetables my dad grew in the garden. It was the epitome of farm-to-table."

"You grew up in the middle of nowhere Wisconsin, surrounded by farms. It's not quite the same when you live in suburban Chicago. Maybe we could start small? Shop at the farmers' market, find a good butcher, that kind of thing," he reasoned.

"How hard can it be?" I snipped, frustrated by his practicality. Honestly, sometimes his pragmatic sensibility could be really annoying. "I just want to make sure the cows are humanely treated and ethically slaughtered...though I suppose 'ethically slaughtered ' is a bit of an oxymoron, isn't it?"

"Okaaaay," he said. "But you're not going to make us all go vegetarian, are you?"

"Oh, hell no!" I laughed. "I like bacon too much to ever be a vegetarian."

He looked at me sideways, with a raised eyebrow, and sighed.

"Just a few small changes..." I called as he left the room, and I poured an after-dinner bowl of Doritos. *I wonder if Doritos are non-GMO*, I thought.

Like any wanna-be hippie raised on a steady diet of American free market capitalism, I didn't just want to be environmentally conscious—I wanted to be the best damn eco-friendly hippie this side of the sixties. I wouldn't just try to waste less water, I decided I needed to get the biggest rain barrel I could find and display it prominently in our yard so the entire neighborhood could see how eco-friendly we were. I wouldn't just buy organic produce; I would buy locally-grown organic produce with a CSA share, slipping the acronym into casual conversation and acting surprised anytime someone asked "What's a CSA?"

I resolved to eat eggs from free-range chickens named Millie who had plenty of time to laze in the sun and weren't forced to socialize with the mean hens. I would eat only grass-fed, holistically-raised beef from cattle that were given their own private living quarters, massaged daily with essential oils, and read a bedtime story each night.

I bought a rain barrel so big that it stuck out the back of my minivan. I ordered a luxe, compost bin so that I could humblebrag about our so very eco-friendly compost bin while pretending that it wasn't a giant box of garbage and worm poop.

I walked around under a halo of good intentions for a while, basking in the glow of my wholesome plans to live in a more environmentally responsible way while self-righteously letting the whole world know about said wholesome plans and showing off my inner hippie. When people asked about the large covered bucket in our backyard, I smugly answered, "Oh that old thing? That's just our rain barrel made from recycled byproducts." When people talked about making a trip to Costco or Whole Foods, I haughtily thought to myself, *at least I buy LOCAL organic produce*. And even though I had never been a particularly enthusiastic carnivore (aside from bacon, of course), I proudly shared our Meatless Monday recipes and asked if anyone knew where I could buy organic, grass-fed beef made from happy cows that did yoga and meditated.

And much to my husband's chagrin, as he had fearfully predicted based on my incapacity for moderation, I soon thereafter decided to go full-on vegetarian after being an accomplice to the massacre of a family of squid. You see, shortly after I decided to bust out my inner hippie, I joined my dad and brother on a business trip to Korea. While there, our hosts took us to interesting restaurants and introduced us to all kinds of new foods. One night we went to an upscale restaurant where our dinner hosts ordered *shabu shabu*, which is a lot like fondue, except instead of dipping veggies in cheese, you cook your food in a seasoned broth.

After the waiter brought plates of veggies and sliced meat, which I timidly dipped in the boiling water between large sips of my *soju*, he set down a bowl filled with a family of small squid in front of me. *Live squid.* Now I loved calamari as much as the next person, but I generally preferred my food to be dead before it hit my plate and to not look like the animal it had once been.

"What the fuck are we supposed to do with this?" I whispered to my brother, who was sitting next to me.

I didn't want to offend our hosts, but there was no way in hell I was going to kill the wiggling invertebrates in a pot of boiling liquid. Before I knew it, however, the waiter reached over my shoulder, grabbed one of the squid with a pair of tongs and tossed it in the boiling pot. I stared, paralyzed, as its tentacles crawled up the side of the pot in a desperate attempt to flee. *Help! Help!,* it seemed to be saying to me. I stared agape at my bowl, horrified.

Just when I didn't think it could get any worse, the waiter returned to pull the limp squid from the pot. He set it on my plate and pulled out a pair of large scissors, which he used to cut it into tiny pieces. Blue-black ink pooled on the plate while bile pooled in my mouth. That was enough for me. Hippies are vegetarian, aren't they? I could live without bacon.

Armed with a slew of good intentions, a compost bin that looked like an army tank, a rain barrel the size of a water tower, and plans to only buy meat for my family from pampered animals, I basked in the glow of self-righteous hippie-ness. I had visions of eating only the heartiest of homegrown vegetables that were grown in dark brown composted shit-dirt and watered with collected rain water. In short, I was the perfect little hippie. In my mind. For about five minutes.

As it turns out, good intentions will only get you so far. These days our warped rain barrel no longer stands upright and, instead of collecting water, it is used as a hiding spot for the kids' backyard battle games. Occasionally I need to remind them not to use it as a weapon. As soon as I open the back door, I'm blasted by a wall of stink coming from the compost bin and when I holler out a *"Stop hitting your brother with the rain barrel!"* (in the calmest hippie kind of way, of course), one of the fruit flies swarming around the composter lurches into my mouth. After spitting it out, I stomp back inside to finish cooking pre-packaged hot dogs for my family.

As much as I *wanted* to be a good little hippie—in a suburban kind of way, of course—my enthusiasm was thwarted by reality. Phone calls to a few local butchers in search of happy-cow meat for the rest of my family (who hadn't joined me on the vegetarian train) revealed that their meat products were shipped to Illinois from faraway and exotic places like Texas and Kansas. I didn't even dare to ask if they were fed a non-GMO diet and given a long hug before they transitioned to their next life as ground chuck. And when the "CSA" I had mortgaged the house for delivered a box of bananas and kiwis—which, last time I checked, are not native to suburban Illinois, especially in the middle of winter—I realized that our "CSA" was really just a fancy organic grocery delivery service.

Our conspicuous rain barrel saved approximately seventy-three cents on our water bill before winter hit and we forgot to release the water it had collected, leaving us with a giant five-by-three foot cylinder of ice rolling around in the backyard come January. And it only got worse from there. When spring arrived, the tube connecting the rain barrel to the gutter broke, damaging it beyond repair, regardless of how much duct tape, swearing, and fist-pounding I applied. Eventually, the rain barrel became makeshift backyard playground equipment, with kids climbing on it and filling it with sand, rocks, and inflatable pool toys.

And don't even get me started on the compost bin. I ordered a couple of starter kits—with Amazon Prime, of course—but even those were too difficult to understand. I threw in a few piles of dirt, some banana peels and coffee grounds, along with some dandelions for good measure, but there were no worms so it was basically just a giant spinning pile of stinky garbage dirt. I thought about revamping my efforts, and even bought some worms to kick start the worm pooping process, but every time I looked on the internet for some advice about composting, my eyes glazed over reading words like "oxygen infusion" and "heat retention." We're talking about dirt and worm poop, right? I stopped putting food waste in the bin two years ago—the fifty foot walk from the kitchen was too far—but that didn't stop hordes of fruit flies from making it their meeting place.

I did eventually find a real CSA that delivers a box of organic produce each week during the summer. Of course, we nearly had to pull our son out of preschool to pay for it. Most weeks, our share includes a small portion of the most delicious fruit you have ever eaten, along with the largest bag of greens you have ever seen— mesclan, kale, mustard greens, and usually some kind of leafy green plant I'm pretty sure I could smoke if I wanted to. But after making a couple of burned kale chips, the greens usually sit in the bottom of our crisper drawer until I find them swimming in a pool of shit-piss liquid and I immediately toss them in the garbage because it is fifty feet closer than the compost bin and rotten produce stinks like a mother fucker.

I tried to keep up with the charade for a while, telling myself that I had just "taken a break" from my ecological wholesomeness and I would get back on the wagon soon. When friends commented on "how cool it was that we had a rain barrel," I didn't admit that it hadn't actually held water for a few years. When neighbors offered suggestions on how to use our compost to grow exceptionally red tomatoes, I responded with "That's a great idea!" even though I was thinking, *No fucking way; whatever is festering in that thing is probably poisonous.* And I offered greens, beets, and other produce to friends, telling them that we "had more than we could use" — which wasn't actually a lie since we weren't eating any of the greens in our CSA box anyway.

It didn't take long for me to realize that, while part of me is a little hippie-ish, there is also a part of me that is a perpetual half-asser. And given the size of my ass, half of it is more than enough to take down the hippie side. In fact, I may be more of a hippie in theory than practice. The unused rain barrel still sits in our backyard, rolling around in heavy windstorms, because we can't figure out how to fix it and we're too lazy to put it out by the curb. The compost bin remains unused by the side of the house, where it stinks up our backyard and collects fruit flies. And each week I have to clean out the unused produce I had good intentions of using in some new exotic recipe I found on Pinterest before I remember that I don't use Pinterest.

But there is one change that stuck. As it turns out, being vegetarian fits quite nicely with my half-ass attempts to be more eco-friendly because finding organic, grass-fed beef made from locally-raised, blissed-out, yoga-practicing, meditating cows rubbed with essential oils every day is much harder than you'd expect.

CHRISTINE ORGAN is a writer whose wanna-be Zen patience is tested daily by her two loud kids and ill-behaved dogs. She likes naps, happy cows, and swearing. She dislikes cleaning, angry chickens, and wearing regular pants. She abhors yoga. When she isn't putting flowers in her hair or singing Kumbaya, *you can find her in front of the computer or sneak-eating cookie dough in the bathroom. She is a staff writer for Scary Mommy and her work has also appeared in* The New York Times, The Washington Post, *and* Babble, *among others. She is the author of* Open Boxes: The Gifts of Living a Full and Connected Life, *co-author of a forthcoming photography coffee table book, and co-editor of a forthcoming anthology. You can find her wasting time on Facebook, Twitter, and Instagram.*

Pizza Party From Hell
By Suzanne Fleet
Toulouse and Tonic

"What's wrong?" I say to Gabe as he comes into our bedroom, flings himself across the bed on his stomach and releases a dramatic sigh like a teenager. I lay down beside him and rub his back.

We'd been married about two months—and just days after our wedding, we'd moved seven hours away from all of our family and friends so really, all we had was each other. Gabe was consumed with the intensity and uncertainty of the initial year of law school and for the first time in my life, I had no job, no friends, and too much time on my hands. With little else to do, I threw myself into my new role— the perfect wife.

"It's nothing," he says in that way that means it's very much something. "It's just that we've been here two months and it just sucks because I don't have any friends."

He was right. We were in kind of a weird position, caught between two worlds. We were older than most of the other law students who'd come to Vanderbilt straight from college. We were also married, and most of them were single. Their beer pong and sticky-floored lifestyles and ours didn't always mix so well.

Not that we hadn't tried. Gabe had dragged me to crowded keg parties in various students' apartments—but I was so far removed from that lifestyle, it was impossible for me to have fun squashed onto the corner of a couch with a bunch of people I didn't know, trying not to fall asleep while ninety percent of all conversations around me involved law, law school, law class, law students, law cases...

On one such night, we'd been to a couple of apartment parties and when we got back into the car with two other law students, there was animated speculation about where to go next. This person's party or that person's party? Or a bar? Or another bar? I'd been miserable and playing the "supportive wife" for hours by that point so when Gabe asked me what I wanted to do next, I erupted. "All I know is I'm not going to another person's fucking apartment."

So while I clearly wasn't achieving total success at being a perfect wife, I was putting a lot of effort into my new role. I cooked, I cleaned (this depends upon your standards), I did laundry, I shopped carefully for our needs on a limited budget, I listened attentively to Gabe's problems and tried to help. And I prepared for the other role I hoped to tackle soon: the perfect mother.

"I think I've been going about this the wrong way." Gabe switches from pouty to planner. "I've been hanging out with single people so long that I gravitated towards those guys. But it makes a lot more sense that you and I would probably hang out with the other married people instead, right?"

It doesn't surprise me at all to see him shift into a strategy for achieving his goals. After all, somewhere around a year after we started dating, he came clean to me that he'd listened very carefully to my complaints about men during some of our early phone conversations when we were just friends, and after hearing me mention several times that it seemed like men mostly wanted to talk about themselves and rarely listened to anything I said, he set out to win me over by being a listener. And it worked.

"I guess so," I say. "That does make sense."

I'm a person who lets things happen organically. If I run into you three or four times and we seem to have a good connection, then I'll think about trying to get together. It can be a long process. It can also be no process, because it's based on total randomness.

But my super-social, extroverted, planner of a new husband was out to find himself some friends. And I knew he would do it. The chihuahua sinks his teeth into something and never lets go.

"Are there any married couples that seem cool?" I ask, not because I'm interested in proactively courting these people—or any people— but because I'm pretty sure my primary job right now is trying to make my husband happy.

"Yeah, maybe. There are actually a couple of married Mormons..."

Our eyes meet, skepticism prominent on both of our faces. Neither of us are religious. We're rarely seen without a drink in our hands. We curse like sailors. All I can think is *this seems like a match made in hell.*

"I know. I know," he says. "But they seem pretty nice. And they have kids—and we're trying to have a baby—so we'd have some things in common with them. It might be OK."

I bite my lip and perform an exaggerated shrug as if to say, "Not likely but ya never know!"

"There are a few other married couples too. I'm gonna check 'em out."

He rolls over onto his back and pops up off the bed. At least he's in a better mood now that he has a plan.

Relieved, I say "Okay, babe. Do your 'hey buddy buddy hey buddy buddy' thing and see what you think."

A few weeks later, after Gabe has drinks with another married law student named Ralph a time or two, we receive an invitation to join them at their house for a pizza party. I have no idea what an adult pizza party is as I am more used to cocktails and hors d'ouvres, but know they have three little boys, so I figure this is what married people with kids do for fun. Make pizzas and hang out at home with other couples. Since we hope to be headed in that direction soon, we should probably learn about these "pizza parties."

However, I am trepidatious, because Gabe had let slip that Ralph spent a good portion of their beer time together talking about how unhappy his marriage is. The last people I want to hang out with are a miserable, fighting couple about to get a divorce. I envision the two of us sitting there, exuding awkwardness, while the couple throw passive-aggressive missives all around us.

But Gabe's friendless misery is enough to convince me that we have to take a chance on spending an evening trapped in *The War of The Roses.* He assures me Ralph said he was having a group of people over—and that we wouldn't need to stay very long. I figure as long as there are other people there, it will diffuse whatever tension may be in the air.

After a pretty detailed discussion about the appropriate thing to bring to a grown-up pizza cook-out (Is it BYOB or are they providing alcohol? Is wine or beer more appropriate for pizza? If beer, how much do you bring without seeming like you want to turn their cookout into a keg party?), we stop and buy a six-pack of nice beer on the way.

And what a way it is. As it turns out, the couple doesn't live in Nashville, but in a suburb called Franklin which is about a forty-five minute drive from our house.

"Where do these people live?" I ask Gabe about twenty minutes into the trek. "I should've packed us a lunch!"

"We're almost there, I think" Gabe says, tensing up on the steering wheel, leaning forward and squinting at road signs, unsure of where he's going.

I look at the directions in my hand again.

"It just says 'Take exit 41' but is Exit 41 in Alabama because it feels like we should've crossed state lines by now." Sweet wife is a helpless newborn baby. She is powerless in the polished presence of Super Snarkess.

Gabe finally eases the car off the highway at our exit. Only six more vague turns and who knows how many miles before we're there.

When we finally find the house, we pull up to the curb and look at each other without turning the engine off.

"This has to be the wrong house," Gabe says. "What's the street number again?"

"3505," I say as I look at the little piece of paper in my hand and then up to the door. "That says 3505. Maybe we're on the wrong street?" I say hopefully.

"Noooo, I think this must be it." He gives me a look and I see a bit of an apology in there already.

"This can't be it. There are no cars here. Not one." A frothy head of panic is rising in my throat.

The garage doors are closed so I assume the family's cars are inside but otherwise, the driveway and the curb are empty. And we are anything but early. We've purposely arrived fashionably late to ensure we won't have to hang out with this unhappy couple alone.

It quickly becomes obvious to us that there is no pizza party. We are the pizza. I shoot daggers at Gabe with my eyes.

"Just keep going. They haven't seen us yet. Drive down the street, turn around, then we'll just get back on the interstate and go home," I plead desperately.

"We can't leave! There's no one else here! We have to go in or no one shows up for their party!" Gabe is speaking in exclamation points and all I want is to escape, even if it means I have to carjack my own husband.

"JUST DRIVE!" I say. "GO!"

Then Gabe bites his lip and rotates his head like Stevie Wonder a few times in a gesture I will eventually come to know intimately in stressful situations. He exhales deeply and puts both hands out in front of him in a "calm down" gesture. I don't know if he's asking me to take it easy or if he's gone into some kind of prayer state.

"It's gonna be fine. We're just going to go in, have a piece of pizza and then we'll say we have to go. We'll say you're not feeling well." His eyes are still closed, but he's pleading with me, not because he wants to go in but because he thinks he has to. "Thirty minutes. Just give me thirty minutes and we'll leave."

I'm stuck and I know it. I also intuitively know that his promises are bullshit. We are entering Dante's inferno.

We step out of the car carrying our six-pack. I shoot him a *You are so dead* look over the hood of the car as we walk towards the house.

We climb to the top step, look at each other and each take a deep breath. Gabe rings the doorbell.

There is a chaos like I've never heard before from inside the house. Like a herd of mountain goats running from a cougar—and then the door opens and there are three small boys with crooked smiles standing there blinking up at us. Their mother, who looks as though she was due to give birth three weeks ago, catches up to them and smiles warmly.

"Hi! I'm Molly, come in, come in! This is Brandon, Drew, and the little one is Mark. Please come in."

I look at Gabe as she turns her back and leads us into the house. We shrug our shoulders. She was not what we were expecting from Gabe's talks with Ralph.

Once inside, we are quickly divided and conquered. Ralph swoops Gabe into pizza preparations in the kitchen and Molly and the boys give me a tour of the house. The boys are all talking over each other, except for the little one who mostly waves a toy in my direction and says "twuck" over and over again. Molly is warm and gracious and panting from the exertion of simply existing.

As our tour moves past the kitchen, I see that Gabe and Ralph are each having one of the beers we brought. Gabe swiftly hands me one before Molly, the boys and I move on outside to see the swing set.

We are separated for most of the night, Gabe and I. He cornered in the kitchen with Ralph. And me, I am sitting on the sofa reading *Harry Potter and the Sorcerer's Stone* to three eager little boys. Our only communication is exchanging occasional wide-eyed looks that are incapable of saying more than "OMG."

So we both know that we are each in our own "OMG" states but neither of us knows exactly why.

The first really terrible thing to happen is that the beer runs out about forty minutes in. Gabe has two, Ralph has two, I have two and then there is none. We were invited to a party that included no alcohol and our precious six-pack has quickly been consumed by us and one of the hosts.

No one offers to get more. Normally one of us would immediately head for the store but in this case we're unsure how they feel about alcohol in the house (after all, there was NONE when we arrived) and are also hoping to eat pizza and leave as soon as possible. We need to be drinking to be here, but at the same time, we don't want to extend this fucking fiasco any longer than we have to.

Another hour or so passes and the next terrible thing to happen is that no food of any kind appears. Not even goldfish crackers. These children must be starving.

The only communication Gabe and I have is when we pass each

other in the hallway coming and going from the bathroom and Gabe quickly whispers that the first thing Ralph said to him when he arrived was "Well, I think I'm going to get a divorce."

"WHAT?" I mouth dramatically.

"That's all he's talked about the whole time we've been here."

"Oh my God, oh my God! She has no idea! She's so sweet! They're about to have four little boys and she has no idea he's planning this!"

And then we have to go back to our stations as three little voices ping-pong down the hallway, "Come on, come on, we want to know what happened to Harry Potter!"

Finally Ralph calls us dinner, offers us Kool-Aid or water and then casually slides two *turkey* pizzas onto the table. Gulp. I've never seen sadder pizzas in my entire life. They are like two deflated beige balloons with a heap of chopped up, leftover, dried out Thanksgiving turkey on top.

I lock my eyes on my plate. I know if I even look at Gabe, I won't be able to disguise my disgust. The entire group is in close proximity.

We politely choke down a couple of pieces of the Devil's dried meat pie then quickly make our excuses.

Three hours after we'd arrived, Gabe finally opens my car door for me. I climb in and reach over to open his. Not so much because I'm being the perfect, polite wife but because his door no longer unlocks from the outside.

As soon as we close our doors, we each fall back against our car seats and release the sighs of a thousand awkward moments held inside.

"You are never in charge of making plans for us EVER again," I say, letting perfect wife dissipate into the night like a bad fart and welcoming back the real me permanently.

Gabe nodded. "That was utter hell."

It remains as the worst "party" either of us has ever attended and has been a regularly told story at gatherings for a good decade. Gabe and I now frequently attend parties that include children, including our own two boys, with our many married and single friends who wouldn't dream of inviting people to a dry turkey pizza party (neither the turkey nor the party would be dry). But just in case, you can always count on us to show up with alcohol AND back-up alcohol.

And yes, all plans still go through me.

SUZANNE FLEET *is the writer and humorist behind the award-winning blog, Toulouse & Tonic. Suzanne is perhaps best known for her Honest Wine Labels for Moms and Sexy Halloween Costumes for Moms as well as making a lot of plans and never wanting to do any of them when the time comes. A contributor to the* The Huffington Post *and* Today.com, *Suzanne's work has also appeared on ABCNews.com, Yahoo.com,* The Daily Mail, *Jezebel,* The Stir, PopSugar, Scary Mommy *and more.*

Suzanne appears in 5 humorous anthologies, one of which made her a New York Times *bestselling author (*I Just Want To Pee Alone*). She's currently working on a funny book about sick kids. The only way to figure that one out is to put it on your future reading list.*

Mom to 2 stinky boys and wife to a very self-assured man, Suzanne makes fun of them, herself, and everyone else on Facebook and all other social media @toulousentonic.

A Pantry Is Just a Closet with Food in It
By Nicole Leigh Shaw

"You mean the pantry?"

That's one of my kids. Doesn't matter which of the four, they are all word police. I've just said something like, "Put the cereal back in the closet." They can't let that pass without reminding me, stupid cow that I am, that I should have said "pantry," just like I should have said "yes" to a tubal ligation after my first was born. Instead I have four human autocorrects following me around to alert me when I misspeak.

I misspeak a lot. Either my aging brain is failing or I just live with too many people with too many simultaneous activities and needs and so my brain is deleting unnecessary bits like the last four digits of my social security number and the right word for things to make room for the dates and times of sports practices and school events.

So it's true, sometimes "English muffin" comes out as "toast." The kids can see it's not toast and they cannot allow that I could have mistaken one kind of hot bread for another. "Toast, Mother, is not an English muffin. See the nooks and crannies, Mother?"

As if I asked them to use a penis instead of a pencil to do their homework.

A favorite slip up is when I tell them to put food back in the "closet" when I mean to say "pantry," they know exactly which teeny room within a larger room I'm talking about. Still, they correct me every time. I can only assume that's because either their father or I have passed on an asshole gene, so they, like, are genetically motivated to remind me that it's a *fucking pantry, Mom*. They don't say "fucking" pantry, but they want to. I know this because I don't say, "It's a fucking 'closet' for food, you insufferable shits," but I want to.

As my children age they scrutinize my every deed and word, marking every mistake. I may as well unhinge my jaw and devour my own face before my children should suffer my wrongness. And I just might because I can't stand to have them correct me. The irony, of course, is that I've spent the better part of their lives correcting them.

Once, my kids were little and thick-tongued and toothless. I encouraged them to say "free" instead of "three" when they were still toddlers, slurring through language like booze-soaked party goers. Now that they are in grade school, I tell them "ain't" ain't a word. I remind my son that I'm not his "bro." I tell them when they write their letters backwards. I tell them that wiggling shoelaces into a tangle isn't the same as tying shoes. I correct them and try to perfect them.

Looking at all that unasked for tutelage kind of makes me look like the insufferable shit.

But I've earned my overbearing righteousness. I've earned my errors. Not only am I entitled to do as I please and say whatever word comes to mind ("head rest" when I mean "pillow"), I also expect to be understood. I shouldn't have to translate because I'm done growing my brain and it's their turn for nimble-mindedness. Plus, I said so. Plus, I buy all the things. Money is power and I think twenty million (roughly) dollars in birthday parties and braces gives me leave to recreate the English language at my leisure. It's in my parental bill of rights to say "Put it in the place with the thing," and have that thing be done.

They do not have the right to walk away, mumbling to each other, "She means iPod. She says 'iPad,' but she means 'iPod'." But they do.

Enter irony. If I didn't make mistakes, they wouldn't correct me. If they didn't correct me, how would they recognize the same behavior, in all it's glorious comeuppance, when their own children do it to them? That's what I'm banking on, a cycle of revenge that got rolling outside the gates of Eden when Eve's child asked her, "Lizard, I thought you said it was a snake?"

God bless that cycle. Our parents erred; we survived. Still, somehow we've gotten it into our heads that perfection is not only the best, but a viable parenting modality. We all buy in to the idea that there's a thing we must always or must never do, and every child will turn out okay. Maybe they'll become a pharmacist or a successful Realtor or a comptroller—they don't all have to be doctors and lawyers. But if we do it really perfectly, they might be better than okay! They might be incredible.

Shun perfection and you get, who knows? Maybe a politician or a televangelist or a Ponzi schemer.

But, statistics seem to indicate that the investment we are making in our kids is very unlikely to produce Nobel Prize winners nor serial killers. We try our best, but still raise up young adults who surf the internet for porn, sample illicit drugs, date (and marry!) losers, and get heavily into social justice bumper stickers on their electric cars.

We should lower our expectations, not of our kids, but of our ability to parent so well and so perfectly that we will raise the next Einstein or Gertrude Stein. Most of us just aren't that capable and the genetic material our kids are saddled with is okay at best. After all, we did once try to skateboard off a roof…in college.

Accept that the vast majority of our kids will be good enough humans. They'll be kind to most animals, extraordinarily important to a select group of people, have reusable shopping bags they always forget to bring into the store, and sometimes wear socks with sandals. Mostly, they'll be embarrassingly relieved to learn that life has turned out to be pass-fail.

So it's okay that we correct each other, up and down the generational ladder. Parents help little ones to fly right. No nose picking, chew with your mouth closed, tattoos are permanent, that sort of thing. And then they come and fix our remotes, but instead of remotes it will be a chip injected into our forehead and our kids will laugh and laugh when we say jowly old person things like, "But is it safe?"

That's what living is. It's a series of mistakes we correct or don't. Parenting isn't immune from life. That's how Democrats are born to Republicans, wild children are born to prudes, and Yankees fans are born to Red Sox families. Somewhere along the way we try to instill the right and good and proper things in our kids (sunscreen!) and they go test drive our rules and corrections and make devastating mistakes anyway (permanent lip liner!).

Later, when we parents can't suspend disbelief long enough to trust a self-driving car, our kids will teach us the ropes. We'll go out and try their rules and suggestions on, and finding them entirely annoying or unsatisfying or not elastic enough in the waist, will ignore them and get perms or reverse mortgages or date that guy from the senior center with the wobbly dentures because he still likes to dance. Also, we'll put their babies "back" to sleep, because, dammit, they loved napping on their backs in an armless fleece Snuggie, and they turned out fine.

Mistakes will be made. You're probably making one right this minute—I bet it's artificial sweeteners or ignoring the lice letter that came home from school. We've been saying "to err is human" since antiquity. Screw-ups are proof of life. That's why perfection isn't living. Perfection is holding still. Perfection is what happens when we stop growing.

And our kids deserve the fallible, human version of us, the insufferable shits.

NICOLE LEIGH SHAW began writing as a newspaper journalist in 1999, but has been moving through all the metamorphic stages of the modern writer, except "tortured novelist." Soon she'll emerge as a butterfly or a vlogger. Nicole writes for the Internet, which does not offer a 401k. She also writes in print periodicals and periodically contributes to anthologies, including this one. Don't believe her? Then read her essay in the New York Times *bestseller* I Just Want to Pee Alone. *In addition to her four kids, two dogs and one husband, she also maintains a blog at NicoleLeighShaw.com, a Facebook page, and a Twitter account.*

Gladys Doesn't Live Here Anymore
By Lisa René LeClair
Sassypiehole

Gladys was a proud woman with a ruddy complexion and thin white legs resembling that of a pelican. She had eyes of fire that complimented her charred sense of humor and the temperament of a sleeping tiger that just got poked. She also liked to talk—a lot—about all the people she despised and why. And if you *didn't* want to hear what she had to say, she would gladly add you to her black list and find someone who did.

The first time I met Gladys, I was living with my (soon to be ex) husband in a two-bedroom apartment in midtown. I knew upon meeting his mother that she was the kind of woman you wanted to keep on your side: a conflict enthusiast who clearly fancied drama. So, whenever she came to visit, I would drape her in sympathy and pretend to care about whoever she was keen on tearing down. But he and I were only friends back then, so pleasing his mother was easy, and because I had no interest in his pathetic attempts at wooing me, she seemed to admire me even more. She wanted her son to settle down but needed to make sure it was with someone to whom she saw fit and, eventually, her eyes turned to me. Why not? I was intelligent, attractive, funny, and kind; everything she was hoping for in a daughter-in-law. The only thing I *wasn't* interested in was her son.

"Oh sweet Mary and Joseph, I wish my son would hurry up and find himself a nice girl already. What the hell is wrong with you? Why aren't you dating my son?"

They call it a *web of narcissism* because once you are in, you can't get out, and a spider with fangs should have been my first clue. When her son and I married, I was on the best of terms with his mother. She liked me. She even told me so once; stating that if she *had* to choose a partner for her son, I would have been her *second* choice, which was big news coming from a woman who disapproved of everyone. It was also another life ago because one day, I said something I shouldn't have: an innocent statement taken out of context, but my fault nonetheless.

Her granddaughter was about to sign a contract on her very first home. It was a two-bedroom condo near our house that Gladys knew little about. She wanted to make sure that the place where her granddaughter was going to live would exceed her elevated standards, so she called to get my opinion. I told her that I loved it and that I thought it was an ideal opportunity for a young girl in a new town. And then, without thinking, I made the fatal mistake of sharing the irony between my niece's extensive wardrobe and the limited amount of closet space in a potential new home. Regrettably, the satire of my response seemed to rub Gladys the wrong way because, instead of laughing with me, she paused and insisted that *her granddaughter* would be just fine. "Oh shit," I whimpered, "that did not just happen."

You would think that a person like me would be smart enough to edit her words before saying something that might piss off a snake, but I must be addicted to venom. The gargoyle was on high alert, and I knew that no matter how hard I tried to tame her with apologies and remorse, there was no subduing the beast. So instead, I covered my larynx and confronted my husband the second he walked in the door.

"Well, I did it. I managed to piss off your mother."

Unscathed by my anxiety, he rolled his eyes and proceeded to shove a slice of bologna into his mouth. "Shheeelll getovvret!"

Over the next few weeks, I did my best to salvage the dying relationship with his mother. I called, left messages, and followed up with heartfelt emails, but my efforts went unnoticed. At one point, I even sent her an out of print book about forgiveness, along with a hand-written letter of apology, but she never said a word. And then one day, a few weeks later, I received a gruff email advising me that she was in agreement. It wasn't *forgiveness*, but it was a start. Desperate for acceptance, I continued to keep up with our weekly phone calls: speaking only when spoken to and not a word of the incident. But mostly, I just listened.

"Oh, Jesus, Mary, and Joseph—who in God's name dresses like that?

You should have seen her. She looked like a goddamn streetwalker! It reminded me of those outfits YOU used to wear before you started dating my son."

By the time she came to visit, I had convinced myself that the buffer had done its job. I was an attentive and polite listener who could stroke an ego with the skill of a surgeon, and nothing was going to stop me from repairing the damage. Oh sure, things were going to be sticky for a while, but over time I was certain I could ease the blow with false compliments and thoughtful behavior.

Hello, Gladys—I know how much you like wine, so I bought you an ENTIRE PALLET!

But I was wrong—dead wrong—and soon learned that *once you burn a bridge with Gladys*, you're pretty much screwed. I went from being a *perfect wife* to the controlling bitch married to her *poor son*, and in the blink of an eye, he became a victim just like her.

Her first two post-traumatic trips to our house were harsh and defiling. She was out for blood, like a vampire with burnt yellow hair. But by her third visit, I was ready. I knew she liked having coffee in the morning with one egg and a side of toast. I *further* knew that my normal sized coffee cups were far too encompassing for her dainty claws. So, like the good (bad) daughter-in-law that I was, I ran to the store to buy a set of espresso cups *just for her*. While I was out, I also purchased a petite French press as a token of my commitment to the cause. I remembered her telling me once that my four-cup press was three cups too many, and I wasn't looking forward to hearing that story again. When I finished paying for everything, I called my husband to talk condiments.

"What does your mom take in her coffee?"

"Huh?"

"Does she prefer whole milk? Two percent? Half-and-half—what??"

"Whole milk."

"Are you sure?"

"One hundred and ten percent positive."

"What about sugar?" I pleaded, "Does she like plain sugar? Equal? Sweet'N Low?"

"No idea."

"Great. That's helpful."

"Don't worry about it," he signed, pecking at his keyboard, "It doesn't matter."

"Doesn't matter? Do you *know* who your mother is? Whatever, I'll just get them all," I sighed, and hung up the phone.

The next morning, I sprang from my bed to show off my thoughtful response to her disapproval.

"Good morning, Gladys, may I offer you some coffee?" I asked, while exhibiting a thirty-five dollar French press; still in the box.

"Oh, how lovely. Thank you for doing that. Yes, I would like some coffee, please."

"Great! Would you like an egg and some toast as well?"

"Why, yes I would. Thank you very much."

Relieved by her optimism, I began to prepare the morning meal. I had never been so nervous about cracking an egg in my life, and the fear of burnt toast was overwhelming. She was watching; waiting for me to drop a yoke when my husband walked in to grab a plate and her undivided attention. I listened as she complained to him about everyone who had wronged her in the past and nodded in agreement the way you do when you're trying to avoid confrontation.

Things were going well, too well, and I knew there was no way to keep that plastered look on my face for much longer. I placed her breakfast on the counter and smiled. Then I laid the French press down beside it, along with a decorative espresso cup, some whole milk, and a variety of sweeteners to choose from.

"Bon appetite!" I smiled.

"Perfect!" she beamed, "Now hand me my half-and-half and I'll be good to go."

Half-and-half? Shit. He *specifically* said whole milk. One hundred and ten fucking percent sure, he said. And, of course, he was no longer in the room.

"Umm—your son told me that you liked whole milk in your coffee, so—"

"WHAT? Whole milk? Who told you that? I despise whole milk. I *only* use half-and-half in my coffee. That's all I have *ever* used!"

"Well, I asked him what you liked and he swore up and down that you *only* used whole milk. He was sure of it: one hundred and ten percent sure to be exact. We can run out later and get half-and-half if you'd like, but for now, this is all I've got."

I wanted to kill him right there on the spot. How could he do that to me knowing the severity of her rage? Didn't he know how hard I was trying to please his impossible to please mother? Didn't he care? I had been so careful, and everything was going so well. Why was this happening?

The rest of the day was a series of adventurous tales on how *not having half-and-half in her morning coffee had ruined her life*. It was incredible: in just one night, I had gone from being a shitty Realtor to a fucking dairy farmer and I sucked at milking cows. The last one came around eleven o'clock that evening. We were sitting in the living room, staring at her catty disposition, when she whipped out a story about traveling abroad.

"*—and I told the guy, I said, 'If I don't have half-in-half in my morning coffee, it's a terrible start to an even worse day.*"

Gladys may have been wrong about a lot of things, but she was right about that—what a day, indeed. Imagine my surprise ten years later when her daughter informed me that her mother has never used half-and-half a day in her life.

LISA RENÉ LECLAIR is a writer, humorist, social media junkie and mom who shares childhood stories and bad advice for your amusement at Sassypiehole. She is a co-author in several anthologies and a contributor to various online publications, including Scary Mommy, Woman's Day, Good Housekeeping, and The Washington Post. *She is currently living the dream in Atlanta with her beautiful daughter and a shitload of thankless pets.*

You can follow her just about anywhere on social media, but the majority of her shenanigans happen on Facebook, Twitter, and Instagram.

The Suburban Dress Code
By Kelcey Kintner
The Mama Bird Diaries

There came a moment when my husband and I knew we would have to leave our charming west village apartment in New York City and move to the suburbs. It was about the time they told us our daughter's first year of private school would be roughly ten million dollars (I may have rounded up but I'm pretty sure the number was close to that.) For a pre-K program. Like where they learn to tie their shoes.

And that's how we found ourselves, along with our two young children, meandering around Westchester looking at homes in great public (AKA free) school districts. I wasn't sure how I would adjust to life in the suburbs. We had lived in New York City for a long time. Still, I had grown up in Connecticut so surely I could get the hang of this again. But then I would hear words like cookie swap and Bunco (a dice game that is popular with the housewives of everywhere) and think, whoa...I'm not made for this. Still, we forged ahead.

Within a few months, we sold our New York City apartment and found a place in Westchester with grass, trees, and that thing people seem to love so much: "peace and quiet." Before we moved, a friend (who had recently made the suburban crossover) came to visit me in the city. She said the following words which I will never forget..."All the women in the suburbs wears yoga pants."

"What?" I said. "You mean to the gym?"

"No. They wear them wherever they go. To school drop off, on errands, out to lunch, everywhere. I mean, not at night. At night, they change. But during the day, it's like a dress code."

That could not be true.

"They must wear jeans sometimes!" I insisted. Surely she was exaggerating.

"Not often," she said.

After she left, I let this incredible news sink in as I surveyed my own outfit which consisted of a t-shirt with the 1970's Tab soft drink logo and a pair of corduroys.

Not long after, we made the move and I'd like to tell you that my friend was crazy. That she had made the whole damn thing up. But honestly, the town really was a sea of yoga pants. With the occasional tennis skirt or two thrown in to keep it spicy.

In fact, one day as I was buckling one of my children into the backseat of the car, a lady opened the driver's seat door, got in and attempted to start my SUV.

Was I getting carjacked? In the suburbs? Umm no. Definitely not. You know how I knew? Car jackers don't wear yoga pants. This woman has simply mistaken my car for hers and after realizing the error, laughed, apologized and went off to find her own black SUV.

As I adjusted to this life of peace and quiet, I knew I would need to assimilate in some way. If I couldn't be a city mom any longer, I'd be the perfect suburban mom. Since cookie swaps and Bunco didn't sound all that appealing, I decided I'd invest in the best yoga clothes out there. That meant a visit to the holy grail of lounge wear... Lululemon.

I had actually been carrying a Lululemon gift certificate in my wallet for three years and it was about to expire. It was clearly given to me by a friend who had some kind of psychic vision that I was going to embark on an athletic clothing journey.

I drove to the store and immediately went right to the rack with the yoga pants. Now these pants seemed very similar to the ones they sold at Target but judging from the price tag, they must have magical superpowers. Superpowers that would undoubtedly catapult me to suburban stardom.

After choosing some pants to try on, I then grabbed a bunch of athletic tops in my size and made my way to the dressing room. These dressing rooms just had a curtain. You know—to give you the illusion of privacy, but the truth is that anyone can pull back that curtain in a hot second.

I tried on a couple of the pants which looked super cute and I could already imagine sashaying around town in them. Then I tried on a bunch of athletic tops. I was looking for one that masked my post-too-many-babies stomach but instead I found a lot that accentuated it. Which is slightly different.

As I tried on one particular top, it felt a little snug going on but I wasn't concerned. These were athletic tops. They have some stretch.

And then I attempted to take it off.

There was no stretch.

I tried pulling it down to my waist in some misguided attempt to move it over my butt and down my body.

It didn't work at all.

I tried to pull it over my head again.

My head had gotten bigger.

And then I started sweating which of course made it completely stick to my body with the suction strength of a 1,000 vacuum cleaners.

Full panic set in. It reminded me of the time a zipper got stuck on one of my boots and my foot started getting so claustrophobic, I attempted to cut the boot right off me. Obviously, I'm prone to panic in these sort of situations.

I peeked out of the dressing room.

"Hi! I'm sort of stuck in the top I'm trying on."

"They run a bit small," the sales girl informed me about fourteen minutes too late. "Try pulling it over your head."

Really?!! Try pulling it over my head? What does she think I'm doing in here? Trying to levitate myself out of the top?

But I responded with a big smile, "Okie dokie! I'll give it a go."

More tugging, pulling, sweating. And the sudden realization that I had forgotten to put on deodorant.

My mind was racing. Should I call someone? Who would I call? A friend? And what would they be able to do for me? Talk me out of the top? And how long could I live without food and water in this dressing room anyway?!

I felt like baby Jessica. Remember that little girl? She was only eighteen months old and tumbled down a well in Texas. It took fifty-eight hours to free that poor baby.

I did not have that kind of time.

I peaked my head out of the dressing room.

"Hi. Me again. You know, the one stuck in your top. I hate to bother you. But I'm totally going to need some assistance. Do you offer that sort of service?"

In she came. Her little blonde young self pushed and pulled and finally helped wrangle me out of that shirt which must have been mismarked because I'm pretty confident it was a 3T.

I bought a few pairs of yoga pants that day. I didn't have the courage to try on any more of those tops. Having extricated myself from a web of Lycra, I cherished my freedom too much.

But even as I left that store, I knew I would never be sporting loungewear at school pick up or at the farmer's market. I was a jeans girl. Sometimes a corduroys girl. But not a yoga pants girl. Unless I was doing a downward dog which was never. I'd wear those yoga pants at home, mostly for TV watching and napping. If I learned one thing that day—trying to be something you're not—will just leave you a hot sweaty mess, trapped in a dressing room.

I would have to conquer the suburbs without fancy lounge wear.

But I knew I'd be just fine.

Just like baby Jessica.

A former TV journalist, KELCEY KINTNER writes the humor blog, The Mama Bird Diaries and works as a freelance writer. You can find her at US Weekly Fashion Police, The Huffington Post, *Alpha Mom, and other outlets. She has also been published in numerous anthologies including* Moms are Nuts *and* Blogher 2012 Voices of the Year.

Kelcey has a journalism degree from Columbia University. She has been nominated for an Emmy, won numerous awards that weren't Emmys and won best typist her sophomore year of high school.

Babble named Kelcey's blog, The Mama Bird Diaries, one of its top 100 Mom Blogs and Kelcey one of top 50 Moms on Twitter. Kelcey was one of Blogher's Voices of the Year in 2012 and 2014.

Kelcey has five kids. She is still trying to figure out how to fit them all on a Vespa. You can find her on Facebook and Twitter.

Vintage Dreams and a Modern Reality
By Shya Gibbons

I could proudly type on a resume: perfect wife and perfect mother. Cooking and cleaning; perfectly groomed and always put together. You know those people that have it all? Well, hi, you are now acquainted with one.

Then I actually became a wife and a mother and realized that I. Know. Nothing.

While most children aspire to be astronauts, doctors, or veterinarians, I always wanted to be a mother. I am one of those intrinsically maternal people—you know, the ones who always have everything you could ever need somehow packed away into a purse. At one point in my life I even carried around individual packets of sunscreen and would hand them out to the workers corralling carts at the supermarket. Who the fuck does that?

But I digress. I found the perfect man. He really is perfect in every single way. No flaws at all with this man. My dreams were starting to come true; I was going to be a wife! I should mention that I have a bachelor's degree and at twenty-three I was the recipient of a first-place award handed out by my state for my investigative reporting. I had a kickass career that I loved, so I wasn't just sitting around at coffee shops dropping napkins and daintily picking them up to try to get a man to notice me.

My bridal shower theme was vintage housewife. Yes, I had a themed bridal shower so judge me if you must. I had the perfect a-lined dress with a lace overlay and donned a custom-made apron that had my soon-to-be married name on it. I also rocked a pearl necklace that hung around my neck in layers. No, you perverted petunias not *that* kind of pearl necklace. I have been rocking pearl necklaces long before bitches started clutching them over everything posted on the Internet.

We had a beautiful shower where guests brought their favorite recipes and placed them into a binder so I could have dozens of new recipes to make to satisfy my husband.

Fast forward a few months after our perfect wedding. I was settling into my role nicely. Cooking and cleaning, taking care of my husband. It's what made me happy. Then, after our first time trying, I became pregnant with a little baby- here forth to be called Chicken Nugget. This was it. Perfect wife, perfect mother status: locked and loaded.

I daydreamed what it would be like once the Chicken Nugget announced his arrival. I had my entire day planned out. Wake up, smile because life is so good, brush teeth and brush hair, do subtle makeup. Once that is completed I will pick out a nice, but sensible, outfit. I will begin cleaning the house at six am. My husband is a police officer so he usually will be coming home by that time to a home cooked meal, I assumed.

Hark! What is that melodious sound? My sweet cherub is awake and he is singing the song of his people. Give kisses galore, tell him his positive attributes: you are smart; you know to stop eating boogers that you find up your nose, and you have not tried to spice up your wallpaper with homemade paint in a few days. Rock on, Chicken Nugget, you've got this.

Next step: begin meal preparation. Lunch can be homemade macaroni and cheese with whole wheat pasta and cheese and milk from our local barn. Chicken Nugget eats every last bite and asks for seconds. This parenting thing is easy.

While my ray of sunshine eats I will prepare for dinner. A nice roast with potatoes and vegetables from my garden sounds delicious. I fly around the kitchen collecting everything I will need. Dinner is prepared in ten minutes. An errant hair has fallen out of place, that cheeky bastard. I find a bobby pin and pin the rogue hair back.

After lunch would be playtime and arts and crafts. I had a theme set out every day for our crafting, with lesson plans included. As an example, today we will paint his feet, press them onto paper that I picked intentionally for this project, and they will form a butterfly's wings. Lessons taken away from craft hour: the letter b, the paint we used was blue, and the insect we painted was a butterfly, which starts with b.

After crafting there is a quick bath and then a two hour nap. He awakes for dinner-time looking famished. I will feed him delicious beef from the local butcher shop with mashed potatoes that came from our garden. For desert I have a homemade pumpkin pie and homemade whipped cream to add on top.

That is how I wanted it to all go, friends. I ate, slept, and breathed this routine in my mind. It had no flaws. It was going to be perfectly executed.

Chicken Nugget, apparently not getting the note I shoved up my vagina that listed the plan, decided to come six weeks early and throw everything out of whack.

So here we are today. Chicken Nugget is now a two-year-old chicken tender and our days go a little something like this.

"Mommy." I am being summoned by my spawn. He has awoken from his long hour and a half slumber. He is rejuvenated and rested. He is ready to take on the world despite the fact it is four am and neither of us slept.

I go and get him. He stays in pajamas. I still tell him three of his positive attributes: you make me happy every day, your laughter is melodious, and you not have ruined anything in a week.

He gets his teeth brushed then he decides what cereal he wants to eat that day. Some days we have French toast and watch cartoons. I have done absolutely nothing to myself. I have remnants of make-up on my face from one—maybe two days ago? I am wearing a pair of my husband's basketball shorts because they are comfortable. I am wearing one of his cotton shirts because they are comfortable and he has dozens more shirts than I do and all of mine are in the laundry.

The laundry that should have been started days earlier still sits there. It's fucking glaring at me. I swear it mocks me. It is like washing machines and moms have started a turf war over laundry rooms. You try to enter and all of a sudden you've got a cashmere sweater throwing up a Do Not Wash symbol and yelling, "Don't make me shrink a bitch."

A sock is calling out that I am a loser and good luck finding clothes to wear because all of our clothes are shoved into a basket and tumbling off the top and over the sides. I mutter angrily to myself, "Fuck the laundry."

We need necessities at the store, though, so we will have to venture out at some point. Chicken Nugget will be dressed perfectly. Usually in name brand clothes I have found at a well-known clothing store that is known for their fabulous sales and coupons. I have one pair of skinny jeans that I rock, and a tight rotation of a few shirts I feel comfortable wearing. I have yet to lose the baby weight I gained. Even at a higher scale number, I like myself more physically now than I did when I was on the lower end of the scale.

When we venture out, no matter how messy my hair is (usually in a bun and hasn't seen shampoo in days), or how awful I think I look in whatever I am wearing, I still wear my pearls.

That vintage girl with perfect dreams is still stuffed deep down inside me.

I have been pounding away at this parenting and marriage thing for close to a decade now and I don't think I am any closer to cracking the riddle. How the hell is one person/one team supposed to get this all down with no hiccups. I know there are people out there that run a tight ship and adhere to the schedule I always dreamed of implementing. That is not me, though. I've learned to accept that what I want me to be and what I actually am are vastly different, but there is beauty in the space between the two and that's where I lay, floating.

Maybe it's not the immaculate house that makes the perfect mom, or the length of time she spends readying herself. Maybe it is true that there is beauty in your imperfections. Embrace them. Love them. Love yourself. Spend hours playing outside and making memories and stop stressing about the laundry. Those piles will never end, but the high-pitched giggle/squeal from Chicken Nugget will someday be replaced with a teenager telling me to get out of his face.

Be you and do what makes you happy. Find something, anything, that gives you a little glimmer on days where you look in the mirror and think, "How did I get here?" And if, at the end of the day, the thing that makes a little light shine out of me is wearing a string of pearls around my neck, then I'll wear those fuckers until the day I break them by clutching them too hard from something I see online.

SHYA GIBBONS is a full-time CEO (also known as a stay-at-home-mom) to a precocious, blue-eyed two-year-old. She is happily married to a gorgeous man who doubles as her best friend who loves her even on her worst days.

She was born, raised and still lives in a picturesque small town where she has stacked up hundreds of bylines at the local newspaper. She has won first-place in her state for her investigative journalism and now she spends her time investigating where that mysterious stain came from.

When she is not writing she likes to cook big dinners and bake. In her free time she loves to binge watch seasons of shows at a time and becomes far too attached to fictional characters.

Putting the Wrong Foot Forward
By Ellen Williams and Erin Dymowski
Sisterhood of the Sensible Moms

You know what takes a lot of perfectly orchestrated energy to perfectly maintain? The stance of staunchly rejecting perfectionism. My dear friend and writing partner, Erin, has this persona, and I'm not going to lie, watching it slip is one of my favorite spectator sports. I just have the sort of personality that's allergic to all things Pollyanna. Of course, now this paints my persona as shiny asshole, but hear me out.

Ask even a casual acquaintance of Erin's and they'll describe her as fun-loving, spontaneous, and charitably generous to a fault. This is all true! Ask her to describe herself and she'll pretty much ramble out of the same thesaurus, minus the Mother Teresa claims because she does have a decent helping of humility bubbling in her personality cauldron. But, BUT, if you want to join me in the bleachers for the "Erin Show" as a true fan when it all unravels, ask her about perfectionism.

Oh, she'll say things like, "With five kids, there is no perfect, there's just getting through the day while enjoying life." So true. Who can argue?

And she'll wax poetic, "I was a perfectionist my entire school career until I hit high school and then I *decided* perfect scores were just not something I was going to put myself through." Um, okay, seems like a sound approach for mental health.

To take my own little spin in the roasting pan, I, Ellen, am a recovering perfectionist. Anyone who has befriended me in the last seventeen years during my stay-at-home-mom life may spit-take their Diet Coke at "recovering." However, ask anyone from my kindergarten to medical school era and you'll get "Sweet chestnuts, she's so much better." I cultivated a tedious row of achievement to hoe during my primary education, was the group partner from hell in high school, routinely broke out in hives in college, lost weight in medical school, and as an OB/GYN resident made medical students cry. During my parenting career I've tried to adopt the mantra "If there's no blood splashing on the floor, we can take a breath;" but let's just say, no one is surprised when I snap.

So there you have it. Two business partners and friends: one with vibrant shades of perfectionism flying for all to see and one who not only hides her freak flag, but protests robustly that it even exists. So who cares? We're all onions with different layers to peel. Trust me; the fun comes when you stress Erin enough for her bubble of bubbly laissez-faire to pop. For full disclosure, I am no fun when I detonate, but Erin? She is such an effervescent soul she even melts down delightfully. At least it's delightful to me.

There has to be perfect conditions to trigger the "Erin Show." You need a combination of utter chaos (and it has to be A LOT, she has five kids), a steady drip of irritation, and the secret sauce perfectionism trigger: a staged photograph. If you add sleep deprivation, you've got yourself some lighter fluid to get the party raging.

How often could this very specific perfect storm brew you ask? Thanks to our insanity that moves us to take a multifamily camping-ish trip every summer, well, EVERY SINGLE FREAKING YEAR.

For these shenanigans, five moms and thirteen kids descend upon a state park conference center for three days. By the way, when you're picturing this conference center, I guarantee you're doing it wrong. Think more of a basic two-story house—perched on a beautiful canal—that was gutted and remodeled by a lunatic with major deficits in his spatial reasoning skill set. The first floor is a split level jumble of kitchen, utility kitchen, and living area with a bathroom and two postage stamp bunk rooms shoehorned over to the west side. The second floor is an enormous space complete with blackboard and podium with two bedrooms and two baths (hallelujah) pushed off to the east edge. These two bedrooms are connected by a hallway impersonating a closet, and just to crush any lingering delusions of "glamping," that windowless space is where I set up my air mattress to hunker down.

Getting back to our perfect storm, let's look at one particular year where the atmospheric conditions were just right. First, we always have chaos. There are thirteen kids in a cavernous space with no carpeting. Cacophony doesn't touch what it sounds like in there. Getting shoes on and sunscreen applied in preparation for canoe launchings would make Houston Ground Control weep. Never mind that blisters and hardships with chain store knock-offs have forged us all as Keens true believers; making the hallway look like a homogenous mountain of rugged, waterproof hiking sandals. (This right here folks, is what is known in the biz as foreshadowing.)

Secondly, Erin had irritation. Getting her five kids plus one friend packed up for this trip had been particularly trying. Hard to believe, right? But this time, her crew had outdone themselves. They were missing whole categories of items from sleeping bags to toothbrushes, and the Greek chorus of "Mom, where's my...?" was moving from background noise to center stage vexation. Erin was as irritated as an oyster snacking on a sand buffet with no hopes of a pearl on the horizon.

Erin also had sleep deprivation in spades because she has the circadian rhythms of a toddler. For camping, it's GREAT to be up at the crack of dawn! She's hiked, stacked kindling, whistled zippity-doo-dah, and procured kayaks before I've even slithered off my air bed. At 7:30 am. While she's always an early bird, she's usually not catching *that* many worms before breakfast so she is toast a good two hours prior to her usual 10:00 pm bedtime. When Erin is ready for bed, it's not a typical adult-like stretch, yawn, and "I'm ready to hit the hay." No. Think dropped and forgotten popsicle melting on the edge of an asphalt parking lot at high noon. Think hot fudge sliding down a sundae into a puddle of melted ice cream. Think baby past her bedtime minus the tantrum. Erin never causes a scene, she just slowly fades away. We'll all being sitting around enjoying girl talk and sangria at the-kids-are-finally-in-bed o'clock when we'll notice Erin has melted down on the couch to commune with the backs of her eyelids. You can always tally her in the sleep deprived column one night into our adventure.

This brings us to the best part: The Trigger! Erin always has fun and funky photography ideas. It's kind of her fabulous thing. Remember the Keens hiking sandals? On this particular trip, Erin got it into her head that it would be the coolest picture ever to line up all eighteen pairs on the dock outside our house. Since all five moms strive to document this precious time together on five separate DSLR cameras because we don't trust each other to share photos (it's not like we're bad people, we're just busy), we were all at least half-heartedly in. The kids were playing happily after dinner, so us moms scooped up the jumbled shoes from the hallway, schlepped them outside and dumped them at the foot of the dock for sorting. How hard could it be to match up eighteen pairs of unisex shoes in identical shades of navy and beige in nearly identical sizes? Well, we got the moms' shoes sorted out pretty quickly because, well, we're adults. The kids' were a bit more challenging, but anything is fun with your best girlfriends—or at least that's the lie we told ourselves. (It was still a bit too early for sangria.)

We chugged along laying the pairs out in an artsy serpentine pattern coiling down the dock into the imminently setting sun. It really was going to be a great photograph.

"Wow, look how far down the dock these stretch!"

"It's like a growth chart."

"Anyone have a left blue size four?"

"Right here!"

"Did anyone get the cameras? We've got about thirty minutes of good light."

We lined up those shoes from largest to smallest, oh, we lined 'em up real good. Until there were two. That didn't match. Okay, no biggie, just time to double-check. Five efficient moms scoured the hallway and checked the line-up in thirty seconds flat, and yup, still two odd shoes.

"So two kids are missing shoes? Are you kidding me?" I said.

"Well, whose are they?!" asked Erin.

We all just looked at each other. It's not like our seventy-eight combined years of parenting gave us the forethought to write our kids' names in the shoes with permanent markers. Sheesh.

"It's time to get the kids. We'll match them up with the shoes," Erin said.

"Oorrrrrr, we could just take the photo with sixteen pairs of shoes and sort this out when the kids are done playing manhunt," one of our friends suggested.

"No. We are straightening this out NOW. We have eighteen pairs of Keens and there will be eighteen pairs in the picture," said Erin.

Hear that clank? It's Erin's perfectionism gremlin rattling its cage door.

Now it sounded so super fun to disturb a gaggle of kids who were playing happily and cooperatively together for them to try on shoes, but like I said, Erin is usually easy-going and the kids did need their shoes for tomorrow. Someone let out the rebel yell, "Hey kids! Come to the dock and find your shoes."

And everyone joyfully and immediately scampered over to honor the request, all the sandals miraculously matched, gold and chocolate rained down from heaven, and we all lived happily ever after admiring our framed copies of the most awesome photograph ever.

What really happened: kids trailed out like we were calling them to statistics camp. Children in hiding had to be called out by name and reassured they were not losing the game. Older siblings convinced younger ones that they were indeed tagged out of the game no matter what mom said and a general wail was heard throughout the land with a background beat of "Why are we doing this?" and "If all the shoes are here, what the hell do the kids have on their feet while running around in the woods?"

It was like a game of "Cinderella," without winning a life of royalty if the shoe fits. As the kids milled around like lobotomized sheep, the gate to Erin's perfectionism creaked further and further open. She started to stomp. She began to huff. She just wanted one, ONE, flipping picture. We all forged forward, until all the shoes were on all the feet. Wait, what?!

"We had two shoes that were not the same size. How do you all have shoes on your feet?!" Erin said. "Everyone take off your shoes and stand behind them!"

Nothing says good times quite like a prison-style inspection. At this point her beast was fully out of the cage and it was either revolt or comply, and since we had lost all will to live, onward we went.

The kids lined up with as much enthusiasm and cooperation as cats going to the vet, but there was one who protested a little louder than the others, one who had a little more difficulty prying one of his shoes off of his mosquito bitten foot.

But wait, a red herring had washed up on the pier to stink up the joint! Can you feel the suspense? You could definitely hear my delighted laughter because the deconstruction was in full swing. Erin was convinced one of her younger sons had on the wrong shoes. While a snappy round of "These are my shoes! Those aren't your shoes!" was gaining a full head of steam, we kept checking sandals because seriously this had to end somehow. That's when the child standing behind the mismatched sizes was pegged! Hooray! Mystery solved! Let's move on! Sangria time!

That would be nope squared to the hell-no power. As odds would have it—since Erin was the guardian of forty-six percent of the youngsters there—the culprit was birthed from her loins. The show was on! There were hands flapping and voices screeching up a couple of octaves.

"How could you have gone ALL DAY yesterday with your foot jammed into a too small shoe?" Erin asked. "Are you kidding me?" (This from the woman who earlier rolled with the discovery that there was one pillow packed for her whole family.)

"You know, he never complained about it, so maybe we should just get on with the picture," I said in between poorly suppressed snorts.

In the middle of gearing up to read the riot act for not listening when she was trying to get everyone packed up to even come on this stupid trip, the winds of the perfect storm stilled and Erin tucked in her sails. Her perfection beast passed out from the unmitigated overstimulation of it all. She trailed off in mid-rant because like I've said before, she's pretty swell. She told the kids they could line their shoes back up on the dock and be on their ways. I've seen dropped marbles scatter slower than those kids did.

It so happened the lighting was perfectly gorgeous as we snapped our shots of that graduated line of shoes trailing into the setting sun — even the Keen company liked the photo. But look a little closer, you'll see that one pair is not quite right and if you show that picture to Erin, you can definitely still rattle her cage.

ELLEN WILLIAMS and ERIN DYMOWSKI are the two dynamic friends who share the blog, Sisterhood of the Sensible Moms and the podcast, Sensible Moms Soundbites — your sources for sensible parenting advice delivered with humor and heart. But they don't share everything; Erin has five kids with her husband, Steve, and Ellen has two daughters with her husband, Frank. With their combined experience, Ellen's M.D., and Erin's Master of Education, they've got parenting covered — from grade school to college.

While they parcel out a healthy dose of wit and knowledge from their own cozy corner of the internet, they have also been featured or quoted on Mamapedia, The Huffington Post, *In The Powder Room, BonBon Break, Money College Planner and CNN.com. They are freelance writers for Responsibility.org and others, and have been featured in the anthologies* You Have Lipstick on Your Teeth *and* I Still Want to Be Alone. *They presented about podcasting at the BlogU Conference and were BlogHer Humor Voices of the Year Honorees.*

Follow these Social Media Ninjas on Facebook, Twitter, Pinterest, and Instagram to see their latest parenting advice, recipes, DIYs, book recommendations, and travel adventures.

Look into My Eyes: A Theme Song for the World's Worst Baseball Mom
By Julianna W. Miner
Rants from Mommyland

I have arranged my entire professional and personal life in an effort to be a good parent. I'm present and focused and read the things and connect and put my phone away and am full of love and yet... No. I'm ridiculous. To start with, my husband travels a lot for work. That leaves me on my own managing one house, two part-time jobs, three kids, and their exponentially growing list of activities and sports and lessons. I try my best but let me be honest, there have been several times where I've felt very strongly that I might actually be a cartoon bear *pretending* to be an adult human woman.

Let's start by discussing the small person who is most likely to be the tornado to my trailer park on any given day. My youngest daughter is a precious, adorable, fluffy-haired cupcake *baked by the devil*. She always has been. As the youngest of three, she spent her first year largely in her car seat, being carted to school drop-offs, lessons, practices, and trips to Target. She was a jolly, slightly bewildered little creature.

When she realized she could walk, and then run, and then climb with the ferocity of a rabid howler monkey, things changed at our house. There was a stretch of about two years where the act of parenting this child consisted primarily of trying to avert disaster. She knocked over the Christmas tree, ate the dogs' dinner, flooded the the house (well, just the basement), emptied the fridge onto the kitchen floor, took herself for walk-abouts, played with knives, and experimented briefly with nuclear fusion. She would occasionally break for snuggles.

Then she began to talk. That's when things got interesting.

First it was charming. She could tell us how much she loved us and when she wanted more milk. It quickly became alarming. Because she could also repeat everything that she had ever heard and recite song lyrics that someone (her mother) should probably not have played in the van on the way to preschool.

And it wasn't just the things she said. Her specialty has always been timing. We should be grateful. You can't teach timing. She would not sing Flo Rida at home, but at church (during the service). She would see a nice older lady at the grocery store and would smile her sweetest grin and make excellent eye contact and then talk about how much she loved her (very creatively named) toy horse. "MY HORNY IS BIG AND BLACK AND I LOVE TO RIDE HIM", she'd crow.

There is nothing you can do in these situations. Nothing. All you can do is smile and quietly beg your child to stop. You must never, ever laugh. The not laughing is the hardest part of parenting. If you laugh, it's all over. They're going to do it *more* and they're going to *louder*.

Would you like an example? It combines three things my child does really well and three things I do really poorly.

Things My Child Does Really Well
Thing 1: Making up songs with really interesting lyrics that actually make no sense.
Thing 2: Being so exhausted in public that she behaves as if she's really, really drunk.*
Thing 3: Taking any situation and throwing a chaos-sized wrench into it.

Due to her horrible mother keeping her out too late on a school night because of something stupid, like a baseball game that her brother is playing in.

Things I Do Really Poorly
Thing 1: Being an actual adult human woman who makes good choices.
Thing 2: Attempting to be a perfect baseball mom when I don't even really understand baseball.
Thing 3: Trying to do everything myself when that is idiotic and

impossible instead of asking for help or hiring a babysitter because that is what I think perfect sports parents/actual adult human women are supposed to do.

May I set the stage for you? It's an abnormally cold mid-October night. The end of the fall baseball season is upon us. Big brother's team is playing in the first round of the divisional championship. Daddy is selfishly out of town on business. Mommy is on her own for the week. We left the house at 5:00 pm to be on time for warm ups. I'm shivering in a folding chair next to the bleachers, that are filled with parents who are good at this sort of thing. They have thermoses and warm coats and blankets and their children are quietly reading. It is now 9:20 pm and to my horror, it's only the seventh inning. I am kindly told by one of the good parents that the wonder of baseball is that it has no time clock, at which point I silently beg God for another national pastime.

Daughter #1 (*Age ten*): Mom! Mommy! Look! Look! Look at me! I can jump all the way off the back of the bleachers without getting hurt! Wheeeeeeeee! OUCH! My ankle! MOOOOMMMY!

Son (*age eight*): Mommy! Mommy! MOOOM! Did you see that?! I got a hit! Did you see? Did you? Text Daddy and tell him I got a hit. *HE* would really be impressed.

Daughter #2 (*Age four*): Hold me. Hold me. HOLD ME BECAUSE I NEED YOU, AND IT'S COLD.

She is sitting on my lap with my arms wrapped around her.

Me (*age not disclosed*): I am already holding you. Can you move a little? I need to see if your sister is OK. Honey, are you all right? Come here, please. Yes, son! I saw your hit! And Daddy says good job!

I didn't see the hit and the battery in my phone is dead due to letting my youngest play three hours of Angry Birds to kill time. The cold night air is filled with my lies.

Daughter #1: My ankle hurts but I think three dollars would make it feel better.

She points to the snack bar that is filled with exact same things from Costco that we have in the pantry at home that she refuses to eat.

Daughter #2: You're not holding me enough. Hold me more. WHY WON'T YOU HOLD ME?

People on the bleachers are starting to stare. Also, I'm literally holding her, supporting all of her weight, and hugging her tightly. Is she insane?

Daughter #1: I want hot chocolate, please. It's freezing. And a hot dog. And some Cheetos. And some fruit snacks.

Daughter #2: I want all dat stuff, too.

She hops off my lap, holds out a small hand for money.

Me (*stifling my inner Judge Smales from Caddyshack that is yearning to tell them smugly: "YOU'LL GET NOTHING AND LIKE IT," I hand them some money.*): OK. But no candy. And get me a hot chocolate, please.

Son (*playing third base, watches me give his sisters money*): NO FAIR!

The Rest of the Eight-Year Old Infield: Yeah, not cool, that kid's mom!

The two girls return five minutes later, with more crap then they can safely carry, along with a trail of new friends. Lollipops are in all of their mouths. The girls have clearly ignored my no candy rule.

Daughter #2: Here's your hot chocolate, Momma! *(She spills entire cup of scalding liquid down my pants.)* Oopsy. SORRY. Move Momma, I want to sit on your lap. EEEWWW. Your lap is all wet and now it's on my pants. YOU GOT ME WET AND DIRTY, MOMMA. *(She glares at me with crazy eyes. Then turns her gaze to the people sitting on the bleachers. She decides to talk to them.)* I spilled hot chocolate on her and then she got it all over me but I'm not mad.

Daughter #1: Thank you, Mommy! I'm going to eat while jumping off the bleachers! *(runs off)*

Me: NO! That's dangerous. Eat and then jump off the bleachers. Wait. Don't jump off the bleachers. Stop!

Son: Am I going to get candy and hot dogs and hot chocolate when the game is over? Because otherwise that's not fair.

The Rest of the Eight-Year-Old Dugout: Yeah, that's totally not fair, that guy's mom.

Me: PLAY BALL, BOYS!

Daughter #2 *(whispering)*: I haffa tell you a little secret. First, hold all this stuff. *(Dumps all of the snack bar booty into my hands as she climbs back into my lap.)* Now, the secret. Those people are listening to us. *(Whispering.)* They're watching us. *(Turns to the bleachers and smiles.)* Hi people!

Me: Honey, be quiet and eat your fruit snacks.

Daughter #2 *(clapping with joy and laughing for her audience)*: Yay!

Fruit snacks! WOO HOO!

She's twirling a sticky lollipop around while happy dancing on my lap.

Me: I don't understand this. We have the exact same fruit snacks at home. I have some in my purse.

Daughter #2: Wait? Are these the fruit snacks from your purse?

Me: No. You just bought them...

Daughter #2 *(face crumples)*: They are. They're the fruit snacks from your purse. I don't want them.

She starts to cry. Tears fall from her eyes as half-chewed fruit snacks fall from her pouting mouth.

Me: You just brought them from the snack bar, silly.

Daughter #2: I AM NOT SILLY. *(She is now loudly sobbing.)* They're not the same. Not the same!

Me: Please stop crying. These are the snack bar fruit snacks. Calm down.

Daughter #2 *(slurring her words.)*: Do you promise? Do ya swear?

Me: Yes.

Daughter #2: Look inta my eyes and pinky promise.

Me: Fine. Just stop crying.

Son: Mom! Did you see that?! Did you see that?!

Me: Yes! Good job!

I saw nothing.

Daughter #2: I feel like singin'.

Son: Good job? They got a big hit. Are you even watching?

Daughter #2 *(whisper singing)*: Look into my eyes. Look into my eyes.

Me: I was watching. I'm sorry. I'm distracted. I'm watching.

Daughter #1: Mommy! LOOK! Wheeeee!!! *(I look away then hear a loud crunch followed by whimpering.)* I'm OK!

Daughter #2: Look into my eyes. Looky looky LOOOOOK. You're not looking.

She takes her wet lollipop and sticks it in my hair and then uses the lollipop to pull my face around so I'm looking at her.

Me: I'm looking at you.

Daughter 2 *(still singing)*: No, no, no. Look into my EYES. Look into my thighs. MY THIIIIGHS.

Me: Please stop singing.

Daughter #2: Look into my eyes. Look into my thighs. I will *never* stop singing.

Me: That is not appropriate.

Daughter #2 *(singing louder)*: LOOK INTO MY EYES. LOOK

INTO MY THIGHS.

Me: Stop it. I mean it. I will take away those fruit snacks.

Daughter #2 *(singing so loudly that EVERYONE is watching us, probably even the NSA)*: They're purse snacks. Purse snacks! I don't even want that. What I want to SEE is for you to look at ME. Look into my eyes. Look into my THIGHS. We should all sing now!

She then started swinging her lollipop around like she was holding a conductor's baton, but of course it was still attached to a large chunk of what had been my hair. I looked at the people on the bleachers and, to my surprise, they were cracking up. They were all as exhausted and slappy as I was, so they thought it was hilarious. And they were prepared to sing.

This is the point at which I broke my own rule and started laughing. There was nothing else to do. As a result, the song continued until the end of the game (which we lost). We sat there in the cold, and I held her close while she alternated singing about her thighs and angrily telling me to hold her *more*. It was embarrassing and awkward. It was also snuggly and sort of perfect, perhaps because despite my best efforts I'm actually more cartoon bear than perfect suburban baseball parent.

As the team filed by, a bunch of uniformed eight-year-olds looked at me and said, "Cool song, that guy's mom." The squirming little one looked up at me and smiled proudly as we heard various boys walking to their cars singing, "Look into my eyes, look into my thighs..." with their perfect suburban moms yelling after them.

JULIANNA W. MINER is the writer behind Rants from Mommyland, *Parents Magazine's funniest blog of the year in 2013 and one of Babble's Top 100 Bloggers. She's a contributing author of the* New York Times *best-selling anthology* I Just Want To Pee Alone. *Her work has been featured in* The Washington Post, *Parents Magazine, Cosmo.com,* The Huffington Post, *Nickelodeon Parents Connect,* The Washington Times, Washington Parents Magazine, *and Babble.com (a Disney brand).*

Julie is a mother of three and has been married for almost 20 years. In addition to writing, she's currently an adjunct professor of Global and Community Health at a university she couldn't have gotten into because she made bad choices in high school.

You can find her using social media poorly on Facebook, Instagram, Pinterest, and Twitter.

My Sexy Almost Died (And So Did My Stylist)
By Lola Lolita
Sammiches and Psych Meds

"I'm thinking of shaking it up and going with something like this," I said, pointing to the Pinterest image on my phone.

"That short? And asymmetrical?" the hairdresser squinted, head cocked.

"I mean, I don't want to look like I'm trying out for a boy band or anything, but yeah. A little shorter on one side with longer bangs on the other. I like the short cut, but I need to make it a little more badass. I'm bored."

"OK, then," she said, grabbing her shears. She turned the chair away from the mirror, snip, snip, snipping away.

Coming to terms with my increasing oldassery had been difficult. No longer would my students at work ask me if I was going to "da club" on the weekends. Instead, they would ask if my friends and I were getting together to recite Shakespearean sonnets over aromatic cups of English breakfast tea or gathering around the table to play riveting games of pinochle before retiring to our recliners and passing out by 7:00 pm in full-length nightgowns and kerchiefs. They were certain my husband had taken to calling me "Mother" as I inspected the moles on his back for signs of cancer and filled my Monday through Friday pill box with enough medication to outfit a pharmacy. They were positive I was old enough to have survived scarlet fever back when people still died from it, could remember a time when travel occurred exclusively via horse-drawn carriage, and could tell them precisely what the *Mayflower* looked like up close and in person. When I would attempt to join their conversations and connect with them on a personal level, something that had once come easily to me, they would respond with things like, "Oh, we're just talking about this pop star or this song or this movie actor you've probably never heard of."

"I most certainly *have* heard of her!" I would lie, desperately trying to convince them I was cool before learning the "her" they were referring to was actually a "him." If there was one thing I needed in life, it was for everyone to know I still had it. That I could still tear it up on the dance floor while performing the perfectly choreographed dance steps of the latest popular rap song without missing a beat. That I could still make it rain with my swagger and sex appeal. That I was still young, edgy, hip. A new 'do would restore that youthful balance. It would proclaim to the world that I spent my time browsing fashion magazines and frequenting swanky establishments and participating in vogueish nightlife instead of wiping butts and watching old *Friends* reruns and farting myself to sleep. It would scream, "Watch out, people! Super with it, hot mama here!" I was sure of it.

My stylist continued to cut away as visions of once again getting carded at the liquor store tiptoed their way through my mind. But when she swiveled the chair back around in order to concentrate on the other side of my head, I took one look in the mirror and nearly crapped my pants, my weak, pregnancy-abused bladder almost betraying me.

"Oh my God," I uttered, mouth agape. "What? What the fuck is *that?*"

"What do you mean?" she said, puzzled.

"*That.* What is that on the side there? Or should I say, what *isn't* that?"

"I'm not sure I follow," she replied.

"I'm asking what the hell happened to my hair. I'm asking why I don't have any over there anymore. I'm asking how in the name of Christ you interpreted this as what I wanted from the image I showed you."

I got out of the chair and sprung toward the mirror, tilting my head and inspecting the hack job that was now the left side of my skull. This was bad. This was beyond bad. This wasn't the chic look I was going for. This didn't announce to the masses, "Trendsetter here! Enviable fashionista coming through!" Rather, this shouted, "Roadkill walking! Old maid drowning in sadness!" This was what must have driven Sinead O'Connor to declare, "Fuck it!" and order a number two shave all around. This was Britney Spears, the meltdown years. This was what the rotting corpse of a hen looked like after being pecked to death by its fellow chickens. No, it was worse. This was some Nick-Nolte-mug-shot level shit. This was the type of shit one might find on a Pinterest FAIL board, most definitely not the type of shit that would earn me a spot as Most Sexalicious MILF of the Year.

I snatched my purse off the counter and dug through it for my phone, flinging the dirty baby socks and pacifiers and plastic key chains littering its interior to the side until I located the object of my quest. I whipped it out of my bag, pulled up the picture, and shoved it in the hairdresser's face. "Does *this* look even remotely like *that*?" I seethed through gritted teeth, pointing at the hideous reflection scowling back at us.

She stood there, dumbfounded and unsure how to respond as I returned to the mirror and began furiously playing with my part, hot flashes of panic pervading my soul. Maybe if I just grabbed some of this longer hair over here and brushed it over there, I wouldn't look so much like a strung-out crack whore. Nope. Still hookerish. Maybe if we swept the hair forward? Sort of Biebered that shit up a bit? Still nope. Fuuuuuuuck.

"I thought you wanted it shorter on one side and longer on the other," she managed.

"Yes. Exactly. *Shorter.* Not absent altogether," I replied, batting her hand out of the way as she attempted to justify the first degree murder she had committed on my mane. "We need to fix this. Like, immediately. FIX IT," I declared. I returned to the chair and pointed to the disaster that was my head. No words. Just silent demands to do whatever it would take to make me look less like an alley cat suffering from a severe bout of mange and more like the hot thirty-something I had pictured stopping traffic on the street. Meanwhile, I imagined the scene I would encounter upon returning to work Monday.

"Aww, how cute," my colleagues would lie. "You let your five-year-old give you a haircut. We think it's great that you allow your children such autonomy. Uninhibited self-expression is excellent for the developing psyche," they would continue, choking on their coffee and making unspoken plans to gather around the break-room table to discuss my impending midlife crisis.

"Oh, wow," my students would say, terror rising in their guts as they took in the crazy person who stood before them to deliver the day's lesson. *She's officially lost it,* they would think, swallowing their horror in pensive gulps. *Let's just pretend we've heard of VH1's* Where Are They Now? *before and that we know every word of* The Fresh Prince of Bel-Air *theme song so as not to set her off, OK, guys?* they would silently pledge, guarding themselves against what they perceived to be the unbalanced and wild-eyed she-devil with the power to decide whether they lived or died.

I monitored the hairdresser's work closely, directing her every move with menacing grunts and homicidal signs of disapproval, accepting this and vetoing that until there was nothing left for her to work with.

"There," she said, feigning excitement over the butchered comb-over that now rested atop my head. "It looks perfect." Perhaps if it were opposite day, "perfect" would have been spot-on. Alas, it was not, and while it appeared slightly less ghastly than it had before, I envisioned the shrieks of cowering children, clinging to their mothers' legs and burying their heads in fear as the beast my hairdresser had so maliciously transformed me into emerged from the salon and made its way through the shopping center parking lot. She whisked the cape off my shoulders and ushered me to the front desk to fork over my money and my dignity to the receptionist.

"Thanks *so much,*" I said, glaring at her while fantasizing about stabbing her to death with her own scissors, pools of her blood congealing around my feet as I grabbed fistfuls of her long blonde locks and chopped them off before randomly buzzing sections of her perfectly coiffed fringe with clippers. "Really. A-plus job here."

"It's not so bad," my husband assured me after I returned home and burst into tears, clutching my wrinkle cream and withdrawing to the other side of the room to rock in the corner and binge-drink my feelings.

"No?" I pleaded, my eyes searching for some sign of truth in his expression. "Not bad? I look like a fucking shorn sheep. I HAVE BEEN SHORN," I proclaimed between sobs, the salty streams of humiliation running down my face and collecting in the corners of my mouth. I applied the retinol to my puffy under eye area, praying this episode didn't make the deep-set elevens between my brows even more permanent than they had already become.

Dissatisfied with my husband's encouragement, I got up to take my temper tantrum elsewhere and made my way to the basement where I frantically dug through the boxes of storage, finally coming up for air with my old CD collection in hand. I let my fingers trace the outlines of each disc before deciding on a nineties hip hop mixtape and popping it into the dusty boom box resting on a stack of college memorabilia. I pressed play, closed my eyes, and let the sound pilfer my eardrums, first mouthing, then muttering, and eventually sing-shouting every expletive and sexually-charged lyric. Before I knew it, I was doing the Cabbage Patch and the Running Man as though I were in the apex of my youth, my feelings of despair having morphed into something a bit more pleasant. Confidence? Possibly. Badassery? Definitely. I Humpty Danced my way around, navigating past tubs of baby clothes and forgotten keepsakes, my spirits lifting with each Tootsie Roll I perfectly executed.

I stopped when I caught my reflection in the cracked mirror leaning against the wall and ran my fingers through the rat's nest on my scalp, contemplating the image before me for a beat. After a moment, I retreated from its view, Rump Shaking my way back to the boom box. On my way there, I licked my finger, touched it to my rear, and imagined the hissing sound it would make, finally arriving at my destination and whispering through a sassy smirk, "Still got it, bitches. Bad haircut and all."

LOLA LOLITA is the founder and chief editor of the popular parenting and humor website SammichesPsychMeds.com and MockMom, its satirical division. She is the author of Who Pooped on the Corpses? And Other

Pressing Life Concerns as well as a contributing author of I Still Just Want to Pee Alone and Scary Mommy's Guide to Surviving the Holidays. When she's not introverting, determining how cheap the wine has to be before she can't tolerate it, and obsessing about that one embarrassing thing she did in high school, she can be found Facebooking, Instagramming, and trying to figure out the Twitter.

Pain is Beauty. Beauty is Stupid.
By Bethany Kriger Thies
Bad Parenting Moments

When I was twelve years old, I stole my aunt's bra.

I was an awkward preteen; short with an absurdly large gap between my two front teeth. To add insult to injury, I was also President of the Flat-Chested Club for Sad Girls. Where breasts should have been, there was only a deep well of concave disappointment.

My mother and grandmothers, all large-chested women, had provided me with great hope of big-breasted baptism at the font of genetics between the ages of nine and eleven. However, by the ripe old age of twelve, I'd given up completely on puberty and had decided to accept my playground description of, "I'm eighty-nine percent sure she's fifty percent girl."

My aunt was a gazelle; long limbs, long hair and perfect, perky B-cup breasts that didn't drag behind her like the world's most bereaved cape when she walked. She was regal and I was enchanted; the pimpled, pre-pubescent Robin to her Batman.

One morning, clandestine in a Noxzema mask, I snuck into her laundry room to do what all twelve-year-olds, regardless of gender, do - poke around looking for lacy undergarments. There it was, fresh out of the delicate cycle, a pristine white, lace covered bra. I held it up to my chest. Wait a damn minute…this changes everything:

A pristine white, lace covered PADDED bra.

I looked left. I looked right. I looked at my reflection in the mirror. I shoved the bra into my pants.

I was a lady now. And a criminal.

I wore that bra every day for three years. I washed it in the dead of night in the bathroom sink to hide my shame. I dried it with a hair dryer. I wore it to bed. I kept that bra as attached to my chest as actual breasts.

The summer I turned fifteen, I woke up and my breasts had

arrived. And my relationship with suspiciously obtained padded bras abruptly ended.

No longer a perfect B-cup, I'd been cursed to wander the Earth duct-taping my breasts into position and forever swearing off peasant blouses; that look on my frame perfectly mimicked one of a pregnant pirate. My breasts now seductively slide completely into my armpits when I lie on my back.

The moral of this story: There is no such thing as perfection. It's a padded lie. Also, don't steal because there is no karma like breast karma.

When I was thirteen, I started wearing liquid eyeliner.

It was royal blue. As I sashayed to my middle school Japanese class, I was like, "Ohayo gozaimasu, bitches." I was cool. Too cool. My perfectly wing-tipped eyes became my prison tat. They defined me. The blue wave as deep as the ocean...congealed in the interior well of my eye with a hint of poor, white trash and questionable life choices. I brushed my mascara on thick and didn't even bother to blend; I had no problem solidifying what everyone already knew. I had access to make-up and no idea what I was doing.

On the day of "the incident," I wore white jeans; rolled and cuffed. I'd just stolen a drag off of my best friend's clove cigarette in the bathroom. I leaned over the mirror, my Keds hanging in suspension somewhere between reality and middle-school Narnia; believing my cool, cavalier attitude would bust through the mirror with Liza Minnelli jazz hands and "I don't give a shit about your jelly shoes, KIM!" bitch-eyes.

I pulled out the liquid applicator. I put it near my eye. Kim and her jelly-shoes brushed against my back as she exited the stall and the brush went into my eyeball with as much grace as two virgins with braces making out on the town carnival Ferris wheel.

My eye was frankly, mechakuchana. Loosely translated from Japanese? Fucked.

My eyeliner had betrayed me and I found myself with a medical grade eye patch for three weeks while my cornea healed.

The moral of this story is: There is no such thing as the perfect wing-tip. It's a lie. Also, don't think that make-up makes you invincible. There's no karma like angry eyeliner karma.

When I was sixteen, I lost my virginity.

My body had never been more glorious. It was perfect.

I decided that he was the one after my fifth Budweiser. I saw him staring at me from the corner; spellbound by my near perfect lip-sync performance of Eazy E's Gimme That Nutt.

After the second standing ovation, I stumbled toward the ocean to be alone with myself and evaluate this enormous sexual decision. Or, was it because I really needed to urinate and the restrooms, the kind with indoor plumbing, were already full of cheerleaders and toilet bowls full of Zima? Tomato, to-mah-toe.

It could have been the way the moonlight hit the water. Or, it could have been the fresh sand in my nethers, but I was feeling brave. He sauntered toward me. Was this fate? It turned out, it was a quarter of a wayward sand dollar lodged between my thighs.

We made awkward small talk before realizing we had absolutely nothing in common besides too many beers and a propensity toward making ill-thought-out decisions. In teenager, this equaled love.

The walk to the bedroom that was neither his nor mine was the longest of my life...because we were drunk and kept getting lost.

When we arrived, a wall-length mirrored closet greeted us. How fortunate to be my own audience during the most awkward sexual experience of my life. It wasn't too late to turn back. Not even close, but sixteen has a way of making you believe that beer and a stranger's bedroom are as good as you are ever going to get.

I tried to peel off my shirt. It got stuck on my earring. I felt a sharp tug. I ignored the tug and continued Operation Shirt-Off, tagline: All Shirts Left Behind. The mission remained unsuccessful. The shirt was still stuck and the tug was now accompanied by acute pain. My ear was ripping. I was bleeding.

I tried to draw attention away from the cascade of blood exiting my earlobe by improvising what I thought was a strip tease but probably looked much more like a mime being murdered. I lost my balance and fell into the mirrored closet.

Now, my ear and knee were bleeding. I'd also twisted my ankle. My chivalrous date had to help me hop to the bed on my good ankle. It was very fucking romantic.

The next day, we could barely look at each other. It was brutally painful, emotionally and physically. At school, with bandages on my ear, knee and also sporting a sprained ankle, people asked me if I had been in a car accident.

I was a How I Lost My Virginity After-School Special.

The moral of this story is: It doesn't matter if your body is perfect if you're forcing the wrong thing.

This summer, I turn thirty-seven. I have imperfect breasts, a healthy fear of liquid eyeliner, and sex with someone who hates my rap fetish but loves my giant ass.

We give up perfection for the truth. Less glamorous, perhaps even less hopeful.

Beauty is less tangible; we find it more inside of good works and less so in our bra or the lines on our faces.

As a child, my mother would roughly brush my hair and say, "Beauty is PAIN. Pain IS beauty." Frankly, all of it is overrated.

Perfection will always be denied.

BETHANY KRIGER THIES is a writer and the proud mother to four, young Vikings. She is the author of Bad Parenting Moments and screams bloody-satire into space from her perch nestled high atop her Bad Parenting Moments Facebook Page. Bethany once did many things very well but now settles for mediocrity as it best suits her lackadaisical lifestyle. She's quit Weight Watchers more times than she has joined and now simply watches herself gain weight. When prompted by creative urges or promised large sums of cash, Bethany will write for food. She also can be heard on Vermont radio every week. Her children remain, as always, unimpressed.

On Failing to Become an MLM Millionaire
By Jessica Azar
Herd Management

Even though they've been around for several decades now, MLMs, or multi-level marketing companies for the uninitiated (have you been living under a rock?), have skyrocketed in saturation through social media overexposure in the past few years. You can't scroll through a social media feed without at least two status updates about an MLM popping up. Where the Avon Lady had to actually ring your damn doorbell sixty years ago, now she can flood your Facebook inbox and text stalk you into submission. In days of yore, Tupperware parties only pressured the people who had been blackmailed into attending the party to place an order, but these days "virtual" parties prevent people from scrambling out of a party "invitation" due to a schedule conflict, whether it's real or invented. "Nope, your child's swim meet won't prevent you from buying my candles, Sally, you can attend the party online ANY TIME this week! My company's MISSION is to make the homes of our nation smell amazing." Sally is now frightened.

The advent of the internet gave stay-at-home-moms, like myself, a way to expand their at-home business horizons beyond people who were bound by blood to buy SOMETHING. To a sleep-deprived mom of four small children (ages five, four, two and six months at the time) who was scrambling to make ends meet, the opportunity to make BIG MONEY from home sounded like a godsend. I'm no fool, but I lack business sense; Gecko from Wall Street I am not. Creative? Absolutely. Bright and driven? You bet. I'm also adept at persuasive dialogue, but recognizing questionable investments is not my forte. I was mesmerized by the earning charts, and the prospect of being professionally successful was too much to turn down in a time where my days were dominated by screaming, dirty diapers, and around-the-clock thankless tasks. My children were, and still are to a large extent, my world, and I would gladly give up the myriad of things

I've sacrificed all over again, but when you're drowning in a lake of lost identity, a way to reinvent yourself as "more than a mom" can be mighty tempting. MLMs are great at pitching to the insecurities of my demographic, and they snagged me hook, line, and sinker. Without naming names, I can tell you that the company who lured me in specialized in beauty and weight loss aids; we'll call it Skinny 'R Us for discussion purposes.

I was going to be a Skinny Star. Yep, you heard me.

Since the company was new to my geographic area I knew that I would have first crack at all of the people local to me, and I couldn't wait to "sell my way to financial freedom." Nothing would stand in my way; it's all a matter of perspective, right? My transformation to powerful business-owner might not have been obvious to those around me, but I was a rising star in my own mind. Holy moly, my crumb-encrusted family room became an at-home office. Being tied to my kids all day wouldn't stop me from networking, because I could do it ONLINE! I mean, they told me I could work in my pajamas, right? How freeing! Not even my husband, who was unhappy that I joined the company without asking him, could discourage me; I was doing this for my family, dammit. Naysayers, be damned.

Hypnotized by the company's encouraging mantras, I was motivated to work late each night after the kids were in bed, messaging sales pitches to everyone I knew on Facebook and researching ways to make my voice louder on social media. The bi-weekly motivational "team" calls with the company's CEO encouraged us to ignore our inner sense of social restraint and to fearlessly approach everyone we saw, always keeping the mindset that getting them to use our products would change their lives. We were indoctrinated to be world-changers, man, and who doesn't want to wear a cool company t-shirt and shape the lives of everyone around them? Those phone calls fired me up so much I would've stormed Normandy if he'd of told me to do it. Because selflessly, he just wanted me to change lives; saving people from their poor health by selling them unproven dietary supplements and teaching them to join the business to give them the gift of financial freedom. It was my destiny to save others from what they saw in the mirror, and although it nagged at my conscience, I just drowned it out with more motivational calls.

My upline or support team (basically those who had convinced me to join the company and were dependent upon my performance to increase their own financial gain) was several states away, so I was alone in creating my own Skinny Dynasty here. I was a woman obsessed with earning more money with the goal in mind of spending more time with my family, yet I ignored them for hours on end as I prospected, pitched, and managed my team. I put all of my energy into convincing people to have Skinny parties at their homes, and teaching my downline how to recruit more people for our team, because if they weren't making money, neither was I, and I wanted my financial freedom, dammit! I felt like Patton, cracking a riding crop at those who weren't selling enough, and although the power was mildly intoxicating, the ridiculousness of my virtual sweatshop wasn't lost on me.

The kids went neglected at times and did God-knows-what with toiletry items while I was distracted, my house looked like Shrek lived there, Skinny parties in the evenings kept me away from home multiple nights a week, and I was miserable. THIS WAS NOT IN THE BUSINESS LITERATURE, Y'ALL. The gorgeous lady riding in the convertible Mustang she had earned through our company with her golden hair flying in the wind LOOKED NOTHING LIKE ME. I looked like a hot mess, as I sped around town delivering products to customers in my used French fry-encrusted SUV with four kids in tow. There was no section in a help manual on what to do when a Skinny party guest stands up to announce that she had tried out products and they failed to take her from a size twenty-two to a size six like she expected, nearly inciting a riot, or any explanation of what to do when a drive-by shooting happens at another party. It took me two years to realize that I was never going to make a full-time salary selling Skinny products, although I did make a good income by company standards, unless the products came with wine. Which, unfortunately, they did not. I started feeling like a drug dealer, preying on people that wanted to look a certain way, even though I knew they were already tight on cash. Wondering if you convinced someone to compromise their priorities isn't a good feeling, trust me.

A large part of me was terrified of failing; admitting that millionaire status wasn't in the cards for me without some heavy financial investment or owning a storefront like many of the upper level "Skinny stars" did seemed like eating crow and I was on the Skinny diet. I didn't want to disappoint myself, my husband, my kids who had seen me give up everything to chase down a Skinny unicorn, or abandoning the people I had personally recruited. What I came to realize was that no matter how many customers I created, I, along with everyone else selling for the company, were really the company's biggest customers. They had us paying to fly to conventions all over the country to "learn" more and "preparing us to succeed" by selling us company-approved sales aids and clothing. It dawned on me that they were using my own financial and social insecurities to manipulate me into exploiting the physical insecurities of others. I started feeling like a cheap opportunist that made others look at themselves with even more scrutiny than they already did, which goes against my belief of self-acceptance. I felt sleazier than a used car salesman on an oily stripper pole.

A word to women considering an MLM as a way to change your life: eventually people will get tired of your products, your sales pitches and you, leaving you lonely, feeling defeated, broke (or at least not a millionaire), and neck-deep in more products than you can use. People practically ran from me if they saw me in Target and suddenly people were straight up ignoring me online, never commenting on my Facebook posts because they feared I would use it as a hook to sell them something. In the end I realized I had betrayed the good faith people had in my usually altruistic nature; I had sold my self-respect for a company that didn't value me and could never deliver on the pipe dreams it had wafted in front of me. At the end of the day you need to know that you have made the world a better place, and pressuring people to buy things when you know they're scraping together rent money will leave you cold. And feeling like a used car salesman on a stripper pole that gets three percent commission.

JESSICA AZAR writes from home while raising her four children with her husband in the rural American South. Her blog, Herd Management, attempts to find the funny and extraordinary in the ordinary while documenting her attempts at parenting and getting crafty. She co-authored and edited a book on mental illness in 2015, Surviving Mental Illness through Humor, and continues to work for mental health awareness. When she's not refereeing fights between her herd of kids, drinking single-malt scotch, or doing yoga, she writes for other publications like Scary Mommy, marie claire, Country Living, Redbook, The Southern Weekend, and many more.

Follow her on Facebook, Twitter, Instagram, and Pinterest for lots of laughs and an easy way to feel better about the craziness in your own life. Because she's got boatloads.

The Rise and Fall of the Perfect Seductress
By Hedia Anvar
Gunmetal Geisha

When you have willful genes, melded from a dad who was a natural born feminist, and a mom who was so hell-bent on her independence that she froze Tupperware food two weeks in advance in order to go about her German or underwater ballet classes in peace, it's possible you might end up a little headstrong. Here in the West, maybe we consider aspects of those circumstances remarkable since we're talking Middle-Eastern mom and dad in early seventies Iran. But let's leave that where it is, because remarkable Middle-Eastern parents and headstrong me moved to Manhattan, where incidentally, I got to be New York City tough in addition to headstrong.

The remarkable parents never failed to tell me how intelligent/talented/good-looking they thought I was. But they—bless them—didn't do much to cultivate my supposed talents by sticking me in lessons or encouraging sports or any of the stuff a different type of parent might impose on their kids. No one ever made me listen to Mahler while identifying Cubism and reciting Rumi—even though Rumi was Persian just like us.

Maybe they should have, because I grew up a dabbler–not excellent at anything but dipping fingers into everything.

For a little girl afflicted with the sort of perfectionism that dictated every stuffed toy in her room be sitting upright and facing the same direction with their eyes level to one another, never to be touched except for re-straightening and only with washed hands, anything less than "excellent" was physically painful. Yes, physically, because with so much imperfection in life, I was constantly distressed and scowling, which put a massive strain on my tiny brow muscles.

Go ahead, call it undiagnosed OCD.

It doesn't change the fact that my eyebrows have biceps.

The lack of perfection straddling the curse of perfection*ism* is unholy coupling, so being "not-excellent at anything" could've resulted in some gnarly self-hatred. Luckily, I was busy believing my parents' assessment of my (unclear) talents. My self-esteem thanks you, parents, even as my chronic unemployment probably due to the deficit of childhood direction, sometimes keeps my middle-age hand out to you.

Some might admire the gratitude-and-guilt multitask I just pulled off addressing my parents, but its purpose is to profile a madness: the lucky loser. The worthless winner. Take your pick, because that's what would become of me for a long time.

In a way, being forced to endure myself as not-excellent at anything turned into its own exception, so you might say I developed one mastery during childhood. We're talking prodigy status: I became *the* perfect little screw up.

I melted a doll's toy milk bottle on the lit stove and tested it on my baby brother's bare chest. I was six years old and they kept telling me fire burnt, so I had to make sure. They were correct. It was science and not cruelty, but I knew better than to test it on myself. Melting plastic welded to the little boy's skin and he wailed in pain, and suddenly I wasn't a mini-sociopath anymore, now wailing too at the horror I'd committed.

Hindsight or no, I was a perfect asshole and somehow I would grow up to be an unintentional seductress. That comes later.

Fulfilling my screw up duties was the only time I was predictable, meaning, I couldn't be counted on under any other circumstance. As a child, I didn't brush my hair or listen to reason, and if ever there were an important occasion or trip, tears would ensue. Not mine. My baby brother's or my mother's, probably because I hid his toys or unpacked her ready-to-go suitcase if she had turned off the TV before I was done watching.

A word about my hair—I didn't brush it because I hated how I couldn't control its ratty-tendril ways. When I said "headstrong," as in having things my own way, I meant "control freak"—a very tortured control freak in an uncontrollable world. When it came to my hair, denying chaos existed on top of my head helped me cope. You don't take a hairbrush to denial.

Unsurprisingly, I wasn't a well-liked child. I was a loner at school but didn't give a rat's ass. Well, the truth is, I gave *many* rats' asses, but my survival mechanism kept telling me that I didn't.

Spend enough years being strange and collecting bugs (science, again) and pretending you don't care what others think of you, you start believing it. More importantly, *they* start believing it. It turns out people find those who don't give a shit, alluring.

Later, what I had going for me were big eyes and that scowl combining into a come hither glare. Men thought I was dangerous, and danger is sexy. I also had a good brain and a measure of empathy (a happy reversal after my childhood stint as sociopath). Landing guys turned out to be easy and the bug-collector blossomed into an unwitting seductress.

When I didn't finish college as a young adult, instead taking courses on and off for the next twenty years, my parents gave up all hope in me, even the hope of marrying me off. It also never occurred to myself to find a husband to provide for me. The idea of being a wife seemed distasteful–it wasn't like I'd pick up cooking and cleaning. And bear *kids*, run the risk of them doing to me what I did to my parents!? No freaking thanks.

That didn't stop prospective husbands or their families from casting matchmaking nets my way. After all, I came from a nice family and my polite surface did a fine job of hiding the inner hellion. Fortunately, my father–the natural born feminist–was quick to inform them I wasn't the marrying kind. The truth was, he was secretly proud of my non-conformist ways.

Having grown up not excellent at anything or rich or conventional, but cocky about being imperfect, it was something of a shocker for me to end up uncommonly lucky in love. Again and again. That sounds sluttier than the truth, because I was actually a closet prude.

The "perfect" anything, just is, because it's the opposite of manufactured. I grew into the perfect seductress, whether I wanted it or not. But let's be honest, why wouldn't I want it?

In each long-term, live-in relationship, the seductress thing fell off right away because really, I'm just a crazy-haired introvert. But somehow, the men didn't notice it fall off. I was all about being myself, and being myself sometimes meant wearing my bra over my t-shirt when I stayed at home because underwire is annoying. Maybe for the dudes, the ridiculousness of me wearing a bra over my clothes amounted to more I-don't-give-a-shit allure. Maybe the fact that by nature I was no sexual live wire, and generally hard to bed, kept them in a perpetual state of desire. Whatever the theory, I was bewitching and I didn't even have to try. It was ... perfect.

Although we've determined with the gratitude-guilt scenario that I might be good at multitasking, the above ramble isn't me sneaking in a bunch of self-stoking biography. Neither was profiling myself as the lucky loser about guilting my parents. It's all a set-up to a cruel cosmic joke.

You see, at the age of forty-five, I was tired. The inner hellion had worn me down and I was ready to be an adult, maybe. Living in Los Angeles, it had been a few years since my last serious relationship and time to get my shit together. No more casually dating dipshits who were ten to fifteen years younger than me, and worrying if my ass in underwear in their presence had a forty-five-year-old jiggle to it.

I set out to find my next relationship with a man in my own age group, and I was determined to make it my last. The man I ended up picking, picked me back. We met each other's standard of unconventional and decent-hearted, and six months later, he moved in. Apparently I still "just was" the perfect seductress, and that made me feel better about being middle-fucking-aged.

My battle with imperfection and chaos was barely shy of half a century, but I was more comfortable being me than ever. Even though I was a tireless enemy to nicks, specks, lint and stray hairs, I planned on being the perfect girlfriend with a more reasonable attitude toward life's uncontrollable nature.

Here I was, ready to settle down, generally calm the fuck down, be the perfect happy homemaker, maybe even the perfect fiancée for the first time, when *they* marched into our lives. Not even a full week had passed since my maybe-future-husband unpacked his belongings among my arty furniture that had taken me years to collect.

The cruelest of cosmic jokes? Bed bugs. And my maybe-future-husband hadn't brought them. Instead, they made their presence indisputably known as soon as the poor guy moved in. For probably a year, I'd been in denial about them. Chaos wasn't supposed to exist if it weren't acknowledged, just like with my hair.

My building manager had warned me the year before as soon as she had discovered my next-door neighbors' apartment to be a nefarious bed bug hub.

"Those two are hoarders," she had said and handed me test lures to make sure none of the bugs had migrated to my apartment. She joked that my neighbors had been harboring bed bugs "since the eighties."

"How did you find out?" I asked.

"You see them sashaying on the walls like they own the place when you walk in." *Ewww!* I thought those fuckers were supposed to be reclusive, rearing their insidious little heads only after the witching hour, whenever that was.

Between "the eighties" and "sashaying," I had pictured a broken-down disco ball and the hoarders running a bed bug discotheque. Beyond that, I didn't give it a thought. Not even when a cluster of mystery bites appeared on my left arm, or a few months later, on my right boob. I refused to believe I could have bed bugs because you either had to be unlucky or gross to get them.

In fact, a few weeks before my maybe-future-husband moved in, I discovered a teeny baby cockroach on my bathroom sink, which happened to be attached to the wall adjoining my hoarder-neighbors' bathroom. It must have been my former bug-collecting soul and my grown-up measure of empathy kicking in, because I decided to catch and free the icky thing.

Yes, between my naked thumb and forefinger, I voluntarily picked up a miniscule baby cockroach *that turned out to be no cockroach at all* and gently carried it down the long hall to throw over the building's fire escape. *Be wild and live free, my young friend.*

That night, I even bragged about my generous heart to my maybe-future-husband over dinner. He already knew I was weird, so it was okay.

Soon, he moved in with me even after I let him see me wearing my bra over my shirt, so for his sake I took to washing my hated curls more regularly than I liked. It's all about give and take. On one of these excessive hair-washing occasions, while I dried off in the bathroom, I noticed a dark speck on my foot. The speck had legs.

There was no denying bed bugs now.

This one was a teenager, and teenage bed bugs are less cockroachy in appearance than the babies. The next-door teeming bed bug discotheque must have bred them to be *bold* for this repulsive mofo to hop on my wet foot in the bathroom and attempt to suckle my blood in the middle of the day while I was awake. Such a huge number of them had bred that two wretched human hoarders no longer amounted to enough blood meals, so the creatures branched out my way just in time to ruin my perfect homemaker inauguration.

Hence began the undoing of the tough New York City girl and the fall of the "perfect" seductress.

All attempts at presenting myself as reasonable when it came to uncontrollable life events joined the teenage bed bug I picked off my foot: right down the flushing toilet. Even though it was spring and eighty degrees in Los Angeles, I began sleeping with socks on my feet and hands, wearing leggings, a hoodie with the hood drawn and tied, a bandana around my face, and finally, a sort of dog cone fashioned out of paper towels tucked into my hood. Other than the cone barricading my face, all of these items were black, so essentially I slept in a neurotic ninja costume.

My maybe-future-husband lay next to me, staring at the ceiling and not finding any of it sexy. Bra over shirt was one thing, but *this*?

It didn't help when I took to spraying a natural bed bug repellant with cinnamon oil all over our red bedding. Now we were trapped in a package of Big Red gum while not falling asleep.

In some ways, this was the worst thing that could happen to a psyche like mine. This was *imperfection,* multiplied and mobilized among my precious belongings and leaving shit dots on my pillows. It was a great big fuck you to my sense of order, lack of control gone amuck and rudely parading on my body when I was asleep and most vulnerable. Chaos had physicalized into living specks with skin-piercing proboscises, not just for a few drops of my blood, but to smear the soul underneath.

To be honest, I resent that one baby bed bug I released. It could've shown some gratitude and dispatched bug telepathy to the rest of his kind:

"Let's leave that one alone, she's cool." And for the first time in her life, she was considering marrying someone, so she would've liked to make a good homemaking impression, dammit.

Sure, we got rid of the exoskeletal terrorists in a few weeks. But it was more of a draw than a win, because memories of our first days living together in what was supposed to be perfect homemaker bliss are permanently bed bug-speckled.

As for my accidental seductress persona, things might change a little once you see me wearing a paper towel dog cone.

Writer, filmmaker, actor HEDIA ANVAR is a New Yorker transplanted to Los Angeles by way of Tehran. Somewhere in between, she lived in France and Italy, which either expanded her world-view or culturally befuddled her.

As a writer, Hedia has been featured in Narratively and The Huffington Post, *and is currently working on a novel. She is a 2016 "Listen to Your Mother" cast member and a 2015 BlogHer Voices of the Year honoree. Hedia has written and directed over a dozen short films in the last several years, many of which have won awards or reached finalist levels in various competitions.*

Priding herself on doing what she loves doesn't always translate into square meals, but that works out because chewing can be time-consuming and she'd rather put the effort into creative endeavors. In addition to starving artist jokes, Hedia writes about her severe case of "chronic dichotomy" at gunmetalgeisha.com. She's @ravnah on Twitter, Gunmetal Geisha on Facebook and loves visitors.

Bikini Wax By Nadia
By Meredith Gordon
Bad Sandy

"Hi, I'm Meredith and I'm a pube-a-holic," I said to myself in the bathroom mirror. There was no one there to answer me back. No one to offer me encouraging bumper stick slogans like, "You can do it," or, "One pube at a time, friend. One pube at a time." I was alone, naked from the waist down staring at what can best be described as the self-inflicted scalping of my vagina. No, I hadn't trimmed my own hedges. I would have at least felt better about that. This, I paid for. I even tipped her despite the tears streaming down my face as I repeated, "I asked for a regular bikini wax, not a pre-pubescent American Apparel ad."

Just then my three-year-old daughter Margaux walked in, took one look at my bald vag, started to cry, and said, "Mommy, something happened to your penis!" It was then that I realized things had gone too far. I had less public hair than a toddler and I had just traumatized my own toddler, all because I had to have perfect pubes. In fact, I had to have the perfect everything. Children notice things. They comment on them. And worse yet, they try to emulate them. I didn't want my own daughter to grow up plucking, exercising, and waxing herself into perfection like I had. She was already perfect. I could no longer deny the truth. I was a pube-a-holic. I needed to get help. But first, I had to put on pants.

* * *

From the time I was a small child growing up in the suburbs of the San Francisco East Bay, I knew that keeping a tidy trim was going to be important to me. Summers were spent at our local swim club, which was not to be mistaken with a Club. A Club with a capital "C" was where the wealthy and elite went to swim when they were not lounging by their own pools feeling happy and superior.

Ours was a club with a lower case "c" for non-elite people whose best hope of staying cool during the blistering California summers was to park themselves and their children around a giant pool, which boasted an equal chlorine to urine PH-balance. There, at the swim club in Pleasant Hill, California, I witnessed what can best be described as a visual assault on my senses that forever changed and defined my opinion of pubic hair.

I was five or six at the time. My friend Kendall's mom had driven us to the club where we were going to spend the day swimming with friends, playing Marco Polo, and eating tuna fish sandwiches which had been packed and prepared by Kendall's mom. Secretly I always hated Marco Polo. I never wanted to be "it." It wasn't that I had to win, but as a kid my sole goal was to get through life totally unnoticed and ideally not embarrassed. The group nature of Marco Polo could thwart my goal. In my mind when it was my turn to be it, I'd close my eyes and everyone else would sneak away leaving me alone in the pool screaming, "Marco" to an empty pool of giggling Polos.

So when it was my turn to be Marco, I swam around the pool, straining to keep my eyes shut, while screaming, "Marco!" and I heard nothing in response. Positive that all the Polos had left the pool, I sneaked a peek. I wasn't trying to cheat. I was just checking for proof of life. What I got was something much different.

At the very same moment I opened my eyes, the ash from the Parliament Kendall's mom was smoking dropped from her cigarette to her chest. Kendall's mom bolted into high alert from her previously reclined position soaking up the sun. As she sat up in the lounge chair, she straddled the chair, one leg on either side while she brushed the ash from her skin. As she straddled the chair, one side of her lady garden escaped out of one side of her swimsuit. The inmates had made a break for it just as I looked their way. I had never really seen pubic hair before, or at least I hadn't noticed it. My mom wasn't a shower in front of the children kind of gal. My parents were conservative by nature. They were Republicans who thought things like family nakedness was for hippies and Democrats. So pubes were kept private. Now it was clear why.

There at the pool, Kendall's mom's short and curlies were out in full display making that one side of her bathing suit look like it had eyelashes. I couldn't stop staring. Her inner thigh looked like an Orthodox Jew with long curly peyos.

As Kendall's mom realized her bush was out, she made eye contact with me making eye contact with her exposed bikini line. I immediately looked away, pretending like I was looking for any participating Polos just behind Kendall's mom. But the damage had been done; I had been caught catching her. I was embarrassed, on her behalf, and on my own.

I never played with Kendall again for fear that her mom would bring up our embarrassing game of Peek-A-Pube. To this day I've never smoked a cigarette either, nor can I stomach a tuna fish sandwich. It sends me right back to that fateful summer day when I learned just how embarrassing imperfect body hair could be.

So as soon as I went through puberty, I made it my mission to never let my bush embarrass me the way Kendall's mom's had. But when I became a mother, my time became not my own.

Things like manicures, haircuts, and yes, bikini waxes, became harder to schedule. But I was determined not to be one of those women who let her beauty regime go just because she had kids.

I may not have been able to keep up the frequency of my pre-baby beauty routine, but I got close. If I had to find a hair stylist who worked at night, I'd do it. And if I had to nurse my baby through a pedicure, I'd do it. Hell, I even paid my brow girl to come to the house during the little one's nap. I was willing to do anything—anything but let myself go.

As my kids went from infants to toddlers, taking them along as bikini wax plus ones proved more and more challenging. I didn't know how to explain body hair to them in the first place, so I certainly didn't know how to explain why I was taking it off. But, I hated knowing I had an overgrown bush. It made me feel like someone whose house is perfectly clean as long as you don't dare open the closets.

My husband, Justin, didn't care what kind of bush I had. He just wanted to be privy to it. "Oh, the seventies are back!" he'd say without a hint of disappointment or contempt if the time constraints of motherhood had left me days late for my regular bikini wax. But, I cared. Other women stopped showering and had Afro bushes when they had kids, but I wasn't other women. I knew I could do better. I knew I could be better.

The crisis began as Justin and I prepared for a much needed, first time in three years, kid-free vacation. The truth is two kids and two careers had made Justin and me feel more like roommate babysitters than hot and heavy romantics. I feared our marriage was in trouble. I needed the trip to be perfect and I needed me to look perfect on that trip.

I upped my workout game, sometimes exercising twice a day. I scoured all of Los Angeles, and the internet, for the perfect vacation beach wardrobe. I self-tanned. I moisturized. I highlighted. I plucked, sucked in, and didn't exhale.

The day before the trip, the house was empty and I decided to do a test run of my new vacation wardrobe. The summer dresses looked fine. All those spin classes had made my new shorts totally doable. And so with temporary confidence, I decided to try on the new swimsuits I'd ordered online.

I had expected to be horrified by my mom bod in a bikini, but my body image anxiety was overshadowed by the reality that my brand new bathing suit looked like it came with fringe. I had forgotten to get a bikini wax!

And though I hardly had time for one more beautification appointment, I was not going to Mexico with a hairy beaver. I could sleep on the plane if I had to. This was more important.

I speed dialed the Bee Hive, Beverly Hills, and asked for my beloved bikini waxer, Angelica. That's when the receptionist told me the devastating news. Angelica had lost her license for health code violations and was now a barista at a Starbucks just outside of Palmdale.

I was less concerned about the health code issue, which I chose to ignore, and more concerned that I no longer had a go-to waxer. If Palmdale weren't so far and school pick up so soon I would have shown up at that Starbucks and asked for a wax, and a latte.

I began to panic and soon was in a full travel tailspin. My perfect vacation dreams were going to be squashed by images of me sitting poolside with eyelashes on my vagina. I should have called a friend whose references I trusted, but I was drunk with the notion that I couldn't get on that plane without everything being exactly as I'd pictured, pubic hair and all.

So I did the unthinkable.

I went online and searched for bikini waxers.

I highlighted the first name that came up, "Bikini Wax By Nadia." It could have said "Bikini Wax By Helen Keller" and I wouldn't have cared. It's not like I needed a stripper wax. I just wanted an adorable, tamed triangle that wouldn't creep out of my swimsuit. Plus when I clicked on Nadia's webpage, it said she used Italian wax.

I had no idea what Italian wax meant. Was it a wax that smoked tiny little cigarettes, rode a scooter to work, and could metabolize pasta? I didn't know, or care. It sounded European and glamorous and I was a girl who grew up swimming at a lower case c swim club. If Nadia's wax was good enough for all of Italy, it was good enough for me. Sure I was putting my vagina and my marriage in the hands of the first result of my online search, but I was on a mission. I had a higher purpose.

In a frenzy, I dialed the phone.

"He-loooooow!" chirped a woman with a thick Italian accent on the other end of the phone. "This, uh, is, uh, Na-di-ya."

"Hello," I said. She immediately cut me off.

"You are, uh, new client?" she asked.

I told her I was.

"I am, uh, not to taking any new clients," Nadia continued. "Sorry."

"No, you don't understand. I'm going on vacation to Mexico," I said, half-begging. "I'm sure you have the time."

"I am, uh, just too busy," she said again.

Now I was determined not to take no for an answer.

"Please," I said again. "I'll come anytime. I'll make it work."

She paused for a moment to look at her schedule and then said, "If you can to come now, I, uh, squeeze you in."

I looked at the clock. School pick up was in forty-three minutes. Her salon was ten minutes away. If every stoplight worked in my favor, I could make it work. I took the appointment.

Nadia gave me the address of her salon and told me the appointment would take forty-five minutes to an hour.

"An hour?" I thought. What could possibly happen during a bikini wax that would take remotely close to an hour? A bear could be waxed in less time and I was just a fair skinned girl from the suburbs. I don't actually have that much hair.

But time was ticking and I needed Nadia to be as good as her potentially fake internet reviews claimed. I had no time to find someone else. My vacation was just a day away. Nadia was my only hope of having the wax of my dreams. So I ignored the fact that I was going to be massively late to pick up my kid, and got in the car.

I wasn't ten feet out of my driveway when remorse set in. Truthfully, I had always been monogamous when it came to beauty services. I stuck with Eric, my hairstylist of six years, despite him constantly shoving his erect penis into the back of my neck while he stood behind me under the guise of cutting my ends straight.

"It's probably just his cell phone," I'd think to myself as I rationalized not breaking up with Eric. But truthfully, he could cut layers like nobody in Los Angeles. I was willing to endure the veritable sexual assault as long I left with perfect hair.

So despite Angelica's questionable waxing methods—I still have PTSD from the time she had me on all fours like a car getting its tires rotated—I stuck with her. Angelica's waxes were fast. Fifteen minutes if it had been a while, ten if it had only been a few weeks.

She knew what I liked. I didn't have to tell her, "Just a tidy little triangle, please." And she knew better than to try to push a Brazilian on me like other waxers previously had, as if every woman's goal in life was to have a vagina that looked like it was going through chemo.

But without Angelica, I was on my own. I had to start seeing another waxers.

My mind first registered panic when I drove up to the address Nadia had given me on the phone. There was no pale-green painted salon sign or lovely storefront with relaxing waterfalls beckoning me in like a salon usually had. There was only a downtrodden brick building that conjured images of getting a bikini wax in Baghdad. I ignored my instincts, parked my car, and went inside.

The salon was actually a windowless room no bigger than a closet. It may have actually been a closet that Nadia sublet from the hardware store next door. In any other situation, the conditions would have caused me alarm and I would have left without feeling guilty.

I don't want to get waxed in a windowless room where no one can hear me scream. When it comes to beauty services, there's safety in numbers. I want to see other customers coming and going. I want evidence that some other living breathing person has left there without hepatitis or a lawsuit.

But this wasn't any other situation, or any other day. Today was not a day for thorough research or a good referral. Today was not a day for me to be comfortable or to find the best option possible. Today was a day about getting what I needed however that had to happen.

From behind a curtain out popped a middle-aged woman with long thick curly hair and a cigarette dangling from the side of her mouth. She held out her hands like Roberto Bengini going in for a hug.

"I am, uh, Na-di-ya!" she said. "Let's, uh, make you beautiful!"

I half-smiled and put down my purse. I ignored the dust bunnies in the corners of the room and assumed Nadia would put out her cigarette and put up her hair.

Nadia sized me up and said, "Now, what would you like me to, uh, do?"

As I carefully described the tidy triangle I wanted Nadia to create, Nadia walked back behind the curtain.

"Everything off," she interrupted from the other room.

"But I'm not done telling you what I'd like," I said in a raised voice.

"I know what you, uh, want. You want the perfect bikini wax," she said. "Now everything off!"

Most waxers worked around the client's underwear, for their safety and the client's dignity.

"Everything?" I clarified.

"*Si,*" Nadia responded. "We don't, uh, need to be shy. I like to get up, uh, close, so I don't miss anything. Plus, it's very hard to get all the hair when we work around the panties."

Reluctantly I slipped off my underwear, shoved it in the pocket of my rumpled up jeans and lay down on the table.

When Nadia returned, she moved a stool in between my legs and placed her face close enough to my vag that I could feel her hot breath. And her cigarette.

"Now spread!" said Nadia. She pushed my legs further apart than when my babies were crowning and looked at my inner thighs like she was Michelangelo and I was the Sistine Chapel.

"Just a reminder," I said, my voice creaking, "Just a triangle."

Nadia nodded her head.

And then she shut off all of the lights.

Experts say that when adults hear the sound of a baby crying, it feels like they've been hearing the sound for twice as long as they actually have. Seconds feel like minutes. The same can be said for when you're lying alone, half naked in the dark, in a windowless salon with a stranger who is smoking a cigarette within inches of your labia.

Time stands still.

And so when Nadia finally switched on a floor lamp she had moved to illuminate my bikini line, I breathed a deep sigh of relief that bordered on orgasmic. The floor lamp was the only light she used for the entire time she worked. It looked like an inquisition light as if my vagina was a prisoner of war and she was trying to get all the answers.

But the truth is, my vagina was a prisoner of war. I was at war with myself and had taken my vagina hostage.

For the duration of the wax, Nadia did not stop talking. Her favorite subject was herself, whom she'd refer to in the third person. "Everybody loves Nadia's work," she'd say. "You'll see. Nadia will make you beautiful." "Nadia is an artist." "Nadia knows what you need." Nadia. Nadia. Nadia.

I don't know if it was the Italian wax, which I learned is a thick blue wax that looks like putty that gets rolled on and off the skin so it doesn't tear the skin, or the annoying hum of Nadia's never ending chatter, but I stopped paying attention to what Nadia was doing.

Truthfully, it was probably just exhaustion. I had spent the past few weeks beautifying myself into vacation perfection. I had even managed to get a bikini wax with ten minute's notice. This was the first time I had sat down, much less laid down, in weeks.

I closed my eyes, exhaled, and thought, *Everything is going to be perfect.*

Forty-five minutes later Nadia sat back, exhausted as if she'd just climbed Kilimanjaro, and proclaimed she was *fini.*

She proudly passed me a hand mirror. I focused it and immediately started to cry.

To say Nadia had taken off a lot of hair would be an understatement. I hadn't been waxed. I had been sheared.

Seeing my tears, Nadia explained, "You say you want a triangle, but that isn't what you want."

"No," I said. "That's what I wanted. I wanted you to trim my bush, not remove it!"

Nadia was steadfast, insisting that what I wanted wasn't what I wanted. But, the damage was done.

Short of getting a merkin, I was going to have a bald bush for the foreseeable future.

I left her salon in tears, but of course tipped her first. I'd hate for a woman who did a terrible job to think I didn't have manners.

I picked my daughter up late from school, went home, shut the bathroom door, and surveyed the damage.

As if being scalped for forty-five minutes wasn't bad enough, it became clear to me as I looked in the mirror that I was allergic to Nadia's blue Italian wax. Margaux was right, something had happened to my penis. My penis had a receding hairline and an allergic reaction.

By the time I boarded the plane to Mexico, my inner thighs were so red they looked like the hotel walls in *The Shining*. I spent the duration of my kid-free vacation, sipping a Benadryl cocktail, while discretely icing my vag. I never got to wear one of my fabulous new swimsuits. And sex was totally out of the question. Not only were my inner thighs red, they felt like they were on fire. The pain lasted most of my trip.

As outraged as I was that Nadia had gone against my wishes, I knew that Nadia had given me exactly what I needed. I had been in a perfection-frenzy right down to my bikini line. This was not the first time I had pushed my body and myself past their limits, but it would be the last. I knew I needed to recover from this quest to improve myself.

So, as I sat on a soft chair with a bag of ice shoved between my legs, overlooking the Sea of Cortez, I took a deep breath, exhaled, and told myself, "One pube at a time, friend. One pube at a time."

MEREDITH GORDON is a recovered actress and stand up comic who writes the side splitting humor blog BadSandy.com, which was voted one of the Top 50 blogs to watch by Mom.me. Meredith spent two seasons on the writing staff of NBC's The Apprentice *and her writing has also been featured in* Cosmopolitan Magazine *as well as on Today's Parents, In The Powder Room, Momtastic Mom.me and Scary Mommy. Known for her spot-on observational style, Meredith uses her poison keyboard to poke fun at everything from Gwyneth Paltrow's helpful suggestions to her darling husband's inability to wash all of the dishes. Meredith also hosts the smash hit podcast, The Meltdown Moms Show, a humorous look into parenting under the shadow of the Hollywood sign.*

Meredith lives in Los Angeles where she's raising her husband and two children. She hopes someday to fit back into her high school jeans. Follow her on Facebook, Twitter, and Instagram.

Bedpans, Barbies and Busted:
One Nurse's Perfectly Public Humiliation
By Christine Burke
Keeper of the Fruit Loops

I worked my ass off for my nursing degree.

Frankly, if I'm being honest, aside from single-handedly growing two humans, having the letters R.N. after my name is my proudest achievement.

Earning those two letters was no walk in the park, either, I don't mind telling you. When I entered nursing school, I had visions of taking care of sweet little old ladies while I donned adorable, holiday appropriate scrubs as I assisted doctors in finding the cures to cancer and male pattern baldness. I expected to find a job that fit seamlessly with having a family and I envisioned working as the school nurse who handed out kisses for skinned knees and lollipops to children with tummy aches.

I was going to be the PERFECT NURSE and patients would come from far and wide to be treated by my healing touch.

Turns out, I kind of had my head up my ass when I signed up for nursing school.

You see, it's a good thing those nursing school brochures don't include pictures of nurses covered in blood, urine and fecal matter. It's an even better thing the brochures don't have "scratch and sniff" sections to help applicants fully understand what their noses will be subjected to on the job. And it's a really, really good thing that nursing students don't find out until *after* they've paid for their first semester that exactly ZERO men look like George Clooney in a hospital gown.

So, yeah, nursing school was hard. Like, really, really hard. Hours spent committing every facet of the human body to memory, long days spent on my feet emptying bed pans from confused, incontinent patients, nights where I nearly went blind trying to memorize minute details because I knew my professor would level me at clinical rounds the next day. While my friends were getting ready to go to keg parties and off campus shenanigans, I would tuck myself into bed at eight o'clock in preparation for a five o'clock morning shift report at the hospital.

And, as if tedious classes and impossibly long hours weren't enough, nursing school exams are an alternate version of hell. Mere written exams are for the weak. Nursing students are subjected to practical exams intended to ensure little Miss Nurse Suzy isn't going to accidentally kill herself with a defibrillator. You haven't lived until you've had to insert a urine catheter into a decrepit, old lady crotch while your nursing professor pumps you about kidney flow and signs of renal failure. You don't know terror until you are faced with having to learn proper CPR technique on a patient who has just expired and you hear his very last dying breath groan through his lips as you press down on the poor departed's chest. And, we are NOT going to talk about the time I let my lab partner insert a nasogastric tube into my nose so she could pass her clinical exam. DON'T EVEN GO THERE, I SAID.

My point? After four long years, I earned my degree and I was FINALLY ready to hit the floors of the hospital in my holiday appropriate scrubs and meet the nice little old ladies clamoring for my healing touch.

I was going to get the PERFECT NURSING JOB.

Uh huh.

Turns out, I kind of had my head up my ass when it came to first nursing job expectations.

After enduring almost two years on a Migraine Headache Unit (yes, that's a thing. No, I didn't know that, either. Yes, it was as horrible as it sounds. No, I didn't get the good drugs there so stop asking), I had finally gained enough experience to springboard into the intensive care unit. In my early days of nursing school, I had quickly abandoned the notion of being a school nurse for the chance to work in the fast paced, high intensity world of critical care. I realized pretty early on that kids whine A LOT and ICU patients tend to have so many tubes shoved where the sun don't shine that they can't bother you at two in the morning.

So, after six years of preparation, I was finally, FINALLY going to be the PERFECT NURSE.

Yes, you can roll your eyes. I know I am.

What they don't tell you in the intensive care unit is that there's a metric ton of information you must learn on the job in order to not just save a life but to also not lose one. Drips. Tubes. Pumps. Bells. Whistles. Code Blues. Code Browns (don't ASK). As any veteran ICU nurse will tell you, their training began on their first solo ICU day. You don't know fear until you've been talking to a patient who suddenly slumps forward into his hospital food. You don't know terror until you've walked by a patient room and notice more blood than linoleum on the floor. And, you don't know all encompassing panic until you've lifted a hospital gown only to find a busted incision and a real, beating heart in front of your face.

But, for all of the panic and tension in the ICU, I kicked ASS at critical care. I owned my assignments. I was on my A game all day, every day. Drip rates? I could do them in my head. Code Blues? I ate my lunch while I brought a patient back to life. I knew cardiac rhythms inside out and backwards. I could see a Code Blue before it even hit the monitors. Work a double shift after three days on and no pee break for eight hours? BRING IT, BITCHACHOS.

After eight years of hard work, I was there. I was at the pinnacle.

I was the PERFECT NURSE.

And then I got fired.

FIRED.

As in, take your stethoscope home because you no longer work here, Nurse Burke.

Yeah, nothing like getting fired to ruin eight years of hard work, I have to say.

Oh, wait.

There IS something worse than getting fired from your job as the perfect nurse in your dream specialty: getting fired from your job because you wrote an email insulting the Chief of <Specialty Withheld> and his girlfriend.

Oh, how the Mighty and Perfect fall.

In my defense, his girlfriend was a total twit. Big boobs, big blonde hair, next to no brains and I'm convinced the only reason she had a nursing position on our floor was because she put her knowledge of anatomy and physiology to very good use with the male residents of the hospital. She flirted as she rolled patients over, leaned her perky little ladies right up next to a doctor's arm as she received orders and had a sugary sweet, gag inducing laugh that made all the men swoon. It came as no surprise that she was quickly dating the Chief of <Specialty Withheld> and his very severe acne problem (you can see where I'm going and yes, I'm hanging my head in shame as I type).

She was dumb as a brick and I couldn't stand her and her "perfection." She made mistakes; she faltered through procedures and cut corners. I couldn't stand her and I said as much to a friend in an email. Actually, what I **might** have said was that she was dumber than a post and that I suspected that Dr. <Specialty Withheld>'s acne would clear up soon because she must be a miracle worker in bed. Oh, and I may or may not have referred to her as Nurse Barbie. Okay, I totally did.

Not my finest literary achievement, I might add.

Of course, back then, email and social media seemed more private. Facebook didn't exist and emails were choppy and spotty at best. No one really understood back then that emails could be copied. And pasted. And forwarded. And read by the people being insulted in the text. Okay, when I say "no one" understood, I mostly mean that *I* didn't understand that an email could bite me in the ass.

But I wrote what I wrote. My "friend" forwarded what I wrote. The Chief of <Specialty Withheld> read what I wrote. And worst of all: Nurse Barbie read what I wrote.

It did NOT go well for me. Not well at all. Deservedly so, of course, but holy cow: you don't know fear until you walk onto a nursing unit and realize all at once that every single person standing at the nurse's station not only knows what you wrote but is also standing there with their arms crossed behind Nurse Barbie.

It was a public and very PERFECT humiliation. I still cringe to this day when I think about just how loudly Nurse Barbie yelled at me in front of those cardiac monitors.

I die a little bit inside when I think about having to look my supervisor in the eye and tell her that, yes, I did, in fact, write the embarrassing email. It took me quite some time to get over hearing that I was relieved of my duties because I was stupid and less than perfect. I'd like to say that I held my head high as I left her office and walked by Nurse Barbie and her cronies but I'd be lying. I ugly cried like a baby and didn't stop for days.

My perfection was ruined and I had no one to blame but myself.

A funny thing happens, though, when you suffer a PERFECT public humiliation: life simply goes on. Fortunately, my supervisor had mercy on me and gave me a stellar recommendation for my next job. I was back in the ICU after a short reprieve, smarter and wiser. I still brought my A game all day, every day but I kept my comments and thoughts about bimbo nurses limited to my head or my BFF. (And, yes, the irony of starting a public humor blog many years later is *not* lost on me.)

And, that time I ran into the Chief and the now Mrs. Nurse Barbie at a black tie function? Well, let's just say she hasn't gotten any smarter, her boobs were sagging, and his skin was still bad. But you didn't hear it from me …

CHRISTINE BURKE is the Keeper of the Fruit Loops, Manager of the Fecal Roster and Driver of the People Mover. In other words, she's a mom. An Erma Bombeck Martha Stewart with a Roseanne Barr twist, she has the mouth and organized cabinets to prove it. She resides in Pennsylvania with her ever budget conscious husband, two blog inspiring Fruit Loops and her extensive collection of thrift shop shoes. In her spare time, she runs marathons, governs the PTA like nobody's business and drinks cheap wine to cope with it all. Her personal blog is keeperofthefruitloops.com.

The Perfect Wife
By Kathryn Leehane
Foxy Wine Pocket

The invitation to my husband's company Christmas party could not have arrived at a better time. Like a summons from heaven, we were invited to don elegant clothing, dine amongst corporate elite, and spend the evening at an upscale hotel.

I wept tears of joy.

See, at the time, I had a three-year-old daughter, an infant son, two large dogs, and four cats under my round-the-clock care. (Take my advice: just have the baby; don't pretend you're not ready and adopt too many animals instead.) Still nursing my son, I was severely sleep deprived and generally ragged. Showers were infrequent (as was any basic hygiene), and milk, bodily fluids, and other mysterious substances constantly covered my skin and clothing. My best outfit included some capri maternity jeans from Old Navy and whatever machine-washable shirt didn't have stains on it.

I was desperate for an adult night out without anyone clinging to me, needing to be fed, or changed. I was desperate to feel clean and beautiful. I was desperate for a full night's sleep.

Oh yeah, I also wanted to support my husband, Tim. Recently promoted, he wanted to make a good impression with the new VPs and the CEO. Arm candy couldn't hurt. Operation "Be the Perfect Wife in Exchange for a Free Night on the Town" commenced.

The first order of business was to find the Perfect Dress. Because I'd not yet lost my pregnancy weight, I embarked upon a quest for that magical dress to disguise my post-partum pooch and enhance my breastfeeding boobs. It took several shopping sessions and many bribes in the form of lollipops and chocolate to keep the three-year-old quiet. Some trips were interrupted by a howling baby demanding to nurse; some were aborted because of threenager tantrums. Once I even had to run out of the store pushing a stroller with a screaming preschooler foisted over my shoulder. After much agony (for everyone), I finally found The One: the dress that made my breasts look amazing.

I then purchased the perfect shoes and the requisite Spanx and borrowed the perfect necklace from my best friend. In order to complete the package, I scheduled hair and makeup appointments. (I needed an expert to cover those eye bags. Seriously.) Because I absolutely wanted to ~~impress my husband and his colleagues~~ feel human again.

The company hosted the party at a local hotel, so my husband reserved a room for us. The promise of wild hotel sex prompted me to make a deal with ~~the devil~~ Grandma to do the overnight babysitting, including the late night and early morning baby feedings. I pumped before I left, and we had enough breastmilk in the refrigerator that I could drink the free wine and pump-and-dump before bed with no gap in the milk supply chain.

The hair and makeup were a breeze…mostly because I didn't have to do the work. Dressing myself, however, was another matter. Perhaps I should have put on the Spanx before hair and makeup because I tugged and shimmied and labored my way into that shapewear for a good ten minutes. The entire exercise was just that— a workout. After a couple of blotting wipes, I managed to remove the sheen, smooth out the wobbly bits, and adorn myself with beautiful attire.

My husband's jaw dropped when I entered the living room. I was The Perfect Wife.

"Mommy, you wook beawtiful!" my daughter exclaimed as I used my arms to fend off the animals and offspring. No one was going to ruin my perfection.

After dazzling my family and then leaving them behind in the dust, I felt liberated. Entering the ballroom on my husband's arm and immediately being offered champagne by the tuxedo-clad servers, I felt glamorous. Talking to adults who didn't need their faces wiped, their food cut up, or their undergarments changed, I felt like a brand-new person.

"This is what perfection feels like," I whispered to my drink.

That first glass of wine transformed me into an outgoing, articulate person who rocked meeting and mingling with the executives. I was polite, graceful, and witty. They all loved me, of course. (I'm sure it wasn't my impressive cleavage.)

Over dinner, I drank some more wine and befriended my husband's colleagues and their spouses. I politely chuckled at the office shenanigans and politics I had left behind three years earlier. I didn't even cry once thinking about my groundhog-day-like existence back home. It was probably the free wine.

Because I was still breastfeeding my son, I hadn't had much alcohol in over a year. Because I was severely sleep-deprived, I didn't notice the waiter constantly refilling my wine glass. And because I was being squeezed to death by a spandex boa constrictor around my waist, I picked at my dinner like an obstinate child. Still, my mummy wrap was quickly becoming intolerable.

I excused myself to go to the restroom. Maybe a quick trip could relieve some of the pressure building inside of me. Using the toilet with Spanx presented a dilemma that I had never before faced: should I take off the deathtrap to pee freely or should I use the pre-cut hole in the bottom of the shapewear instead? Remembering my spandex aerobics from earlier in the evening, I opted for the later. I awkwardly straddled the toilet, tried to pry open the hole wide enough, and attempted to pee straight through the opening. Between my drunken swaying and the screwed-up nature of my post-partum nether regions, it was like pouring a gallon of milk through the eye of a needle. Though I managed to empty my bladder, I might have peed a little on the undergarment.

Having achieved a small level of relief, I cleaned up the best I could and staggered out of the bathroom, using the wall for leverage. Across the hallway, Tim eyed me with concern. "How are you feeling?"

"Greath!" I raised my arm triumphantly.

"Uh, let's get you up to our room." He secured his arm around my waist to hold me up, and we quietly exited the party.

By the time we arrived upstairs, my head was spinning, I was sweating, and the elastic vice around my stomach and nether regions was going in for the kill. My insides churned, and I could feel saliva pooling in my mouth. "I'm gonna hurl."

I stumble-ran to the toilet. I fell to my knees and heard my nylons rip as the bile rose in my throat. No longer even close to the perfect wife, I became Mt. Vesuvius—spewing vomit everywhere: in the toilet, on the floor, on myself. The sheer force of the eruptions even caused me hit my head on the toilet tank. Also, I might have peed a little. Again.

My stomach flipped. I was panting. Dizzy. Woozy. The Spanx was cutting off my circulation, crushing my internal organs. I was going to die.

When the puke storm passed, I hobbled over to the bed, and face-planted on the mattress. Sounding like my preschooler, I whined, "Can you take off my Thpanx? PLEATHE? It'th trying to kill me."

Tim's initial concern gave way to confusion. "Uh, your what?!"

"My Thpanx! The giant grandma underwear that ith thqueezing me to death!" I flopped over and pulled up my dress to show him. "I'm going to thwow up my inerds."

Horror flashed in his eyes, but he quickly concealed it and ran over. He gave the shapewear a gentle tug; it didn't budge.

"You're gonna have to pull harder. It's like a thecond thkin." I tossed my head back and forth on the bed.

So he pulled a little more. They didn't budge.

"HARDER!" I commanded. Spit flew from my mouth and landed on my face.

Steely-eyed, he crouched down, prepared for battle. He yanked my Spanx...and my entire body down the length of the bed. As my butt crash-landed on the carpet, I realized I was stuck. "Oh fuck. It'th hooked to my bwa by those thrappy thingys. You're gonna have to sthrip me."

Not even remotely sexy, Tim undressed his semi-conscious, sticky, reeking-of-vomit-and-pee wife right there on the floor. Every article of clothing. Probably not what he had imagined when he booked the hotel room. Once he stripped me, he heaved me into bed, very similar to hoisting a giant, flailing octopus into a cradle. My body melted into the mattress, completely exhausted.

Tim's hand touched my shoulder. "Uhhh, Kate? You're leaking."

I was mystified. Disoriented. "What?"

"You're leaking milk." He spoke slowly. "All over yourself."

My hands flew to my hard and slippery boobs. "I need to pump." I started crying. "But I can't move."

"I'll get the pump for you." Tim retrieved my breastpump and set it up for me while I helplessly watched. He eyed me cautiously. "Do you want some help?"

I waved him away. "Nooo. I can do dis mythelf."

"You sure?" Doubt dripped from his words.

"YETH!"

Fortunately I was already naked, so there wasn't much to do except hold the pump parts to my breasts. Unfortunately, between the wine and the sleep deprivation, I kept ~~passing out~~ falling asleep during the extraction. My arms would fall down, dropping the pump parts. Breast milk poured down my chest, on the sheets, on the pillows.

Whether he was full of horror or mercy, my husband finally took over. He propped up the pillows. He positioned me upright. He held the pumps against my chest.

He. Pumped. My. Breastmilk. For. Me.

The gentle tug at my nipples was the last thing I felt before I passed out for good.

I woke up the next morning to the stench of Eau de Sour Milk, Vomit, and Pee. Dried bodily fluids sullied my body. Honestly, I would have been cleaner at home.

The hotel room, however, was spotless. My husband had cleaned and put away the breastpump parts. He had tidied up the mess I made in the bathroom. He had carefully placed my filthy clothing in a bag (to be sent directly to the cleaners). In the end, I was not the perfect wife, but Tim was most definitely the perfect husband.

KATHRYN LEEHANE *is a writer, author, and storyteller. She pens the humor blog, Foxy Wine Pocket, and loves to tell tales that make you spit out your drink. A regular contributor to Scary Mommy, her writing is also published in several anthologies and popular web sites, including Redbook* Magazine, The Huffington Post, *and* BLUNT*moms. Kathryn lives in the San Francisco Bay Area with her husband, two kids, and a ferociously snuggly pit bull. In her down time, she inhales books, bacon, and Pinot Noir, and her interests include over-sharing, Jason Bateman, and crashing high school reunions. Follow the shenanigans on Facebook, Instagram, and Twitter.*

I'm Just Trying To Fit In
By Harmony Hobbs
Modern Mommy Madness

I have a long history of getting trapped in articles of clothing. Strappy items, small(ish) ones, even normal attire—I've been imprisoned in all kinds. I'm also claustrophobic, so the moment it dawns on me that I'm stuck, I *freak*.

Have you ever crammed a cat into a pillowcase? It's very much like that.

In my younger, less experienced days, when I'd get tangled, I was known to rip clothing from my body with my bare hands before making a run for it, never looking back at the dressing room. With age, I have developed more sophisticated methods...like snipping myself free with fingernail clippers. I carry a pair of them with me everywhere I go, and they are especially helpful when I get my hair caught on one of those tiny hook-and-eye closures, or—God forbid—when I zip my own flesh into a metal side zipper.

One time, I got stuck in a bathing suit top with my arms over my head in a T.J. Maxx dressing room. Too proud to call for help, I stubbornly tried to wriggle my way out of it. The movement and the hot lights made me start sweating, causing the material to practically glue itself to my skin.

I eventually managed to escape, but not without pulling a shoulder muscle—which is very similar to the time I pulled a chest muscle trying to remove a pair of boots. Apparently my legs are too big for tall boots, which saddens me both on a fashion level and a human level. Few things are more humbling than hobbling into a living room full of family members and having to ask someone to help you pull off your brand-new riding boots because they got caught on your calves.

Also humbling are the conversations I've been forced to have with people about my clothing-removal-related injuries:

Friend: "Do you want to go to aerobics class with me tomorrow?"

Me: "No, sorry, I can't."

Friend: "Why not? What's going on?"

Me: "I pulled a muscle. It's no big deal, I'll be okay."

Friend: "Oh, no! What happened?"

Me: "Well, there was this evil swimsuit…"

There have been countless situations with sports bras and Spanx, strapless bras and body shapers, most of which I have blocked from memory. Suffice it to say that it's been a constant problem in my life, and after more than thirty years of this, I've had no choice but to wonder if the real issue is *me* and not the *clothes*.

For the record, I am an average-sized woman. When I think with my rational brain, it's clearly the clothing, not my ass, causing the problem. Sizing is all over the place, varying so much that there is no way for me to intuitively know what size to select. Not all bodies are designed to wear skinny jeans, even if they are made of a denim/spandex blend. I have to try things on. And sometimes, I try on things that are too small because I am not psychic and I don't always know what will fit. Sometimes I'm a size ten and sometimes I'm a size six.

Okay, that was a lie. I'm never a size six.

This is probably why I have these problems.

When I think with my irrational brain, which admittedly happens much more frequently, I want to be *smokin' hot* at any cost. And if those skinny jeans don't fit properly—something I realize too late as I am flopping around like a mermaid in the dressing room, trying and failing to remove them from my body—then I need to do something about it immediately.

My irrational brain thinks my ass is the problem, not the clothing.

My irrational brain is a bitch.

The truth is, I have three kids, chubby genes, and a propensity for cellulite, but luckily, the bar is set pretty low for moms. One benefit to being a mother is that you can always blame your appearance on the "baby weight"—at least for awhile. Unfortunately for me, it's been three years since I last had a baby, and I can no longer use that as an excuse. My tummy flap didn't go away on its own and my cellulite is still there and my thighs did not magically shrink and the diet I've been on—the one where I eat whatever I want and hope I don't gain weight—isn't working.

At all.

There comes a time in every woman's life when she has to assess her reflection and decide how many fucks she is willing to give. I consider myself to be a moderate giver of fucks. This means that sometimes I get upset with my appearance and eat nothing but salad for several days, and when I can button my pants again, I return to my usual diet of simple carbohydrates.

Moderate givers of fucks also occasionally eat two servings of cake right before bed. Sometimes they drink unknown amounts of full-bodied wine and can't be held responsible for what they eat after 8 pm. Sometimes they crush Doritos up and mix the crumbs with sour cream, salsa, and grated cheese and then eat it with a spoon like cereal.

Basically, I never end up making it to anything remotely close to my goal weight. I know I'm supposed to embrace my *mom bod* and be proud of it, but sometimes I also wonder what it would feel like to have a gap between my legs. Are those women happier? Are they less sweaty? Do they live a life exempt from clothing entrapment?

I feel like maybe the answer is yes, and that curiosity eventually overtakes me and I embark on a journey that can only be described as an evolution, because it goes from something simple to something very complex. It generally happens about once a year, right after my yearly exam when my doctor informs me that my Body Mass Index is too high. I explain that it's always been too high, ever since puberty, because *what are pounds anyway?* This is me. I'm big-boned.

My doctor does not accept this. I hang my big-boned head in shame before going home to research diets. After much Googling, I find one that sucks slightly less than the alternatives. I promise myself that I'll start on Monday, and thus begins the following seven-day journey:

Day 1: I eat all the things before my diet begins. I tell myself and my family that I'm clearing the house of junk food before I start my diet…and it is DELICIOUS.

Day 2: I begin dieting. I carefully shred lettuce and lovingly slice celery and admire my restraint because there is a jar of peanut butter sitting *right next to me* and I am not eating it.

I'm amazing.

Day 3: I officially hate my life. I hate being hungry. I hate my husband for not caring about his weight. I hate everyone.

Day 4: I decide that I do not wish to give up eating and drinking whatever I want, so instead, I will exercise approximately four hours per day. SHUT UP, I CAN MAKE IT WORK. I go to the gym to begin. I make it through sixty minutes of Spin class before collapsing on the floor and deciding I've done enough.

Day 5: When the alarm goes off, I feel as though I've been hit by a truck. I realize that I cannot exercise four hours per day. Also, I'm tired of kale. Fuck kale.

Day 6: Do I look skinnier? I feel like I look skinnier. I step onto the scale. I've gained two pounds. Fuck this scale.

Day 7: I conclude that losing weight will solve exactly zero of my actual problems, so fuck the Body Mass Index, fuck my doctor, fuck my big-boned genes, and fuck the clothing that I will never look good in. I'm tired.

It is always on day seven that I order a full-fat, triple vanilla latte with whipped cream from Starbucks because that DOES solve one actual problem: exhaustion.

It is plain to see that not only am I incapable of giving enough fucks, but I *am* fucked, because I am not willing to go to extreme lengths (ahem, kale) to lose weight and that means that I'm looking at a lifetime of getting stuck in dressing rooms.

Also, bathing suit season is approaching.

I guess it's time for me to invest in a tiny pair of scissors.

HARMONY HOBBS is a freelance writer who navigates the waters of motherhood without any grace or finesse whatsoever. A fan of strong coffee, red wine, and sturdy undergarments, her work is self-described as "honesty and insanity in one fell swoop." For more—and you know you want more—follow her on Instagram, Facebook, Twitter, and at her blog, Modern Mommy Madness.

A Labor of Love
By Ashley Fuchs
The Malleable Mom

Long before blogs, Facebook, and Pinterest, taught me how to feel superior to other moms by having the perfect birth, I was way ahead of the curve. I was a brand new Pediatric nurse and a certified doula, dreaming of becoming a midwife. I consumed home birth videos, tearfully admiring the tender interaction between the laboring mother and her attentive partner in the dimly lit comfort of their "nest," while high-end spa music played in the background. I argued passionately against the unnecessarily high rates of C-sections in America to anyone who feigned interest. I spouted my "breast is best" and "nipple confusion" beliefs, having had zero days experience with motherhood, while brandishing my *Florence Nightingale Award for Clinical Excellence in Breastfeeding Advocacy* upon graduation from an Ivy League school. (Yes, I was that annoying.)

I apprenticed at a local birthing center to learn the ins and outs of natural labor (pun intended.) I was in Heaven. Birth really is an amazing thing to watch, if you can get past the smell and how truly intimate it gets, and I could. I walked mostly naked women up and down the hallway and taught them how to do "nipple stimulation" to encourage contractions. I held sweaty legs, fetched ice chips, and wiped brows. I helped new fathers cut the umbilical cord and choked up as I handed them their new son or daughter. I basked in the glow of it all. I received handwritten notes from families who said that my compassionate care had forever made a difference in their lives. *Damn, I must be really good at this,* I thought. *My own birth is going to be magical.*

It's OK to laugh at my hubris. I think we all know where this is going.

When I got knocked up, I managed to convince my husband to not freak out when I announced I wanted a home birth. I was thrilled when he didn't put up a fight. That night, I dimmed the lights of the master bedroom in our urban Victorian townhouse, picturing him murmuring softly to me, "Just breathe…" the two of us working as one to bring forth this product of our love. I got misty-eyed just thinking about it! *What kind of music would I play? Could I have a water birth?* The next day I ran to the bookstore, bought a copy of *Husband-Coached Childbirth: The Bradley Method of Natural Childbirth*, and proudly gifted it to him in honor of "our" decision. He glanced at it, said "Oh," and tossed onto his nightstand…

…and there it sat for months, collecting dust. I couldn't understand why he wasn't tearing into this bad boy—this was supposed to be his thing! Why wasn't he chomping at the bit to train up? I would often stare at the book on his table, my resentment building like a clog of slimy hair in a drain. I silently willed it to open up and leap into his hands. Eventually, I began picking it up and reading passages aloud, in an overly excited tone, like I imagined a parent would use trying to convince a toddler to take their medicine. Sometimes, I would say encouraging and passive-aggressive things, like, "So, what chapter are you on?"

He never fucking read it.

As we got closer to Go Time, we were having dinner with friends when the subject of watching the baby crown and cord cutting came up.

"Oh, I'm not doing any of that," the love of my life stated.

"Any of what?" I said in an I-must-be-hearing-you-incorrectly tone. Our friends are smart and recognized the signs of a very pregnant woman receiving shocking news, which looks a lot like a king cobra stilling before it strikes. He was oblivious.

"I'm not looking at anything below the Calvin Klein equator." He chuckled. (He was the only one.) My friends glanced at each other with a "dead man walking" look on their faces.

"You're *joking*, right? You are not going witness your own child being born? Not going to cut the cord, which is your rite of passage as a new dad?" My voice was getting shrill.

"Nope."

To spare our tense friends, I let it go, thinking that I would deal with him later. Oh no, he was dead serious. Two babies later, and I can assure you, he can describe their entry into this world about as well as you can.

OK, so I wouldn't have the birth partner that I had always dreamed of. That's OK. I should have known that it might be this way from our past experience with swing dancing: he always accused me of back-leading him, but I did that because I had more dance experience than he did! If I wanted this birth to go the *right* way, I would just have to back-lead it, and who was more qualified to do that than me? I had this: I had been diligently gathering my extensive, midwife-provided checklist of supplies to prepare my perfect birth nest.

My prep also included the typical expectant-mother rituals: I bought tiny diapers and stacked them on the changing table, washed and folded wee clothes in Dreft and sobbed over how adorable they were, tossed aside anything from my baby shower that was for a human over one month of age, because it was "overwhelming," and cleaned my house like it owed me money. Every ounce of energy I spent doing these tasks brought me closer and closer to my vision of having the perfect birth and being the perfect mom. *If I just worked hard enough, I could control. It. All.*

A week before my due date, I started slow-peeing my pants through my evening shift and bought an early ticket to maternity leave. It was Monday night. I went home, and announced to my husband that my contractions had started, and excitedly waited for the back-rubbing/foot-rubbing/doting that came next. He kissed me on the head, and promptly fell asleep. (Um, okay...) I would spend the next two and a half days in early labor and wide-awake. Not true labor, which is productive and where a baby comes out. But the kind of ineffective labor that is exhausting for both the person and the uterus. But, I was at home! I had my labor "coach" right with me! I didn't have to do anything but bask in the glow of the natural process...right?

Somewhere around 2:00 am on Tuesday night, my contractions were coming every minute (not great for making baby come, and absolutely draining). This had been going on for *hours*, and I was suffering in my bed awake and alone. My husband was, once again, sleeping through it next to me, and my nudging him awake to give me the labor support that I required was gradually moving from shoulder-tapping to temple-punching. The next morning, his eyes fluttered open to face another day, only to find his sweaty, panting wife next to him with murder in her sunken eyes.

"What?!" He yelped.

"You slept all night! I needed you!" I whisper-screamed.

"Not really. It was hard to sleep with all of the yelling."

Oh, he *loves* that joke. He still tells it. I wish I had kept that goddamned Bradley book, so I could beat him with it.

At this point Gerta, the midwife, arrived to determine when the actual labor was going to start. She was not happy with my less-than birth documentary state. "You need to *sleep*," she chided in her thick German accent. "You're never going to make it like this." She gave me a mouthful of bitter herbs and left. I'll admit, my resolve was starting to crumble as I longingly thought of the hospital IVs and the magic they hold. But if there is one thing that you don't do in a hospital, it's get uninterrupted sleep, and that's the only thing I needed to do.

In all of my carefully crafted fantasies about home birth, I missed several key points: I didn't live in some hippie commune in the moss-encrusted woods, where home birth was invented: I lived in a bustling, city neighborhood. Normally, I loved the energy there: it was always buzzing with families, loud music, laughter, traffic—you know, all the noises that one associates with a quiet birth setting. In my mind, labor happened in a magical bubble where the environment is completely controlled: the temperature, the lighting, the noise...Yeah, those places are called Birthing Centers. Not my inner city row house in the middle of the day. For chrissake, I couldn't even darken my room, because my windows were six feet tall and had sheer curtains. The sunlight poured in, burning my eyeballs, mocking me. A dimly lit labor nest it was *not*. I laid in my bed, weary to the point of psychosis, squinting against the sun on day three of little to no sleep. *Why hadn't I thought about this ahead of time? Why weren't darkening shades, ear plugs, and an eye mask on my stupid checklist?*

Miraculously, those mystery herbs that Gerta gave me had just started to work their magic and make my eyelids heavy, when a familiar noise filled the room: "beep...beep...beep...beep..." What the...? It sounded like a truck was backing up in my bedroom. Well, I was close! It was backing up to the house next to mine. What kind of truck? I'm glad you asked: *a cement truck.* I figured this out, because seconds later, jackhammers started ripping up the pavement to lay my neighbor's new sidewalk for the next four hours.

MOTHERFUCKING JACKHAMMERS!

I think I eventually passed out from crying. In any case, actual labor started that evening whether I was sufficiently rested or not. In order to fulfill my "home birth video" vision, I had borrowed a birthing tub from Gerta. This giant, inflatable plastic pool is not unlike something that you would set up in the backyard for several kids to play in, but it has a heating element that you place somewhere into the lining before you fill it with a bazillion gallons of water, so that it stays warm during labor. Gerta was what you would call "laid back." This was great when it came to things like not freaking me out about small risks, or offering me wine for Braxton Hicks contractions, but not so great when it came to things like giving us accurate directions (or any directions at all) about how to set up the damn pool.

As my labor ramped up, I got in the water to begin my dreamy journey into motherhood. I noticed almost immediately that my ass was on fire! Ouch! I tried to lift my butt off of the offending sensation, but I looked more like a manatee trying to do bridge pose in Yoga class. I tried to scooch over to the side, but my huge body took up most of the pool with little room leftover. People were starting to notice my pathetic gymnastics attempt.

"Where did you put the heater?" Gerta accused my husband.

"On the bottom...?" He offered.

She sighed. "It is supposed to go on the side so it doesn't burn her.

Well, there is no fixing it now. It takes hours to fill the pool."

Another piece of my birth utopia chipped away. (*No water birth for you! Come back one year!*) My man looked at me for reassurance. I glared back at him—no dice, buddy. If he wanted my sympathy, he should have read the fucking book.

Labor was a lonely and scary experience for me. It huuurt. I longed for Gerta to touch me or tell me what to do, like I had seen so many times at the Birthing Center. Most of the time she wasn't even in the room with me—she was off in another part of my house doing who knows what. My poor mother bore the brunt of my labor support, and she hadn't signed up for that job. After thirty-three hours of active labor later, including four hours of pushing, our perfect daughter was born; the only thing that I can safely say was perfect about this experience. My husband claims that these numbers get bigger every time I tell the story, and I claim that I have the right to punch him in the junk after everything I just told you. I will concede, he may not have watched her come out of the chute, but ever since he laid eyes on her seconds later, he has been head over heels in love, and an amazing dad.

You might think that this experience turned me off to having another home birth, but three years later, our nine and half pound son showed up in the same bed. My husband still didn't read one damn thing about labor coaching, and he didn't watch this slimy, giant kid crown either. But this time, it was a beautiful and near perfect birth, because this time, I was different. I didn't resentfully force my partner to do something he knew wasn't in him. This time, I hired two doulas and two new midwives (Yeah, Gerta kind of sucked. That's not how it's supposed to go.) I surrounded myself with labor experts, and my husband was free to be himself and Daddy to our now three-year-old who needed him. He came home from work that day, fed her dinner, put her to bed, and woke her up the next morning to meet her new baby brother. It worked out just like that.

I didn't plan every aspect of this birth—I couldn't. I had a toddler who distracted me right up until the end. I had no birthing pool, no militant agenda. I barely managed to get the clothes washed and the tiny diapers piled up in time. When labor started, my body took over, telling me to go in and out of a warm bathtub, on my bed, walking, lying down. My team never told me what to do. "You know," they kept telling me. But they never left my side, and they worked their asses off, God love 'em.

I wish that I could tell you that my birth experiences cured me of sanctimotherhood early on, but that would be a lie. Like many well-intentioned moms with control issues, I have gone through my fair share of holier-than-thou phases over the years. The illusion of perfectionism has reared its ugly head time and time again, and along for the ride, as always, went its faithful sidekick, Judgment. The good news is, we are far from perfect! That house of cards fell down a long time ago. After years of judging others and myself so harshly, as well as feeling judged, I am finally learning to let a lot of it go. What I have learned from experiences like the birth of my two children, is the more I chase perfection, the less I am prepared for the journey and the more exhausted I am by the race.

I've also learned that a good push present can make up for a lot.

ASHLEY FUCHS is an award-winning health activist and humor blogger, and was named WEGO Health Network's Rookie of the Year in 2015. She is a hyper-flexible mother of two bouncing (literally) kids, as they have all been diagnosed with Ehlers-Danlos Syndrome. A lack of collagen may have left them the world's worst superheroes (but don't tell them that). She writes about the wacky things that their syndrome has taught her family with a dash of wisdom and a shot of vodka at The Incredible Adventures of Malleable Mom. You can find her online at Scary Mommy, Club Mid, The Bangor Daily News, I Just Want to Pee Alone, Mamapedia, and BLUNTmoms, and she was in the 2015 D.C. cast of "Listen to Your Mother." Follow her on Facebook, Twitter, and Pinterest.

White Mamba
By E. R. Catalano
Zoe vs. The Universe

"Middle-Aged Mom Becomes the Perfect Weapon." This was the headline that flashed across my mind when a friend offered to teach me Brazilian jiu-jitsu. Technically, he wanted to start training his seven-year-old son, who needed a suitable sparring partner. Enter the Dragon, aka, my five-year-old daughter. And I would need to be my friend's partner so he could demonstrate the proper techniques.

With little in my previous forty-something years to give the impression of athleticism, I still entertained visions of myself as Buffy the Vampire Slayer, or Jennifer Garner from *Alias*, moving faster than the eye could see while delivering roundhouse kicks along with a hefty dose of justice. Never mind I couldn't kick higher than kneecap level. Never mind I was not someone who could pull off leather pants (if I could even get them on).

To be fair, I wasn't completely out of shape. I used to run before my daughter was born, and I still managed to do some sort of exercise three times a week. However, my best sport is probably curling up with a good book, afterwards rising slowly to work out the stiffness in my joints.

I did do hot yoga once. A few years ago. I didn't enjoy it.

However, I was now twenty pounds more than the weight I was when I got pregnant, before which time I'd needed to lose fifteen pounds. (Stop doing the math!) Clearly it was time to get in shape.

Of course, the other reason I wanted to master jiu-jitsu was to be a strong female role model for my daughter. She was at the age where she was dividing the world up into activities for boys and activities for girls, and there was one little shit in her kindergarten class who told her girls could not be superheroes. Grrr! I was about to prove him and his ilk wrong. While also going down a dress size!

My friend, let's call him Sensei Pain, had told me that jiu-jitsu was the perfect workout. And besides the martial arts training, he wanted me to start an intense workout routine as well.

The proof that this would work was the teacher himself who was in great shape. He'd been training since he was a child and was a black belt who'd taught adults and children for many years. Ignoring the "for many years" part, I decided that if I worked really hard, in a few short months I'd see massive results.

I'd be fit.

I'd be healthy.

I'd be deadly.

The perfect weapon. Because who expects a short, forty-three-year-old mom to be a ninja? Only me.

Sensei Pain's school was his basement gym, where he has a mat that covers most of the floor, with weights, a kettle bell, and indo boards lined up at the side. Intimidating. To someone else maybe! But not to me. That first day I stepped up to the mat, took off my glasses a la Diana Prince becoming Wonder Woman —

— and immediately injured myself.

Brazilian jiu-jitsu was not like the martial arts depicted in pop culture. No striking and kicking. Instead, it's heavy on ground fighting. Sensei Pain explained this was good to learn, especially for girls, since the size of your opponent was not as important as it would be in a standing fight.

We began with learning how to fall. Having won awards for clumsiness you'd think this was something I could do, but it turns out all the falling I'd done heretofore had lacked finesse. The idea was to hit the ground with as much surface area of your body as possible to lessen the impact.

Sensei Pain demonstrated and then I did my first ever rollout. Which is when I twisted my neck. The kids did much better being closer to the ground and rubbery, but I sat the rest of class out. Perfection would have to wait.

Over the following weeks Sensei Pain taught us different positions and guards, locks and holds, using me to demonstrate. Here came the next hurdle. I've never been a big fan of sweating, which is one of the reasons I only did hot yoga once, but this was worse than sweating.

This was touching and being touched by another sweaty person. My friend was used to it from his years of training. I was not. I liked it less than hot yoga.

In addition, so many of the positions were up close and personal. Top mount was basic but awkward regarding groin placement. But now imagine wrapping a leg around a male friend's head and squeezing. Awkward. And unflattering. One positive result was that it made me swear off Mexican food. *Perfect* weapon, not *chemical* weapon.

As the weeks passed I started getting down about my lack of improvement coupled with the black and blues I'd acquired from the joint locks and chokeholds. Then my daughter started whining before class each week. "Again? But I already learned ju sitsu."

Hearing her complain renewed my determination to be an example of strong womanhood. I told her mastering jiu-jitsu took continual practice, and that I wished I had learned it when I was her age.

But inside, the doubts were starting to creep in. It wasn't too late for me, was it?

I realized I needed a new model, an older heroine.

I decided on Beatrix Kiddo, aka Black Mamba, aka the Bride from *Kill Bill*. After all, Uma Thurman was probably close to my age when she made the films.

(Fact check. OK, turns out she was a full ten years younger than I am now, but I'm about a foot shorter so it evens out.)

In my brain—the warrior's most formidable weapon!—I became White Mamba.

Pasty but deadly. Instead of Kiddo's Deadly Viper Assassination Squad, I'd be part of a different shadowy organization, made of ass-kicking moms like me, called the Butt Wipers with Stubborn Belly Fat Squad.

All I needed was a revenge-based backstory.

I asked my friend if he could teach me the Five Point Palm Exploding Heart Technique, but he told me that didn't exist.

How about just teaching me that hand-strike technique Uma uses to escape the coffin in case I'm ever buried alive, one of my top-ten fears? I asked.

He laughed like I was kidding, which happens a lot in our relationship.

"Ha ha," I said, not meaning it, which also happens a lot.

Sensei Pain continued to drill us on what we'd learned, pausing from time to time to ask the kids questions and showing disappointment when they didn't know the answers. Especially if they weren't paying attention, instead fidgeting around and playing with their feet.

I'd shake my head at my daughter in rebuke, but secretly I was glad he wasn't quizzing me, since I'd been mentally playing with my own feet.

I was preoccupied with frustration that my bookish nature was not helping me keep track of which submission technique went with which attack. Physical intelligence was never my strong suit, and I worked through each move slowly, often pausing to recall which side was my left and which my right. Plus, each move was actually a string of moves, and I couldn't remember the sequence fast enough. Each technique was meant to be performed smoothly. But "smooth move" was something that's only ever been said to me with sarcasm.

I was so slow, in fact, I imagined someday saying to an aggressor, "Excuse me, Mr. Assailant, could you move your elbow a bit so I can trap your arm in a figure-four, k? Super, thanks much. Tap out when it starts to hurt."

That's another thing we learned. Sensei Pain told us that when your sparring partner starts to put too much pressure on a joint, you're supposed to let them know by "tapping out," which basically means tapping them on the arm or tapping the mat.

I kept forgetting this so when Sensei Pain showed the kids a joint lock using my arm, I tended to yell, "Ow! I mean, tap! The safe word is chocolate ganache!"

So I don't know if I'm getting fit. I lost a little bit of weight but soon after I injured my neck I hurt my right arm, so we could only use one side for sparring and also working out.

Remember I mentioned the working out? Because physical conditioning is all part of the package when you want to become a perfect weapon who can fit back into her pre-pregnancy jeans.

I've never worked out so hard in my life. Weighted squats. Weighted crunches. Leg circles—with weights attached to my ankles. Then, and I don't know if it was the ground fighting or weight-lifting, but I hurt my left arm and my lower back on the left side. Also my pelvic girdle is messed up. Apparently I have overdeveloped quads from my previous years of running, thus putting a strain on my underdeveloped hip flexors. So sometimes my hips click when I walk, and sometimes they cramp up mid ground fight. Tappity tap!

A year in and I'm still no White Mamba. I was sure I'd be well on my way by now. Not still be so slow, overthinking each move. Sensei Pain had said my body would develop muscle memory, but I think the pain is so intense my muscles are repressing their memories due to post-traumatic stress disorder.

When I wake up the morning following a workout, that's when I feel most like Beatrix Kiddo, who, when she woke from her coma, had to coax life back into her atrophied limbs through sheer force of will. (By the way, can I also say I'm jealous that instead of enduring a thirty-six-hour labor like the one I had, she gave birth while in a coma? That right there is the white whale of birth stories.)

Today I still like to imagine myself taking down criminals on the R train, holding them in place till the police arrive using my Five-Point-Harness Chokehold Grip, because I may be the perfect weapon, but I'm still a mom, and I wouldn't want the perp to get hurt if the train comes to an abrupt stop.

I have these fantasies during long hot showers, where I direct the stream of water on my aching shoulders and back, and decide that my bruises are badges of honor, evidence I'm being a good role model for my daughter. Keeping up the good fight, even when, especially when, it takes me to the ground. Because if I can't touch perfection, maybe I can still knock it down a peg.

E. R. CATALANO is a writer and mother of one evil mastermind living in Brooklyn, NY, who writes a humor blog about her daughter at zoevstheuniverse.com. She is a contributor to The Bigger Book of Parenting Tweets *and* Lose the Cape: Never Will I Ever (and Then I Had Kids)*, and her humorous essays have appeared on Scary Mommy, In the Powder Room, MockMom, and HaHas for Hoohahs, among others. She's also working on a novel called* Becoming the Girl Detective *and a collection of stories called* Prove You're Not a Robot. *You can follow her on Twitter and on* Facebook. *She needs all the validation she can get.*

I Tried to Be the Perfect Mom Friend
but My Butt Got in the Way
By Kim Bongiorno
Let Me Start By Saying

Everyone has secrets. Many of us try to hide those secrets when in a new environment, in order to make the best possible impression. This is how I found out the hard way that it's rather difficult to hide a busted butthole.

Immediately after having two babies in under two years, my husband and I moved our family to suburbia. I was already slightly insane from lack of sleep and constantly being touched by two small, shouty attention vacuums, so I knew I needed to make some new friends to feel grounded again. I strongly believed that I would drastically increase my chances of winning friends by slipping into the Stepford Wife role of generous hostess, gracious guest, and skilled small-talker. I dove right in, plastering on a smile while hosting group after group of fellow moms, baking them mini muffins and letting their drooling terrors stain various decorative throw pillows. But it's hard to have a totally chill conversation with a potential new friend when your fleshy back door is a raging inferno of derriere doom.

See, both pregnancies and deliveries wreaked havoc on my hiney. Up until then, I had a healthy, happy wrinkled penny comfortably tucked away in my ham sandwich. By the time we moved house, I was in year three of owning a flaming-hot, broken back door that appeared to have its own very angry thumb. I was in constant pain— and not just when I tried to bring the browns to the porcelain pool. The throbbing of my agitated rosebud shot jolts up into my body at night, waking me up almost as much as my two tots did. The pure exhaustion of being a new mom makes it tricky to remember all of one's social graces. Add in a pissed-off musky mumbler in the back of your pants and it's darn near impossible.

Not long after moving, I met a fellow mom whose son was right between my two kids in age. She was funny, hip, artistic, and so nice. She served dinner on real plates when she had us over, and I did my best to be the charming, respectable gal someone like her would want to hang with. Then the pesky protuberance clinging to my corn hole suddenly grew practically four sizes.

With no family close by and a husband unable to take time off, I had no choice but to ask this virtual stranger to watch my kids for an hour while I saw a specialist. Since she was a lovely, compassionate person, she asked if everything was okay. I could have played it cool and assuaged her worries by saying it was a routine appointment, but instead I blurted out that I had a spare elbow growing out of the hopping mad Hot Pocket that was once a rather amiable anus, back in the day. As I threw down the truth bombs, her eyes grew wider and wider, her lips moving as if they wanted to form an appropriate response, but none exist in this universe. In her silence I gave her a double thumbs-up at which she simply nodded.

That wasn't awkward at all!

She watched my kids for me, as requested, both of us thinking I'd be there and back in no time.

NOPE.

Within minutes of walking into the examination room for my appointment, during which I thought the surgeon would simply take a gander at my out-of-order Lincoln Log maker and come up with a treatment plan, I found myself lying pantsless on my side with a strange lady holding my humps apart as the doctor sliced a swollen serving off my flesh donut without warning.

Imagine the worst pain you have ever experienced. Now sit on that pain and drive.

I barely made it to my new friend's house before collapsing on her couch like a giant felled by a sadistic, rectum slicing and dicing ninja. So dizzied by the shocking pain of my backwards vacuum, I couldn't argue when this new friend—whose last name I hadn't even learned to pronounce yet—called her husband to come home from work early to back her up as she cared for me and my weeping poop chute. As I writhed on her couch, she fed our three kids under three years old and packed them into my car. She then drove all of us to my house, prepped my two for bed and tucked them in, and got me in my pajamas and ready for bed. Then her husband showed up to drive her home. *Nice to meet you for the very first time, sir! Don't mind me and my bleeding starfish—we don't need your wife for much longer.*

Not only did she have a front-row seat to the soap opera that was my mud shaft's medical mayhem, but the carefully manufactured façade of Perfect Homemaker Kim came tumbling down when she entered my home without notice. You see, as it took all my strength to act normal *outside* of my home while in so much constant, burning booty-bubble agony, there was none left to do things like mop, pick up any of the tidal wave of toys and clothes coating every surface of the house, or clear the breakfast table/sink/counters/kitchen island of dirty dishes *inside* my home. She saw that I was both a slobby fraud and a terrible prioritizer when it came to caring for my cantankerous coolie.

I wish I could say that was the end of my tushie troubles, but, alas, the hacking of my pink Cheerio failed to fix them.

Over the next few years, as my kids started school, I had more opportunities to meet/lie to new potential friends. Again, I pretended to be a mom who had her act together. I invited the students from my kids' classes over with their moms, serving a bounty of nuggets, mac and cheese, peas, and fries to dozens of littles in the dining room while us bigs gathered around the kitchen island for goat cheese salads, pull-apart breads from Pinterest, and saucy pastas with plenty of wine to go around. I was always at the ready to heap on another serving, wipe a juice box spill, or pull dessert from the oven. My never sitting down made it seem like I was the ultimate hostess, but it was mostly because my stinging Satan's stink eye prevented me from doing so without the use of my most prized possession: an inflatable donut cushion I had named Mr. Darcy while in a painkiller-induced haze one night.

Soon I began losing weight, and fellow moms who were ready to do the same asked my secret. *Well I mostly can't eat solid food anymore because my hemorrhoids are so bad they caused an anal fissure so pooping feels like throwing a spike-covered subway car down a groundhog burrow, causing me to fear bowel movements more than the Grim Reaper* didn't seem like the kind of thing a perfect mom would say, so I smiled and told them I was a vegetarian, cutting back on desserts, and working out fairly regularly. I refused to admit I was slowly starving to death because I had been putting off seeing a medical professional about my caboose quandary for three years.

Finally, my flaming cinnamon ring got so bad that I went in to see a new doctor (during school hours, of course—I wasn't willing to horrify any more ladies in the 'hood). Thankfully, he skipped the lecture and decided to try a topical solution before resorting to surgery. A week into treatment, there was a terrible storm that knocked out power. All my neighbors hunkered down, but I was discovered dashing about, staying active, shoveling, gathering fallen branches, and building makeshift coffee presses. People were impressed with my ability to stay motivated in a crisis, but it wasn't a choice: in the midst of the blizzard every inch of my great divide bloomed with a raging red allergic reaction to the ointment I had carefully caressed onto my ugly olive. I would have visited my doctor for something to tame the blazing beast back there, but the storm blew down enough trees en route to the medical facility that it was closed for days. Sitting on the smoldering sloppy joe in my sweatpants? *Not an option.* Keeping busy was the only thing that kept me from crying and clawing at my cranky crease.

Once the power came back on and school started again, I began the countdown to the big surgery. I was teetering on the edge both physically and emotionally.

It seemed that every time I tried to pretend things weren't so bad, to appear like I wasn't a complainer, to look like a well-mannered member of the community deserving the respect and companionship of the incredible women I kept meeting, it backfired because of my melodramatic butthole. So, when a few ladies from the neighborhood stopped me, asking why I looked gray, thin and downright awful as I was walking my kids from the car to the school blacktop, I took a breath, gave up all pretenses, and spilled my very imperfect guts to them:

"My pudding pusher is a hot mess so I'm scheduled for surgery in two days. I've barely eaten or slept in ages because the pain is so relentless, and I'm desperately behind on every possible thing a homemaker could be behind on."

After one dramatic pause, during which I figured the confession of my long-held secret would repel these women whose affection I craved, they took my kids' backpacks off my shoulders, turned me back toward my car, and told me that they'd take over driving to and from school until I recovered from the surgery—and it didn't stop there. They kept my kids after school so I could rest before and after surgery day. They brought me (easily digested) food and flowers and gentle hugs. They came to my house as I healed, emptying my dishwasher, sweeping my floors, making me realize that the kind of people you *really* want in your life are the ones who like you exactly as you are—problematic pooper and all.

KIM BONGIORNO is the freelance writer and author behind LetMeStartBySayingBlog.com. She adores her charmingly loud family, who she pretends to listen to while writing everything from tweets to novels and playing on Facebook and Twitter. If she were less tired, she'd add something super clever to her bio so you'd never forget this moment.

Diets, Death, and Shit
By Alyson Herzig
The Shitastrophy

I am a big lover of carbohydrates and craft beer. This combination has helped put forty pounds of extra weight on my five-foot-five inch frame over the last few years. My clothes have become tighter, and then there was that awkward time I became trapped in a swimsuit. I sent my husband a text message begging him to leave work to rescue me from the Lands End dressing room but he refused, *asshole.* I had let myself go from a petite vegetable eating size four thirty-year-old into a squishy bread-pizza-ice cream loving size twelve forty-year-old. It was time to kick my carbs to the curb.

As I stood in the checkout line at the grocery store ogling the svelte models gracing the covers of Cosmo and Vogue I made a cursory glance in my grocery cart at my good friends Doritos and Lucky Charms. A major intervention would be necessary to return to my former self. I longed for the days of pants with buttons, instead of elastic, and an ability to pick out a shirt based upon more than its mid-section hiding techniques. I glanced at the Sports Illustrated Swim Suit edition and noticed there was no tankini or swim dress represented. I had fallen off the skinny wagon and landed right on the chuck wagon. I wanted to turn back time to when I was, in my opinion, the perfect size four, fuck I'd even take a size eight. Since I have a deep loathing of actual exercise I opted for attempting a healthier lifestyle, and by that, I mean a diet. Reaching into my cart I removed the Lucky Charms, knowing I would miss my little Irish friend more than the pot of gold at the end of the rainbow. However, I wasn't quite ready to leave the Doritos on the curb yet.

I considered wiring my jaw shut, which would cut out the carbs but allow me the ability to enjoy my craft beer through a straw. Priorities. Ultimately I went with Weight Watchers, with a twist: I would cut my unhealthy food choices, make food at home, but hold on tight to my love of high-calorie craft libations. I was a little apprehensive at first—cooking and I don't always mix—but as the button literally popped off my pants as I was walked up my staircase I realized I had few options. I could live in yoga pants for the rest of my life, which really isn't that bad, or I could suck it up and learn to cook a few meals.

I embraced the concept of healthy eating with gusto. Every Sunday I cooked my week's worth of breakfast muffins and one-point "cake cookies" to hold me over. I planned my meals and tracked my food. I cut my beer as well to two brews a day. Moderation—the key to a successful weight loss. Or so I had heard.

After a month I was down a few pounds and feeling pretty good about my ability to stick to the plan outside of a few extra bottles of my favorite beer Sierra Nevada. I was measuring and weighing portions for everyone in my family instead of buying fast food or pre-made Costco meals. I'm sure my local pizza place saw a loss to their bottom line when I ended my bi-weekly tryst with the delivery guy's cheesy sausage. And others were realizing the benefits in the house too—my son had lost eleven pounds, and my husband was down a size as well. Of course the men in my house would lose more weight then me without even trying, how is that even fair? Jerks.

But acclimating to homemade foods came at a cost: the death of my adoration for some of my favorite cheat foods. I used to love Doritos nacho goodness like a kid who loves that stupid elf that arrives every December. So I was positively ecstatic ripping open a bag that had been taunting me for weeks. I shoved a handful of caloric wonder into my mouth, crunched and prepared for bliss. Instead of nacho yumminess my fingers were covered in the orange herpes of the snack world. It was as if I had taken a bite of sadness itself.

Then real tragedy struck. My father had gotten the flu and was grievously ill. I traveled to New Jersey to see him in the hospital. He was my first Irish love, and although he couldn't speak when I told him I loved him, he mouthed the words, "I love you too." He had always had very little to say. So when he talked—or tried to talk—you listened. Throughout my trip, I stuck to the diet like white dog hair to black slacks. But after two weeks on a ventilator, it was time to remove my father from life support in accordance with his wishes. To say I was crushed is possibly the biggest understatement of the century.

But I didn't break down. I needed to be perfect. To get the kids. To make dinner. To tell my family that Poppy was dying while staying as stoic as he'd always been. Instead of sucking it up, I sobbed. By the time I had pulled my shit together, gotten the kids from school, and told them the news, I was mentally and physically exhausted. And I still had things to do. I needed to keep my mind off my dad and get through the rest of the day. But as I glared at the chicken I had pulled out to make that evening for dinner, I figured perfection was for assholes.

I texted my husband at work and asked him to meet us for a quick bite before my lip wax that evening. I'm half Irish and half Italian so if I don't tame the beast over my lip I look like a man. Perfection may be for assholes, but I was not going to my father's funeral looking like Burt Reynolds.

Now, my family and I had not eaten a meal outside of our home for over a month and I had the burn marks on my hand like battle scars to prove it. We went to a restaurant that serves a combination of soup, salad, and sandwiches. All the soups were cream based, and since I was on the diet I opted to steer clear. But the Tuscan chicken sandwich was calling my name. I figured I would be okay eating, just a small bit, off the diet for one night. I had not eaten all day due to the stress of my father and realized I was famished. I devoured that sandwich as if I hadn't seen food in years. The cheesy awesomeness of thick provolone, the greasy chicken, the buttery French bread was the perfect combination to quell the rumbling in my tummy.

Bidding adieu to my family I headed to the salon for my appointment. En route my stomach began to churn and I realized my greasy, buttery dinner selection might not have been the best option. I was in trouble. Looking at my gas tank I realized I didn't have enough gas, or time, to drive home, use our restroom, and then drive back to the salon. So I put pedal to the medal and forged ahead.

I arrived at the salon with five minutes to spare, and mentally high fived myself for finally being on time. I had a fleeting moment where I considered using the salon's restroom but I abhor public bathrooms. I decided I would just head home after my waxing. I'd be fine, right? Hindsight. It's a bitch.

"You ready?" my aesthetician asked.

"Yup!" I declared as I felt the grumble in my stomach warning me that time was of the essence.

We chit-chatted on the way back to the room where they do the waxing. I was becoming more and more aware that my decision to deviate from my diet was not a good one. Lying on the table, I prayed for the waxing Gods to please give me a pass. My stomach burbled angrily in response.

I resorted to distraction. "So how was your vacation?" I asked, knowing that my aesthetician had been gone when I tried to make my appointment the week prior. Back when my mustache was just barely at the high school sophomore level.

"Oh good, we went to Florida. It was hard to come back to work."

I nodded, clenching my ass cheeks as I felt the familiar burn of imminent evacuation.

"I tried to get in earlier today but they said you were all booked. I hate having to come this late in the day, but I really couldn't wait any longer with this lovely reminder of my Italian heritage." Sweat broke out on my forehead, as my stomach let out a gurgling noise reminiscent of water down going down a drain. A typhoon was beginning to swirl inside my intestines and once it unleashed things would not be OK.

Gina put the wax on my lip, rubbed, ripped, and repeated for both sides.

"Are you done?" I asked, hoping she wouldn't be as thorough as she normally is with the tweezers.

"I just need to put some lotion on you." Gina turned to get the moisturizer.

My body fired a warning shot, like a cannon exploding from the deck of a ship. Something was going down, either the ship, or me and

I had a horrible feeling it wasn't the ship. I had no time for lip oil. My bowels were liquid. And they were angry like a storm raging at sea.

"That's OK, really!" I declared as I jumped from the table and grabbed my coat and purse from the chair in one swift move. "Where's the bathroom?" I asked in a panic, realizing I had not ever used the bathroom in the spa area before.

Gina raised a perfectly waxed brow at my abrupt end to the session. But the noxious vapors lingering in the room were a sure sign of bigger issues at hand, and from the tight line of Gina's mouth, it hadn't been lost on her.

She pointed. "Through the door right—"

I ran full speed from the room as she yelled, "Don't forget to lock both doors!"

I threw open the bathroom door and hurled my belongings on the bathroom floor. Fuck hygiene. I thanked the lord that I had worn leggings, because I had not a second to spare with a belt or button. Racing across the large bathroom I locked the door, and when I turned towards the toilet it happened: my bowels gave out. I was within inches of a full-on shitastrophy, and I couldn't hold on—or in—for one more second. Bent over in pain, clenching my ass closed I got to the toilet in one stride, dropped my pants and planted my cheeks on the seat before the rest of my intestines betrayed me.

This was no ordinary bowel clearing. This was a volcanic blast of liquid horror that erupted over and over again as sweat dripped over my freshly waxed un-oiled lip. The stench was so awful I could almost taste it. As the contractions subsided, I let out a sigh of relief and kicked off my shoes. Leaning back on the toilet I assessed my predicament. I was trapped in a public bathroom, covered in my own excrement, with no solution in sight. I peeled off my soiled pants and looked around the spacious bathroom realizing I had few options. It's not like I could leave without pants on, what the fuck was I going to do? Gathering all my strength, and swallowing the panic rising in my throat, I took a large amount of single-ply toilet paper and cleaned my leggings as best as I could, thankful they were black. I thought about leaving my underwear in the garbage, but I worried my soiled castoffs would be found when the garbage was emptied at the end of the evening. I would never be able to show my hairy body in the salon again. I couldn't risk it; the underwear would have to come home with me. Realizing I had been in the restroom for quite sometime I rushed to clean up in an attempt to dispel the reality of the situation, but the cat was out of the proverbial bag—and my ass.

On the other side of the large wooden door was an entire salon being vaporized by the fumes emitting from my body. I grabbed the bottle of Febreeze from the shelf, but no air freshener would cover up the atrocity that had just occurred. Picking my belongings up off the floor, hoisting my purse onto my shoulder I glanced in the mirror to take stock of the situation. My hair looked good, and my lip was no longer a furry caterpillar. I leaned over the sink, reapplied my lipstick, and dabbed at the corners of my eye to remove the makeup that had slid from my upper lid during my epic shitastrophy. I turned and left the restroom with my head held high, smelling of a mixture of lilacs and shit, with my underwear wrapped in paper towels in my purse. I dropped a twenty on the counter and left the salon looking a few pounds lighter, a bounce in my step, and probably pretty freaking perfect.

Originally from New Jersey, ALYSON HERZIG lives in the Midwest but has kept her sarcastic cynical Jersey attitude. She has been described as the Andy Rooney of Stay-at-Home Moms. She can be found writing about the perpetual shit storm of her life and random ridiculous observations at TheShitastrophy, or on her popular Facebook page The Shitastrophy. Alyson has had works featured online at various venues including Scary Mommy, The Mighty, Good Housekeeping, and The Huffington Post. *She has also been published in numerous anthologies, including* I Still Just Want to Pee Alone *and is the co-creator of the anthology* Surviving Mental Illness Through Humor.

Volunteering Makes Me Antsy
By Susanne Kerns
The Dusty Parachute

My name is Susanne.

I am a volunteering addict.

No, not the kind of volunteering where you build houses for underprivileged families or dig wells in impoverished countries. I mean the Elementary School kind of volunteering where groups of middle aged moms congregate in their finest Lululemon activewear to organize school fairs or recruit people for PTA board positions with bribes and threats worthy of a mob syndicate.

As with many addictions, mine started off with the desire to fit in with the cool kids. We moved to Austin two days before my daughter started Kindergarten. Volunteering at her school seemed like a fun way to meet new friends and start building a sense of community with the school. Plus, it just seemed like the kind of thing that a good mom was supposed to do, especially a good stay at home mom.

My gateway drug to volunteering was the school Beautification Committee—a group of volunteers who rotate weekends tending to the school campus. This includes picking up hundreds of discarded foil Goldfish cracker pouches and those annoying juice box straw wrappers off playgrounds, weeding gardens, and watering plants. Sure, I haven't mowed or weeded my own yard in six months, but what the heck, it's a good mother's duty to volunteer at the kids' school.

Next came the teachers' work room, where I volunteered a few hours a week completing work orders from the teachers like making copies, laminating and cutting out thousands of seasonal pumpkin and heart shapes with the die-cut machine (and spending too much time pondering why there's a die cut stamp not only for 'lima beans' but also 'tiny lima beans'). Between my high from the rubber cement fumes and the basket of complimentary Hershey's kisses for volunteers, it was pretty much the perfect job.

But from there, it just became ridiculous: Class Photographer, Lost and Found Manager, PTA Communications Director, Class Store Manager (which had the bonus feature of storing six giant Rubbermaid bins of store supplies in my garage for two years).

And of course there are all the miscellaneous "you're a stay at home mom" requests. When you don't have any "I'm too busy with work" excuses, everyone knows your schedule is wide open to drive all over town searching through stores to find the "bat-shaped confetti" requested on the MySignUp sheet the room mom sent out for the Halloween Party.

And I know exactly what's on the list the room mom sent out, because, guess what? That's right. I'm the room mom now too! How did this happen? Did someone slip me a roofie at orientation night? Didn't my husband specifically take all of the pens out of my purse so I couldn't mark any of the boxes on the volunteer form?

Like most addictions, I had to hit rock bottom before I realized it was time to make a change. That rock bottom happened last summer, when my volunteering became physically dangerous for both myself and others. Sure, I have had some close calls with laminator burns in the teachers' work room, and smashed fingers between the plates of the die cut machine. But we're talking Emergency Room dangerous.

A couple times a year, our Beautification Committee schedules a big clean up day, where all eight of us break out our matching t-shirts and power tools and do a mass clean up. We rake, prune, paint, edge, mow, and weed the entire campus. I stay away from the weeding jobs because Texas gardens are full of fire ants, which I am allergic to, so I have a 'get out of weeding free' pass. Instead, my task is to load up our rechargeable lawnmower in the back of my minivan and do my best to not look like a complete lunatic while attempting to mow a ten-acre school lawn with a Black & Decker push mower.

Usually I only have to deal with the curious/sympathetic stares of a few cars that stop at the intersection in front of the school. However, on this particular day, there were a couple of little girls holding a bake sale right in the middle of my mowing path with four of their parents supervising from chaise lounges behind the sales table.

In an effort to gain their cooperation in letting me mow around their bake sale, I pulled my minivan up and cheerfully (and passive aggressively) said, "I'll take a brownie and a cookie if one of you nice dads can help me unload my lawnmower out of my van." (In hindsight, it probably wasn't a great idea to demonstrate for the kids that their parents think it's acceptable to get in a stranger's van in exchange for purchasing baked goods.)

I put my snacks in the car, apologized for any disturbance caused by the mower noise and was on my way. I mowed a strip out to the furthest edge of the grass and turned to head back in the direction of my new bake sale friends when I felt my shoe pinching my foot. I reached down to adjust my shoe, only to discover that my entire foot was covered with fire ants swarming from the giant ant mound I had obliterated with my lawn mower. Because I am allergic, even one bite from an individual ant had resulted in trips to the doctor in the past and now my shoe and sock were completely full of pissed off, homeless, toxic insects.

I immediately jumped over to the sidewalk, ripped off my shoe and sock and threw them like they were live grenades in no particular direction. I have had my share of fight or flight panic moments in my life, and each one reinforces my certainty that I am the last person you want around in a crisis. Until this moment, my least dignified situation was when a bee flew up my shorts in college and I immediately dropped trou in the middle of our living room. At least in that situation, I didn't have an audience to worry about. Fortunately, since I was a good twenty yards from the bake sale, my unorthodox lawn mowing technique seemed to have gone unnoticed by the bake sale crew.

As I stood on the sidewalk in front of the school, I weighed all my options for next steps and decided to collect my footwear and try to find one of my fellow Beautification Committee friends to help me load my mower back into the van so I could go home and chug some Benadryl and cover my foot in meat tenderizer.

After retrieving my shoe and sock, I took the next logical step of repeatedly throwing them against the pavement, like those Fourth of

July firework poppers, hoping to evict any remaining fire ants. Still paranoid there could be some stowaways, I carefully shoved the sock in the shoe and started my walk of shame down the sidewalk holding only the plastic-coated tip of one of the shoelaces as carefully as a bomb technician from *The Hurt Locker*.

I walked past the bake sale families as nonchalantly as one can while walking lawnmower-less, and half-barefoot past the same people who had just seen me walk the opposite direction with a lawnmower and both shoes on my feet only minutes earlier. I smiled and gave them my best, "This is totally how I always mow the lawn," face.

Fortunately, I found the last remaining volunteer, and explained my situation and asked her if she could help me load my mower into the van. Once the mower and my infested footwear were finally in the car, I started having visions of how any remaining fire ants would breed and colonize in the air vents so the next time I turned on the AC they would all shoot directly into my face like a terrifying arthropod fire hose.

At last, I was finally on my way home from this volunteering disaster.

Until…

You know when you hear a familiar sound that's so unexpected and out of context that you can't quite pin down what it is? That's what happens when you hear the sound of a lawnmower running in the back of your van.

In all the commotion, I had neglected to remove the power key so when the mower shifted position as I stopped at the stop sign, it started the mower and the self-propel function so that my lawnmower was now actively trying to force itself into the shotgun position for the ride home.

I immediately stopped the car in the middle of the intersection and hopped out to evaluate the situation. I stood behind my car, opened the back hatch and stared at the ass end of my lawnmower.

Half barefoot.

Ant bites burning.

Car running.

Lawnmower running.

Directly in front of the two stunned families at the bake sale table.

I once again gave both families my best, "I totally meant to do that," look as my panicked brain went into full fuck-it mode and without thinking, jumped into a car with a running lawnmower and yanked the power key out, rodeo calf-roping style.

I returned to the driver's seat and decided to cap off my comedy of errors with an illegal U-turn to head back home. On the half mile drive home, I stress-ate both the brownie and cookie that I bought from the bake sale. I also decided then and there this was a sign that my quest to be the perfect school volunteer was over. Next year I was going cold turkey.

I stayed true to my decision this year and have limited my participation to chaperoning field trips and signing up to only bring party supplies that are available through Amazon Prime.

Of course, next year my daughter will be starting middle school at a brand new school. Volunteering would be a great way to meet some new friends and build a sense of community with the school.

On second thought, maybe I'll stick to volunteering at the school bake sales. The brownies are delicious, plus I've heard the people watching is amazing.

SUSANNE KERNS is a Writer and Marketing Consultant living in Austin, TX. Her stories have been featured in the books It's Really 10 Months - Special Delivery *and* Martinis & Motherhood: Tales of Wonder, Woe & WTF?!, *as well as a variety of websites, including her blog,* The Dusty Parachute.

You can find her on Facebook twenty hours a day and on Instagram, where she posts her tasteful nudes.*

(*Mostly pictures of cats and margaritas, both nude.) You can also find her on Twitter whenever she accidentally opens the wrong app on her phone.

Getting Burned By Old Flames
By Robyn Welling
Hollow Tree Ventures

My college years were good ones—great ones, even, except maybe for those six months when my roommate and I were crammed into a tiny one bedroom apartment in a bad neighborhood next door to a very popular, very vocal nymphomaniac.

But for me (unlike that neighbor, apparently), *dating* in college wasn't everything I'd hoped it would be.

Throughout high school, my low self esteem led to low standards, which made me the low-hanging fruit for any bored boy who needed a date. Therefore, although I wasn't particularly cool, I never seemed to be without some jerk or freak to hang out with on Saturday night.

I'm not saying there weren't some nice guys thrown in the mix, but I definitely dated some dudes that fell somewhere on the "Dud to Dangerous" dating scale.

There was the guy who wrote me a really terrible poem, the last line of which ("I will ALWAYS love you, Robin!") was pretty sweet...except for the part where he spelled my name wrong. Still, that wasn't as bad as the guy who chose to prove the everlasting nature of his affections by writing "I love you" in huge letters—with black spray paint—on the street at the end of my driveway. As you can guess, my parents absolutely *adored* him.

Those boys were harmless, though, if a touch misguided. There were also the liars, the manipulators, the cheaters.

I could go into detail, but suffice it to say that by the time I escaped the drama of high school and arrived on campus, I was beyond ready to move on. I'd recently broken things off with my long term boyfriend (or rather, I'd recently found out he was already dating someone else) and I was fully prepared to find myself a Real Man in college. Things were going to be different!

Hahahaha.

By sophomore year I'd finally figured out that, whatever age it was at which boys matured into men, it was definitely *not* during the early college years. How else could I explain the theater major who played dress up (excuse me, I mean "who enjoyed improvisational role play") and pretended to be a different person every time we went out? Or the beau from biology lab who flew into a jealous rage when I wouldn't trudge through a snowy parking lot into Lowes on a quick errand, convinced I just didn't want to be seen with him in public? Not to mention the guy I caught half naked in his apartment, who actually claimed with a straight face that he and his equally naked "friend" were "studying anatomy." *Really?*

It turned out college was mired in the same old games, the same old lines as high school—just add fake IDs, subtract curfews, and multiply by a thousand eye rolls.

My roommate, a fellow victim of the dating scene, was just about ready to give up, too. That's how we found ourselves sitting together at the dining room table one Saturday evening, sipping our wine (okay, sipping our beers) (okay, *fine*, sipping our Boone's Farm sangria), swapping dating horror stories.

Like most women, we'd both been burned, and we realized that our self worth was influenced far too heavily by the decisions and disasters of the past. Besides, we reasoned, maybe *we* were the problem! Were we scaring men off? Or were we so focused on our mistakes and failures that we were attracting…well, more mistakes and failures? We started to wonder if our fates would change with a clean slate, if we had less dirt to dig up—in short, if our pasts were a little more perfect.

For our dating disasters to end with a happily ever after, we decided we needed to ditch our baggage. In order to move on, we needed to make some sort of grand, symbolic gesture. *But what?*

We started by creating a single list of all our exes, alongside the relationship-killing crimes they had each committed. In no particular order, we added names as they resurfaced from our memories. Old anger and pent-up pain dissolved into giggles as our list grew.

Steve: asked me to move in with him (on the third date).

Doug: believed fluoridated water was an attempt at government mind control.

Ryan: no, you may *not* date my sister and me at the same time.

Dave: kept a collection of other girls' underwear.

Chris: told me I gave him Chlamydia...except *I* didn't have it.

Scott: overheard declaring to a friend, "Her boobs are as flat as her back!"

Mike: found out I was breaking up with him, started sending me anonymous death threats.

Kenny: five percent tipper.

Joey: thought deodorant was *so bourgeois*. Also, used pretentious words like "bourgeois" and didn't wear deodorant.

Brian: claimed that horrible noise was him "jamming out" on guitar.

Matt: played Dungeons and Dragons. In costume. On Valentine's Day.

Thomas: didn't think *The Princess Bride* was funny.

Paul: Bugs Bunny tattoo = deal breaker.

Greg: told me I was "pretty...from certain angles."

And so on. More stories were shared, more drinking was done, more giggling ensued. However, when we were finally satisfied that all the worst offenders, from the clueless to the cruel, had been accounted for, we weren't quite sure what to do with the list. Neither one of us wanted to keep it, and just pitching it in the garbage lacked the dramatic flair that the sangria assured us was warranted.

Finally, we channeled some old-school immaturity of our own and struck upon a glorious plan: we would burn it! It would be like a Boyfriend Bonfire, in which old pictures and tokens from a specific guy are erased from your life in a final blaze—except we would dispose of our *entire collection of boy baggage* in one fell swoop. Our sordid pasts would die in the flames, creating ashes from which the phoenix of our perfect future would arise! We snickered and basked in our brilliance, eagerly awaiting the spiritual cleansing we were about to experience. As the glowing embers crept across the list, they would chew through the names and turn them all to dust. The past would be purged from our minds, FOREVER! Take *that*, boys!

The symbolism! The poetic justice! *The booze is gone!*
What?

For reasons that only the empty bottle of Boone's knows, it was decided that I would hold the list during this ritual. My roommate, suddenly quite somber for the occasion, leaned across the table with her trusty Bic. Her hand steady, she flicked the thumb wheel. There was the brief flash of a spark—then, fire.

It's worth mentioning at this point that, as it turns out, the paper you see slowly smoldering when people burn it on television, with a thin line of orange fire crawling lazily toward the center of the page, is most likely made of thick, high quality cardstock. Or it's paper money, which isn't even really paper at all. Or maybe it's actually cleverly disguised plywood.

Our list, on the other hand, was written on a flimsy white fast food napkin.

As such, instead of slowly smoldering while we cackled with glee as we originally envisioned, our list immediately erupted into a giant fireball—an unexpected fireball, which I was holding in my bare hand—while seated at the dining room table—with enough alcohol in my bloodstream that my body itself was probably about as flammable as a Chinese lantern full of kerosene.

"FIRE!" my roommate screamed, as if there were any possibility that this minuscule detail had escaped my attention.

"AAAAAAAARRRRRGHHHHHH!" I responded.

I had to think fast. Dropping the napkin wasn't an option; we'd probably burn the whole apartment complex down, or at least scorch the carpet, and either way I was pretty sure we'd forfeit our cleaning deposit. Could I smother it somehow? No, not without sustaining serious (and seriously embarrassing to explain) injuries. *Wait—the sink! Of course!* I bolted from my chair toward the kitchen, my arm outstretched in front of me like the burning fuse on an obscenity-filled firecracker, and headed for the stainless steel safety in the next room.

Unfortunately, my sudden movement caused the blazing napkin to dissolve into a hundred bits of flaming shrapnel, and each miniature, floating firebomb hung suspended in the air just long enough for me to run straight into it. They grazed my eyelashes and drifted into my long hair. I flailed maniacally, trying to swat them away before my head went up like a torch, but every effort I made to escape only sent more delicately burning confetti swirling into the air around me.

"FIRE!" my roommate screamed again, this time about four octaves higher.

"AAAAAAAARRRRRGHHHHHH!" I volleyed back, to let her know I was totally on top of the situation.

Finally I tripped into the kitchen and lunged for the sink, somehow simultaneously turning on the water and diving waist-deep into the 0.6 cubic feet of relief it offered. The half dozen molecules of napkin that remained in my hand were thoroughly doused. The list, and all the names on it, was destroyed. The deed was done. The crisis was over.

Or so it seemed.

We did feel better about having a clean slate after we purged the past that night. Nevertheless, I decided to take a break from dating (and pyromania) for a while, to stay home and think about what I really wanted out of a relationship...a decision that only partly hinged on the fact that I had to wait several weeks for my eyebrows to grow back.

Our ritual, to no one's surprise, did not end up making us perfect in the long term. On the contrary, we both stumbled through plenty more mishaps and failures in the years to come, some of which were no doubt in some way related to all that baggage we were still carrying.

However, I did eventually meet the man of my dreams—and it turns out that we're perfectly compatible, in part, because we understand each other's flaws. I love him and he loves me, imperfect pasts and all.

But first we spent fifteen years as just friends, too dumb to recognize that we were meant to be a couple.

Oh well, nobody's perfect.

ROBYN WELLING *is a freelance writer, editor, and humorist at Hollow Tree Ventures, where she isn't afraid to embarrass herself—and frequently does. The awesome team at 22 Words, where she enjoys her day job as graphic designer, makes her enthusiastic about working in a way that isn't solely based on the fact that she gets to work from home in her PJs. She's been named a Must-Follow Humor Blog by BlogHer and co-authored four other hilarious best-selling humor anthologies, one of which is a New York Times bestseller, yet her five kids still don't think she's funny. Her goals include becoming independently wealthy, followed by world domination and getting her children to clean their rooms. Until then, she'll just fold laundry and write about the shortcuts she takes on her journey to becoming a somewhat passable wife, mother, and human being; if history is any guide, she'll miss the mark entirely. You can find her avoiding responsibility on Facebook, Twitter, Instagram, and Pinterest.*

I Just Want Perfect Boobs

By Jen Mann

People I Want to Punch in the Throat

When I was nine all I could think about was *Boobs seem cool. When will I get some?* And then when I was ten all I could think about was *Well, looky there, I got boobs.* And then when I was eleven all I could think about was *Wow, they sure are getting big—like* really *big. I wonder when these things will stop growing?* And then when I was twelve I was like *Is there something wrong, because I've got full-on boobalicious happening here?!* And then when I was thirteen I was like *Knock this shit off, Boobs, you're bigger than my mom's. It's not funny anymore.* And that's when my love/hate relationship with my boobs began.

As a seventh grader, I wanted nothing more than two cute, little perfectly perky pointers. I wanted little ripe plums to sit high on my chest and get just enough attention from the boys in my class. I wanted them to admire them and notice them, but only in a respectful and considerate way. Instead, in seventh grade I had two over ripe cantaloupes that were already beginning to hang low with just enough flop that my burgeoning career as a long-distance runner was doomed.

The boys certainly noticed them. They noticed them a little too much, in fact. It started with snapping my—enormous granny bra—bra strap and running away cackling like the pre-teen idiots they were. Then it moved up to the sneak a peek. Being a short girl, most of the boys were taller than me, so it made it very easy for them to look down my shirt. Now that I'm a forty-something lady, I understand what actual cleavage is, so I realize now that they really weren't seeing anything, but they didn't know that and I didn't know that. A simple glimpse of a fleshy collarbone was enough to send them into a tizzy. "I saw your boobs! I saw your boobs! *Bewbs!*" they would shriek while I died of embarrassment and tried to melt into the floor as quickly as possible.

After a while it escalated to the casual "bump and grab." You know what that is, right? Let me set the scene. It's the four minutes between sixth and seventh period and thirteen-year-old Jenni runs to her locker get her science textbook. A group of thirteen-year-old future rapists (Fine—*alleged* future rapists) are hovering around the locker too. Jenni pauses but the clock is ticking. Her teacher is a dick and if she's even one minute late she's going to get a detention, so she takes a deep breath and pushes through the cloud of Drakkar Noir and starts spinning the combo lock furiously. She grabs what she needs and as she slinks by the boys, they all manage to accidentally-on-purpose bump into her. Their biceps gently rub up against her Bahama mamas and the braver ones actually manage to get a full-on palm on her meat puppets. "Oh! Excuse me," they say, giant shit-eating grins erupting across their pimply faces. "I think I accidentally touched your bazooms." That's when Jenni looks at her watch and realizes that she's got exactly thirty seconds to get her butt into science and she doesn't have the time to Hulk out and kill these boys in the slow, painful ways that they deserve. Instead she pretends like they don't bother her. She high-tails it to science class with two seconds to spare, and then she spends the rest of the hour dreaming that she could be like Stephen King's Carrie and burn them all to the ground during prom their senior year. This is also why Jenni isn't Dr. Jenni today. She was too busy honing her murderous telekinetic skills instead of her biology skills.

That's when my boobs went deep underground. Well, under oversize sweatshirts and giant cardigans. I tried to pick articles of clothing that closely resembled tents. I wanted fabric that flowed over and barely grazed my breasts. If a top showed any sort of definition of my lady lumps, it was immediately discarded for being "too revealing."

It was many years later that I finally took notice of the rolling hills of Jen again. Yes, by then I was Jen. I had dropped the adorable "i" and I'd found myself and decided to embrace my curves. I took off my kaftan and inspected my mounds of joy. Imagine my surprise and shock when I realized that they were twice as big as they'd been at thirteen. Suddenly, those "enormous" thirteen-year-old boobs that I once considered jugs were now juggernauts. Even without sunlight, those suckers had managed to double in size. They were bigger than my head (each one, not combined, mind you). They weren't perky when I was thirteen, but oh, how the mighty had fallen! I think those erotic novels my mother keeps under her bed would call them full and lush and buxom. They were the ideal size to heave. Personally, I thought they resembled Ziploc bags of mashed potatoes. They were nowhere near perfect, but I was a new woman. I was strong and confident! I didn't need to worry about what society said was beautiful! As long as *I* thought my Ziploc bags of mashed potatoes were beautiful, then they were, dammit!! Besides, mashed potatoes are delicious!

I was still wearing the granny bras, because Victoria's biggest secret is that she actually hates mammaries bigger than a bad reaction to a bee sting. The average boulder holder couldn't handle my situation, so I was still shopping in the big and plenty section of the lingerie department. There isn't a lot of choice on that one lonely rack. I had an exciting collection of beige, white, and black bras made from what I can only assume must be decommissioned parachutes, medical-grade elastic, and military-grade hook and eye closures.

I also had a boyfriend.

A boyfriend who liked me for my brains and my wit. A boyfriend who thought I was fun and interesting. A boyfriend who was a breast man. What? Did you really think I was going to attract a leg man with these stubby stilts?

My boyfriend didn't care that my fun bags were a bit bigger than the average bag. He thought that meant they were more fun.

Eventually that boyfriend became my husband and badabingbadaboom I was pregnant with our first kid. I don't want to brag, but the Hubs and I were both pretty certain that I would be a world-champion breastfeeder. I mean, how could I not? They're not called num-nums for nothing. I felt like breastfeeding was exactly what Cagney & Lacey were designed for. I'd suffered through twenty years of the opposite sex accidentally-on-purpose feeling me up. I'd given up my running (and medical) career. I walked hunched over from carrying twenty pounds of ta-tas. I hadn't seen my feet in a decade. But now that I was pregnant, it was all worth it, because finally the dairy barn would be open for business and it would all make sense why I had been hauling these honkers around. Not only could I feed MY kid, I fantasized about curing world hunger with my hard-working hooters. I imagined that I would nourish my precious babe until he was stuffed and then I'd pump so I could bottle the rest and distribute it to the hungry world.

I think it was about the time I was picking out what I'd wear to accept my Nobel Peace Prize when God said, "Calm your tits, Jen. Sometimes I only create giant globes so that you could have chronic back pain in the future and for no other reason."

Yup. That's right. My oversize udders sucked at suckling. At first I blamed my baby. Yes, I know. I'm not proud of that admission, but hear me out. He was premature and he only weighed five pounds. He didn't have a suck reflex and his baby bird mouth couldn't open wide enough to fit my silver dollar-size nipple in his mouth. Surely, it was his fault. But I refused to let him stop me from fulfilling the destiny of my door knockers. I hired a professional lactation consultant who took one look at me and promptly charged me double. She also sold me a forty dollar breastfeeding stool (Yes, there is too such a thing. Or at least I *think* there is. Shit, did I buy a made up breastfeeding stool??), ten dollar nipple shields, twenty bucks worth of lanolin to keep my nipples from chafing under the shields, and she suggested I somehow conjure a third hand.

"It's kind of hard to keep your breast from suffocating the little guy, isn't it?" she asked me after my one millionth attempt to hold my baby and my boob and a nipple shield all while balancing my feet on my special breastfeeding stool (It does too exist! Shut up!) and instead of giving him life-sustaining nectar, I was freaking out because he was turning blue every time. "Here, let me help you." That's when the lactation consultant put her cold, clammy hands on my not-so-fun-now bag and lifted it off my child's face. "There!" she exclaimed. "That works. You're just going to need to have your husband or someone else there to help you when you're breastfeeding."

Ohhh! Was that all I was going to need, expensive lactation consultant who I'm pretty sure sold me a bogus stool? I just need to have another person willing to man-handle my naked boob and hold it in the most uncomfortable position for both of us every thirty minutes *for* twenty to thirty minutes while my premature infant who didn't know to fucking suck tries to learn how to suck before he dies from malnourishment? Easy peasy! Great advice. Thank you for that. Where's your bill? Because I'd like to shove it up your ass.

Before my son was born, I had big dreams of going back to work right away after his birth. I worked a commission-based job and didn't get paid maternity leave, so I needed to be back to work as soon as possible so I could pay the lactation consultant's outrageous bill. I'd bought a Baby Bjorn and I was positive Gomer would love cozying up to his mama all day long while she showed houses, made prospecting calls, and filed paper work. I had it all planned out: every thirty minutes I would take a break from my work, I would lean back comfortably in my office chair, throw a hooter hider over the both of us, and calmly and naturally feed my son while catching up on some light reading or hear the office gossip or get my meal plans done and schedule an appointment to get my hair cut and highlighted.

Instead, I never left house, because my child and I never learned how to work together properly. So, if there wasn't a third hand around to help me, I stripped down and hooked myself up to an industrial-strength breast pump and cried while liquid gold dribbled out of me. Yes, dribble, is the right word. You see, the size of your breast does not determine the quantity that it holds. I was lucky if I could get two ounces at a time. I drank my weight in water, I ate oatmeal, garlic, fennel, and any other random thing someone suggested to help increase my milk production. I would have eaten garlic cloves dipped in Pixie Stix if someone told me it worked for their cousins' wife's sister's neighbor. I was like a crazy woman when it came to breastfeeding. And the drama!! Oh, the drama. I worked so hard for such little returns, so I was a bit on edge. You've never seen anyone lose their mind like I did the day my husband accidentally (probably on purpose) knocked over one of my tiny bottles into the sink. I wailed over that drain for an hour. I tried to sop up the remnant milk with a breast pad so I could wring it out into my baby's mouth.

At that point my husband had had enough. My fun bags were no longer fun and they were making me bonkers. He sat me down and calmly explained, "Maybe—just hear me out—please stop crying, Jen—maybe it's time for you to stop trying to breastfeed."

"I'm not *trying* to breastfeed. I *am* breastfeeding," I sobbed, pushing my lank and dirty hair out of my tear-stained face. I couldn't remember that last time I'd showered.

"No," he said. "You're breastfeeding a machine, not our baby. And when you're not hooked up to those suction cups, you're chewing on fennel while you wander around the house topless because you need to 'air out' your nipples. You've given it a good try, Jen, but I would support you a hundred percent if you stopped. It's better to be a sane mother, don't you think?"

At the time I wasn't sure if the Hubs was really worried about Gomer having a crazy mother or if he didn't like having a crazy wife. When I first started walking around topless, he enjoyed the show, but when he quickly realized that I was oblivious to my surroundings, he took steps to control me. For instance, I almost opened the door for the UPS man topless. I figured what's the big deal? He's probably seen it all. Surely I wouldn't be the first topless woman to sign for a box of diapers. The Hubs pointed out that just because other women might have done it, doesn't mean I should.

Fair enough.

So, after much more wailing and gnashing of teeth, I finally put the girls away and learned how to make formula.

It's been ten years since that conversation. I've still got my boobs— and my chronic back pain. I look at them and I start humming that song, *Do Your Ears Hang Low?* Only I swap word breasts for ears. Of all the different stages my breasts have gone through, this stage is upsetting me the most. I'm pretty sure I can throw my breasts over my shoulder like a continental soldier. A few months ago I noticed that once again, they've morphed. Instead of two Ziploc bags of mashed potatoes, I've now got two loaves of French bread.

But.

One loaf is a little bit *longer* than the other.

Since I'm in my forties now, I know it's all downhill from here and I feel like my jiggle jams have already gotten a head start down that hill and one is going faster than the other!

I've never been a very vain woman before, am I really going to let my lopsided lollies bother me now? What is the big deal? Why am I so worried about them now? Probably because I can't stop aging, but I can maybe stop sagging?

So, I looked at my bank account and then I considered going under the knife. Let me say that again. I considered going to a doctor and standing naked in front of him while he flopped my beamers around, tsk-tsking over them, weighing them, and sighing heavily about how much work they'd require and why didn't I come earlier before they required so much work? I would let him draw on them with permanent marker and photograph them (all while telling me that he could totally do something about my nose and my neck and since I was already going to be on the table I might as well let him). I considered letting a doctor carve up by body on purpose. I didn't need a kidney. I didn't need cancer cut from my body. I just wanted better boobs (and less of a turkey neck).

But then I looked at my daughter, who at nine, was looking like she'd been cursed with my endowments. She got my love of writing, my sense of humor, and my early-deploying breast buds. What message would I be sending her if I decided that my breasts needed fixing? How could I look her in the eye and say, "You're perfect, no matter what. Love yourself. Don't ever change," and then go under the knife to have my chest remade into something "better?"

Nope, nope, nope.

My breasts are not perfect. Not by a very long (droopy) shot. But they're close enough. They're mine. They've been with me my whole life and they've never been perfect. I've hated them. I've loved them. And now I'm just going to have to accept them. I'm not about to start rebuilding them now just because I'm starting to feel mortal and I have the overwhelming urge to control something—anything—since so much of aging is out of my control.

That's when I got out my gorgeous beige bra with five rows of hooks and the minimizer feature and wrangled my torpedoes into their proper tubes, I smoothed one of my many fitted-but-not-too-fitted tops over my bosom, and promptly forgot that the left one hangs about half an inch lower than the right one.

JEN MANN is best known for her wildly popular and hysterical blog People I Want to Punch in the Throat. *She has been described by many as Erma Bombeck—with f-bombs. Jen is known for her hilarious rants and funny observations on everything from parenting to gift giving to celebrity behavior to politics to Elves on Shelves. She does not suffer fools lightly. Her blog received a Bloggie Award for Best Parenting Blog. Jen is the author of the* New York Times *bestseller* People I Want to Punch in the Throat: Competitive Crafters, Drop-Off Despots, and Other Suburban Scourges *which was a Finalist for a Goodreads Reader's Choice Award. Her latest book is* Spending the Holidays with People I Want to Punch in the Throat. *She is also the mastermind behind the* New York Times *bestselling* I Just Want to Pee Alone *series.*

Jen is a married mother of two children whom she calls Gomer and Adolpha in her writings—she swears their real names are actually worse. Join the almost 800,000 people who follow Jen on social media here and here, Twitter, and Amazon.

NOTES FROM THE EDITOR

Thank you for reading this book. We appreciate your support and we hope you enjoyed it. We hope you will tell a friend—or thirty about this book. Please do us a huge favor and leave us a review on Amazon and Goodreads. Of course we prefer 5-star, but we'll take what we can get. If you hated this book, you can skip the review.

Every contributor to this book has more material for you to read. Please check out their blogs and books.

OTHER BOOKS AVAILABLE

I Just Want to Pee Alone
I Just Want to Be Alone
I STILL Just Want to Pee Alone

People I Want to Punch in the Throat: Competitive Crafters, Drop Off Despots, and Other Suburban Scourges
Spending the Holidays with People I Want to Punch in the Throat: Yuletide Yahoos, Ho-Ho-Humblebraggers, and Other Seasonal Scourges

Made in the USA
Middletown, DE
29 May 2016